MW00561834

Wil Lou Gray

Wil Lou Gray and Wil Lou Gray II, 1958. Author's collection.

Wil Lou Gray

The Making of a
Southern Progressive
from New South to New Deal

Mary Macdonald Ogden

THE UNIVERSITY OF SOUTH CAROLINA PRESS

Published by the University of South Carolina Press
Columbia, South Carolina 29208

www.sc.edu/uscpress

Manufactured in the United States of America

24 23 22 21 20 19 18 17 16 15
10 9 8 7 6 5 4 3 2 1

Library of Congress Cataloging-in-Publication Data
can be found at http://catalog.loc.gov/.

ISBN: 978-1-61117-568-4 (cloth)
ISBN: 978-1-61117-569-1 (ebook)

This book was printed on recycled paper with
30 percent postconsumer waste content.

To my daughters, Anabell and Mary Laci Motley
My parents, William and Lou Ogden
My great-great aunt, Dr. Wil Lou Gray

We live in the past by a knowledge of its history, and in the future by hope and anticipation. By ascending to an association with our ancestors; by contemplating their example, and studying their character; by partaking their sentiments, and imbibing their spirit; by accompanying them in their toils; by sympathizing in their sufferings, and rejoicing in their successes and their triumphs, we mingle our own existence with theirs and seem to belong to their age. We become their contemporaries, live the lives which they lived, endure what they endured, and partake in the rewards which they enjoyed.

Daniel Webster, "First Settlement of New England," 1820

CONTENTS

Foreword

I am Wil Lou Gray Ogden, and I am the oldest child of Kea Council and Albert Dial Gray Jr. and the great-niece and namesake of Wil Lou Gray. Daddy was determined that his first daughter be named for his beloved Aunt Wil Lou, so my arrival was simultaneous with my naming—Wil Lou Gray II. This unusual name was derived from both of Aunt Wil Lou's parents, Wil for William and Lou for Louise. For me it was a difficult name. My mother admitted that for the first few months of my life she called me *Baby*. In new situations I was always asked to repeat my name. "What is your name? WillieLou? Walou? Willalou?" Although my difficulty with the name was never uttered in earshot of Daddy, I thought, "Why couldn't my name be one with an easy ring, like Anna, Genie, Mary, or just Lou?" I was finishing high school before I fully realized the dignity and respect associated with my name. I was president of the Future Teachers of America Club, and my faculty adviser was a contemporary of Aunt Wil Lou. When Aunt Wil Lou accepted an invitation to speak at our FTA Banquet, the excitement that accompanied rivaled a star, and I began to grasp the importance of my name.

How fortunate to have grown up in a time when we not only had expectations but in a time when expectations were met. During my childhood, in the '40s and '50s, our great expectation arrived in early June. School was out, and we were on our way to my grandmother Mama Lyl's house for six joyous weeks. Mother packed a trunk with our clothes, and Daddy readied the station wagon, often pulling a trailer filled with our bicycles and skates and even a wagon. We were ecstatic to begin the five- to six-hour journey down two-lane highways with no air conditioning from our home in Whiteville, North Carolina, to Laurens, South Carolina. My family totaled nine and filled the seats of the station wagon, but this did not quell the excitement. About an hour and a half into the trip, we expected to stop at the drugstore in Florence, South Carolina, where Daddy treated everyone to ice cream, leaving us sufficiently sticky! Then the questions: "Have we got to stop in Columbia?" Situated exactly halfway between Whiteville and Laurens was Columbia, the home of Aunt Wil Lou and Uncle Coke, the loved and respected siblings of my Granddaddy Gray. Daddy never responded to our pleading, as the answer was always yes. We knew Uncle Coke (married to Aunt Virginia) as the cheerful, elderly uncle who always gave each of us a dollar. We knew Aunt Wil Lou as the short, fat, unmarried aunt whose conversation was always about her "work" and the progress being made in South Carolina. By the time we were children, she owned the old army barracks in West Columbia and was well into running the Opportunity School for adult education. During much of her career, she lived in an apartment at the Opportunity School, rather than on Devine Street, and visiting her at the school meant a later arrival in Laurens. We were adults before we understood her honored place in the family, but we understood fully that we were expected to behave during the Columbia stops. Through the years those repeated stops in Columbia familiarized us with Aunt Wil Lou in such a way that we understood her expectations for the family. We learned early that she expected her family to participate in her work either with time or money. Several of my cousins did summer internships at the Opportunity School. When money was not readily available, Granddaddy contributed a sack of flour for her to sell. My aunts typed letters, and her dear first cousin, Marguerite Tolbert, accompanied and assisted with speaking engagements. Aunt Wil Lou never presented a job as optional, so rarely did anyone refuse. At seventy-six years old, I am ashamed to say when I was a student at Columbia College, when a call came from Aunt Wil Lou, I wanted to run and hide. I knew that the call meant she had a job for me!

Her family was her closest circle. The Grays and the Dials settled in Laurens County in the 1700s and were respected, influential citizens with whom Aunt Wil Lou was very secure. Her father, William, and his brother Robert married Dial sisters, Sarah Louise and Emma. She lost her mother at the age of nine. She, Granddaddy, and Uncle Coke were sent to Gray Court to live with relatives, and there were surrounded by double first cousins (mostly boys). Traditionally the large family gathered for Sunday lunch at Aunt Emma's. Uncle Coke's wife, Aunt Virginia, told the story that while the women cleared the table and cleaned the kitchen, the men sat on the large porch discussing politics, the church, farming, and economics. When the women finally joined them after the long cleanup, the men ceased the conversation and asked, "What's for supper?" This lively family interaction with expectations for all was normal for Aunt Wil Lou. It is understandable that she continued to expect help from Daddy's generation as well as from my generation, and she expected her expanding family to share her passion for progress in South Carolina.

Aunt Wil Lou grew up in Laurens and was a childhood friend of my grandmother Lillian Caine, affectionately known as Mama Lyl. Mama Lyl used to tell the story that Wil Lou as a child expected that life should be better for the less privileged. They always played outside, and when Wil Lou would swing on the garden gate, she showed more interest in the poor person walking across the street than in their dolls. She often asked, "Why do we have so much more than they?" Although as a child Mama Lyl paid no attention to her concern, she recognized in time that Wil Lou expected to make things better for the person across the street.

I was forty-three years old and married to my college sweetheart, Billy, when Aunt Wil Lou died. Looking back, I remember that when my domestic interests overrode my interest in her work, she turned her attention to my academic spouse. He was a doctor and held strong Republican ideals. While Aunt Wil Lou failed to convince him that in the Democratic way government was the vehicle for progress, their debates created a bond that lasted until her death. It was obvious that she expected more from me. When I was awaiting the arrival of our twins, children numbers six and seven for us, I received a package in the mail from Aunt Wil Lou. It contained a letter stating that she was on the president's committee for Planned Parenthood. It contained pamphlets on how to care for a family, and it contained a personal note that Billy and I had enough children and that it was time to stop!

Aunt Wil Lou was completely selfless, as she never lavished on herself. Even now my memory is of her in a black, navy, or light blue dress. Her apartment was unchanging. The blue sofa was never reupholstered, and the furniture never rearranged. One Christmas, thinking that her apartment needed a punch, I made her some colorful sofa pillows as a gift. Her thank-you note, while gracious, ended with her request: "Now, Wil Lou, the pillows are lovely, but you should take the $5.00 you spent on fabric and contribute it to the scholarships at Columbia College, Wofford, or the Opportunity School." With age I realized that the decorative aspects of Aunt Wil Lou's home were not as important as the people who passed through. During our stops in Columbia, we often met people whom Aunt Wil Lou had helped who stopped by to thank her. The impact of her work became more personal to me when a friend from Gaffney told me, "I want you to know how grateful my family is to Miss Wil Lou. She taught my grandmother to read." Let me add that while her apartment lacked the touch of a decorator, Aunt Wil Lou's lifestyle always reflected the refinement of her heritage. When our Columbia stops coincided with lunch, the meal, whether it be at her home on Devine Street or at the Opportunity School, was never hurried. The table was set with silver and linen napkins (to be placed in one's lap).

We sat at attention while Aunt Wil Lou made announcements, introduced her guests, and called for a blessing. I remember feeling tense when she called on my reserved daddy to return thanks. My quiet father obediently repeated the brief blessing that had graced the Gray-Dial tables for generations. Aunt Wil Lou taught and shared this mealtime practice with students, and she expected each to pass it on to their family and friends.

Aunt Wil Lou was an incurable teacher. She had a way of pointing her finger in the air as she gave instruction. A humorous lesson was when she taught me to scramble eggs. Although I had scrambled numerous dozens for my family of nine, she lectured that my whipping and beating made for tough eggs. Thus I watched attentively as she gently pushed the eggs from one side of the pan to the other until they were properly done. The most memorable instruction took place during my visit to introduce Billy. In 1958 he joined me from Presbyterian College to visit in Whiteville. We stopped in Columbia to meet Aunt Wil Lou and my daddy's sisters, Monkie and Rosa. It happened that they had all started a weight-loss regimen. When we arrived Aunt Wil Lou was giving instructions on the latest exercises. Billy has never let me forget his impression of my dignified relatives doing toe touches and waist bends long before aerobics were fashionable!

Aunt Wil Lou's very existence was a testimony to her Christian faith. She expected her church to welcome people from all walks of life. She was a devout Methodist and gave generously to her Methodist alma mater, Columbia College, and to her father and brother's alma mater, Wofford College. When I was a child, I remember sitting beside her in church and not having money for the offering. She slipped me a dime and later said, "Wil Lou, you must never let the offering plate pass without giving—no matter how small." I have never forgotten that lesson and find myself today passing offerings down the church pew to my grandchildren.

It has been thirty years since Aunt Wil Lou's death. Our family still speaks of her accomplishments, and our children and grandchildren are still writing school reports about their "famous" ancestor. Recently Mary Mac asked me, "Mom, if Aunt Wil Lou were alive would you ask any questions to her?" My answer was no, although I still feel her impact on my life. I see that finger pointing in the air and hear her biblical instruction ringing out: "To whom much is given, much is expected."

Wil Lou Gray Ogden
MONTREAT, NORTH CAROLINA

PREFACE

The career of a typical woman in my family history followed a simple trajectory: teacher, wife, mother, and homemaker. She taught school for one or two years, married, had kids, and then devoted her life to mastering the art of home economics. The daily tasks of cooking, sewing, setting a table with fine china and linen, arranging flowers, and attending church revolved around the needs of her husband, the sole breadwinner and head of the household. Only in recent decades have women in my large extended southern family modified this standard and discovered the significant achievements of the one woman in my heritage who chose the path less traveled—Wil Lou Gray.

She was the first female in a long line of South Carolinians to devote her life to public service. Nothing in her background prepared her to complete a graduate degree in New York, craft the field of adult education, practice a profession for more than fifty years, or devote herself to a very public career that played out over a century of incredible transformation. Puzzled by her devotion to the needs of the less fortunate and her incredible stamina for work, few of her relatives could relate to what she did each day. Despite their dismay Gray loved her close and extended kin. Her letters to family members always included an invitation to visit, an appeal to help others, and a check to buy a little something during the holidays. By the end of her life, she was the matriarch of a family far removed from Laurens County, the place her ancestors called home for generations. When she turned one hundred years old in 1983, most of her peers and close relatives were dead and few kin lived nearby, her extended family dispersed by geography and differentiated by economy and lifestyle. Despite the changing nature of her family and the transforming world in which she lived,

Gray passionately conveyed to those she loved a system of beliefs and values that grew from her heritage and defined her politics.

I remember clearly the visits to her home on Devine Street, my six siblings and I packed together on her Victorian couch struggling to behave as she offered us saltines from a mason jar. The brief stops in Columbia were often spent exploring the apartment complex she owned and wandering between her apartment and that of her cousin, Marguerite Tolbert, who lived across the hall. My most vivid recollection was when I was five years old and had to spend the night with her while my parents and older siblings slept nearby at my Aunt Monkie's house. I was scared all alone with her, and the mirror in the bedroom reflected my terrified face as I sat beside her in the bed as she read me a Bible story. She was barely done with the introduction when I begged her to return me to my mother. She complied, but I made her cry. I was fifteen when she died in 1984. I regret that I never apologized for acting so ugly and that I lacked the wisdom to visit more often or interview her before she died that March, five months before she turned 101. A decade later when I chose her as the subject of my thesis in graduate school, Dr. Melton McLaurin served on my committee and told me he had rented her attic apartment while a Ph.D. student in history at the University of South Carolina. That he knew her and agreed she was a good topic of analysis was a sign I was writing far more than a family history.

Twenty years have passed since I first began to study her. Completion of this manuscript was a journey that took me from my early twenties to my mid-forties, and in the process I acquired a deep appreciation and respect for Gray's incredible foresight and idealism. She passionately believed in equality of opportunity and the capacity of humanity to create a just society. Her story is all the more real because time has finally caught up to her. We need only to look at her accomplishments in a marginal state filled with poor black and white people, violence, illiteracy, and numerous idiosyncrasies to realize how important her efforts actually were. I combed through hundreds of newspaper articles, personal letters, professional papers, and pictures to build the narrative, and I found a far more complex Wil Lou Gray than either the literature at present conveys or the family stories reveal. Although the sources did not expose any mysteries that may have added a degree of sensationalism to her story, the evidence shows that she impacted the lives of real people and made real change at a time when many people of her background turned a blind eye to the needs of the disadvantaged.

Gray was a southerner, and southerners are complicated. The vast array of literature on the mind, culture, and history of the region attests to this. She was a refined, sophisticated upper-class South Carolinian who played Canasta, loved tomato aspic, and served meals at the South Carolina Opportunity School on china with cloth napkins. She was also a lifelong Democrat, a passionate supporter of equality of opportunity, a masterful politician, a workaholic, and a supporter of government programs such as Medicare and nonprofits such as Planned Parenthood. If she disagreed with you, she simply dismissed you. In 1964 when my father told her about reading *The Conscience of a Conservative*, she cared not to discuss Barry Goldwater or any conservative matter, ever. She had a remarkable grasp of the problems that plagued her state and, with deep faith in the power of government to foster social justice, developed innovative ways to deal with them despite real financial, political, and social limitations that governed everything she did all of the time. Her life is an example of how one person's tenacity and conviction in the transcendent goodness of humanity and progressive government can impact society—a good lesson to consider today. Although I bring to the analysis of her life harsh critique, I am confident she would give my interpretation a stamp of approval.

Acknowledgments

This manuscript is a product of many earlier drafts carefully read and revised by a number of people to whom I am deeply indebted. Completion of this manuscript was possible because of the guidance, patience, and critique of my work by Dr. Wanda A. Hendricks of the University of South Carolina. She provided constant support and questions during the construction of the story and devoted countless hours to reading and discussing the material during the revision process. Her analysis of the manuscript expanded the scope and possibility of the work, and her example as a teacher and mentor made this journey a rewarding and meaningful experience. To her I extend my deepest thanks and gratitude. I give equal thanks to her peers at the University of South Carolina, Dr. Marjorie Spruill, Dr. Marcia Synnott, Dr. Lacy K. Ford, and Dr. Lynn Weber, who offered generous suggestions, asked important questions, and recommended specific direction for this work. I am forever grateful to these exemplary scholars. Likewise I thank Dr. Kathleen Berkeley at the University of North Carolina at Wilmington for shaping the questions I initially asked about Gray's life and work. Her expertise on the history of women set me on the right course. Additional gratitude is extended to Dr. Melton McLaurin and Dr. Alan Watson, both graduates of the University of South Carolina, who many years ago believed Wil Lou Gray to be a worthwhile topic of scholarship.

Special thanks is extended to the South Caroliniana Library Manuscripts Division at the University of South Carolina for their assistance with the Wil Lou Gray Manuscript Collection, to the South Carolina Department of Archives and History for assistance with state records, and to the Wil Lou Gray Opportunity School director, Pat Smith, who gave time, materials, and support to this project. I am also grateful for the forum provided at the annual meetings of the

South Carolina Historical Association, where I presented aspects of this manuscript to inquisitive and often critical peers. Additionally I owe deep thanks to Dr. Alexander Moore of the University of South Carolina Press. At the encouragement of Dr. Wanda Hendricks, he read this manuscript and agreed to publish it. I know Wil Lou Gray would be proud that this distinguished press in her beloved state published her story.

This project was completed with the love and support of my family. I thank my parents, William and Wil Lou Gray Ogden, who over countless conversations evaluated what I had to say about my most famous relative to date and often reminded me to personalize the narrative since I actually knew her. With their guidance I won the Daughters of the American Revolution essay competition in fourth grade by writing about Aunt Wil Lou, and two decades later chose her as the subject of my graduate thesis. Their personal insight refined my understanding of her life and work and provided clarity when I lost perspective. I thank my daughters, Anabell and Mary Laci Motley, who were toddlers when I began this narrative and young women when I finished. Their love, immense creativity, and intelligence inspire me always. My academic journey defined their entire lives while it reshaped mine. When they were small children, I often caught myself thinking about the daily rituals of Wil Lou Gray as a motherless young girl at age nine who was forced to define herself on her own terms without the constant oversight and insight of a mother. I thank my dear friend and colleague Dr. Anne McKibbin, who spent fifteen years listening to me discuss what I was trying to say about Gray and helped me flesh out the details that mattered. Finally I thank my husband, Greg, who endured many years of revisions, disruptions, and stress; my five sisters—Kea, Gray, Anna, Genie, and Kathryn—who were engaged in discussions about this project every visit home to Asheville; and the dozens of extended Gray relatives, especially my aunt Mardy Choate, who shared their collective memories and array of letters, pictures, and artifacts that tell in part Gray's story. Without the Gray family and their valuable recollections, the story of Wil Lou Gray is incomplete.

For One Beloved

The years have passed, but she has conquered them,
Denying obstacles that blocked her way;
As though related to the Cherubim,
Her face is shining as the August day
Which saw her birth. Her words are always kind,
But do not let mild syllables deceive you,
For once made up, no one can change her mind;
Yet she is very willing to forgive you
If your thoughts are at variance with hers.
She hopes someday that you will look at things
The way she does, that you will pluck sharp burrs
From faltering flesh although your finger stings. . . .

God bless this woman who has done His work
With faith where ignorance and darkness lurk;
God bless her who has opened a locked door
To knowledge, letting earthbound spirits soar.

    Harriet Gray Blackwell

Written for the eightieth birthday celebration of Wil Lou Gray, August 29, 1963

Introduction

THE POLITICS OF PROGRESS

On a stop in South Carolina during the presidential election of 2008, reporter Tom Baldwin of the *Times* (London) observed, "Although the election has become all about 'change,' precious little of that commodity can be found in this corner of the Old South. This is where the Confederate battle flag from the Civil War still flutters outside the state capitol in Columbia, next to a large statue of Ben 'Pitchfork' Tillman, a former Governor who justified and even participated in lynchings."[1] In a state where women could not sit on a jury until 1967, there is plenty of past proof to support his view.[2] Despite its colorful past marked by Yankee occupation, xenophobic racism, and political demagogues, South Carolina has changed due in part to the work of reform-minded citizens who envisioned a progressive, just, and competitive state and worked to lead the region into the modern age. Wil Lou Gray (1883–1984), a native of Laurens County, was a leader among them in the twentieth century. Former governor and senator Fritz Hollings said, "When history makes an analysis of South Carolina in the 1900s history ... might well summarize Miss Wil Lou by saying her life is a life of service dedicated to her fellowman—she is an inspiration to the South Carolinian of this century."[3]

Gray devoted her career to the eradication of illiteracy in South Carolina, and it is by virtue of this work that she is today recognized as a pioneer in the field of adult education.[4] Former governor Richard Riley claimed Gray "did far and above more than any other individual" to improve the state and "had a personal impact on thousands and thousands of South Carolinians."[5] "The genius of Wil Lou Gray was that she knew how to get things done," he said. "She didn't wait for the system to respond to the needs that she clearly observed."[6]

Gray was a powerhouse of ideas, an energetic advocate of social justice, and a passionate South Carolinian. Dr. R. Wright Spears, former president of Gray's alma mater, Columbia College, described her as the "American version of William Wilberforce, who in England was known as the Attorney General of the Poor and Dispossessed."[7] The South Carolina General Assembly acknowledged Gray as a public servant who "championed equal education for both races without being dismissed as an idle dreamer or revolutionary."[8] Known by such interesting sobriquets as "little Napoleon," Gray was persistent in her efforts to remedy the social problems that limited state progress. South Carolina senator James Henry Hammond expressed her determination as "worse than chewing gum in your hair."[9] Fellow educator Mabel Montgomery claimed Gray to be "a strange combination of the idealism of a saint, the loving kindness of a good mother, and the pragmatism of a tough-minded businessman."[10]

Many institutions and organizations in South Carolina recognized Gray's commitment to create opportunities for the underprivileged. The University of South Carolina awarded her the Algernon Sydney Sullivan Award in 1937 for her service to humanity.[11] She received honorary doctorates from Columbia College, Wofford College, and Clemson University, and when Winthrop University awarded her a Doctor of Humane Letters in 1970, the school acknowledged her as the "Jane Addams of South Carolina... for like Jane Addams who gave up a life of ease and comfort to serve the down trodden, she relinquished a life of comfort to serve the less fortunate of South Carolina."[12] In 1949 she received a certificate of merit for outstanding service to the black race from South Carolina State University in Orangeburg, known at the time as the State A&M College for Negroes.[13] She was the only woman among thirty-four nominations for the South Carolina Man of the Half Century Award and received the Sertoma International Service to Mankind citation in 1961. She was inducted into the South Carolina Hall of Fame alongside state leader John C. Calhoun in 1974.[14] The following year she received the International Woman's Year Citation by the National Retired Teachers Association, one of just eighteen citations given in the United States.[15] She died in 1984 at the age of one hundred, ending a public career that spanned eight decades.[16] In an epitaph marking the event, Governor Riley proclaimed, "During her 100 years on earth, she dealt with other people's problems day by day, hour by hour, and person by person. ... I wish she had lived to be 200."[17] As a testament to her century of public service, the Wil Lou Gray Opportunity School in West Columbia bears her name, and her portrait hangs in the South Carolina State House gallery beside one of African American educator Mary McLeod Bethune.[18] An admirer of Gray wrote, "If ever anyone has reason to ascend the stairway at the Capitol

... he will pass a portrait of this lady. Pause a moment and look into the face of greatness."[19]

Born and raised in Laurens, South Carolina, Gray attended Columbia College and began her teaching career in 1903 at Jones School in Greenwood, South Carolina. She attended graduate school at Vanderbilt in 1905, taught English literature at Martha Washington College in Abingdon, Virginia, in 1907, and received a master of arts in political science from Columbia University in 1911.[20] In 1912 she served as the supervisor of rural schools in Laurens County for the South Carolina Department of Education.[21] In this position, in 1915, she started the first rural night school program in the state to provide elementary instruction in reading, writing, and arithmetic to illiterate adults in the community.[22] The statewide acclaim she earned for this work led to an appointment as the field secretary for the Illiteracy Commission of South Carolina during World War I. In January 1919 the General Assembly appropriated funds that made permanent her position, and she served as supervisor of adult schools for the South Carolina Department of Education from 1919 until her retirement in 1947.[23] From this position of leadership, Gray cultivated adult education from an obscure idea few people knew anything about to a tax-funded division of the state educational system. "She contributed a tremendous amount to this state, particularly in adult education," said former South Carolina superintendent of education Charlie Williams. "The basic program we have today had its beginning with her."[24]

The milestone event in Gray's career was the creation of the opportunity school in 1921.[25] The opportunity school was a four-week vacation boarding camp held in late summer that provided instruction in reading, writing, arithmetic, domestic arts, health education, etiquette, and citizenship to illiterate and semiliterate white adults.[26] Gray developed this unique, adult-centered summer school at a time when there were limited public options for adults to acquire a formal education in South Carolina. Historian Norfleet Hardy explains that adult education in South Carolina originated in the colonial era but that these efforts were private ventures. He identifies an 1896 law in South Carolina that forbade anyone over the age of twenty-one from attending free of charge publicly funded schools as the reason why many adults received no education. Public support for adult education in the state began in 1916 when the General Assembly allocated one thousand dollars for night schools and authorized the state superintendent of education, John Swearingen, to increase this appropriation up to five thousand dollars with any money left over from a state school tax levied in 1913. Adult night schools were the primary mechanism for adult illiterates to obtain any schooling after 1916 in South Carolina until Gray obtained state funds to augment her opportunity schools.[27] The first opportunity school summer program enrolled white women only, but by 1923 it included men and, by 1931, black male and female students. Between 1921 and 1947, numerous state colleges hosted summer opportunity schools including Anderson, Lander, Erskine, and Clemson, where camps for white men and women were consolidated in 1931. Though segregated by race, the opportunity schools by 1931 were not segregated by gender. Men and women attended school together at Clemson and in Seneca, South Carolina, where a concurrent opportunity school for black adults opened at the Seneca Institute.[28] Although racially segregated, both the black and white opportunity schools used common educational testing and training materials, and the success of the Seneca program served as a precedent for the establishment of subsequent opportunity schools for African American adults held at Voorhees School and Junior College (later Voorhees Normal and Industrial College) in Denmark, South Carolina, from 1934 to 1937. In 1938 and in conjunction with the Works Progress Administration, a summer camp was held at Benedict College with seventy-two black students in attendance.[29] In 1947 the state endorsed the creation of a year-round opportunity school, the South Carolina Opportunity School, for white adult students, and Gray served as the director until her retirement a decade later.[30] Former director of the South Carolina Opportunity School W. T. Lander said, "Few South Carolinians have made greater contributions to their State than has Dr. Wil Lou Gray. From the time of her college graduation in the first decade of this century until this very day . . . she has unleashed her great energy and intelligence toward the upbuilding of her State and its people."[31] Why Stop Learning is the simple motto inscribed on the gates of the school, renamed the Wil Lou Gray Opportunity School in 1976, and although adult education is no longer the school's focus, today it functions within the state educational system to assist at-risk teenagers complete high school.[32]

In the preface of Well Behaved Women Seldom Make History, historian Laurel Thatcher Ulrich writes, "People not only make history by living their lives, but by creating records and turning other people's lives into books and slogans," processes anthropologist Clifford Geertz labels "constructions of other people's constructions."[33] Wil Lou Gray's role in state educational history is documented in hundreds of newspaper and magazine articles, book chapters, and two biographies. Most accounts of her life reveal a passionate and determined public servant devoted to the improvement of her state but do not address the complex and controversial nature of her work and social vision as they played out in the early twentieth-century South. The literature does not bind her private and public work together to reveal how each informed the other and minimizes rather than illuminates how incredibly important Gray's life and work is to the history of South Carolina, education, women, race, and the narrative of national progress in the interwar years.

This book offers a new interpretation of Wil Lou Gray's early life and career. Here the emphasis is placed on her role as a state worker in the early decades of the twentieth century when reorganization, centralization, and expansion of state departments into local rural communities aimed to improve social and economic conditions in the region. Historian Joseph Kett suggests that in the South reform work that pertained to the welfare of children, the family, and the community—often referred to as social progressivism—was primarily an educational movement led by individuals who saw the consolidated school as an agent of socialization and the means to impart progressive values to the rural population.[34] Progressive women used education and philanthropy to forge new institutions and occupations through which they could play a part in social reform. Gray's job as the supervisor of adult schools, specifically created for her, was a "new" occupation through which she worked to effect change in her state. This gave her a position of influence that differed from the club and church activism common among southern women at the time in that her reform efforts started from within the structure of state government. As a clubwoman she used her connections in clubs and church groups to rally an army of volunteers to assist in her efforts, but she was unique as a state agent who forged reform from the top down. From her early work as a rural supervisor in Laurens County (1912–16) to her work as the supervisor of adult schools (1919–47), Gray used her position in state government to unite rural schools and communities and forge the infrastructure that enabled the state by World War II to assume control over areas of community life where localism and individualism of rural people had traditionally resisted the intrusion of the state into local affairs. As a government representative, Gray at once effectively used her state position to advance the agendas of voluntary organizations and used voluntary networks across the state to strengthen and promote state programs at a time when there existed a general attitude of resistance to government regulation. This was brilliant considering that the status of women in the state and region at the time remained marginal. It would be the New Deal that would radically alter the presence of women in the public workforce in South Carolina, and Gray forged the way.

This book posits Gray as a state agent who used the emergent field of adult education before and specifically after World War I as a portal to carry out a sustained, shrewd attack against the illiteracy, sexism, racism, and political lethargy commonplace in South Carolina in the interwar period. With the assistance of hundreds of teachers, civic groups, academics, and volunteers, Gray transformed the campaign to eradicate illiteracy in South Carolina from a plan of eradication to a program of adult education.[35] Rural communities, charitable groups, and the state benefited from Gray's sophisticated organizational methods and social vision. Illiteracy obstructed social conduct, civic participation, and morality on one hand and economic and social progress on the other. Gray worked to diminish local influence and strengthen state and county supervision and funding of public education by establishing professional standards for teachers and inspiring citizens of the state to embrace literacy as a civic responsibility.[36]

The scope of this manuscript spans a period (1883–1935) of the establishment of Jim Crow, the emergence of Progressive Era reform movements, the growth of the southern textile industry, the influx of immigrants into the nation, the presence of professional women in the public workforce in fields such as social work and education, the proliferation of government agencies as the state expanded the scope of its influence, and the rise of the Americanization movement to combat pernicious antidemocratic ideologies such as Bolshevism and fascism.[37] In the same period, the region was burdened by epidemic pellagra, hookworm, tuberculosis, bank failures, poverty, economic depression, race violence, political resistance, localism, illiteracy, and cotton dependency. In response to these ills, experiments in educational reform were common across the South. Settlement houses, industrial education, and folk schools in the mountains of Kentucky, Tennessee, and North Carolina and in Deep South states such as Alabama addressed the needs of southerners living in the troubled region.[38] In South Carolina Gray's adult night school program and opportunity school concept contained elements of each of these types of experimental schools and resembled the work of Kentucky educator Cora Wilson Stewart, who developed adult "moonlight" schools in 1911 to fight adult illiteracy.[39] Her programs provided a testing ground for theories of learning growing out of the southern education movement and teaching institutions such as Teachers College at Columbia University, where Gray attended in 1916 and established an enduring relationship. As a trained social scientist aware of trends and methods in the field of education, she used her state position and adult school models to test new ideas and, in turn, to alter radically the understanding of the learning capacity of groups of students differentiated by age, race, economic status, and gender. This was a critical step in democratizing education because it challenged age-old assumptions about the intellect of groups labeled ignorant, specifically African Americans, mill workers, and dirt farmers in South Carolina.

Here the spotlight is cast predominantly on the first three decades of Gray's professional career (1903 to 1933) as it played out nationally against the movements for rural reform and state expansion and locally against regional race and gender politics. It is in this period that Gray's innovation as an educator, her progressive philosophy, her role as one among a cadre in the burgeoning state bureaucracy, and her part in the shift from volunteerism to state control in the field of education are revealed. South Carolina's illiterate population, white and black illiteracy combined, was among the highest in the nation between World War I and World War II.[40] Gray's work in adult education provides a vantage point from which to reconsider the political, economic, and social vision of those regional leaders in the New South who promoted reforms that facilitated government expansion in the interwar years.[41] The textile industry governed the economic climate of the state in this period, and both industrial leaders and workers shaped the dynamics of the region's political culture.[42] It was in this arena that Gray concentrated her efforts to provide basic literacy skills to illiterate men and women. She was part of a combined effort by state, civic, and industrial leadership to improve South Carolina's economy and political culture by transforming the ignorant masses into literate, efficient, and enlightened workers, citizens, consumers, and political constituents. Although Gray did not eliminate illiteracy in South Carolina during her long and exemplary career, she did transform the state's educational system in ways that impacted the economic and political landscape of the region.

Additionally the principal focus on the pre–New Deal period of Gray's work reveals how her efforts to develop adult programs were organic, creatively funded, and dependent of material support from voluntary, civic, and religious organizations. In the first three decades of the century, Gray—with support from teachers and voluntary agencies—forged the infrastructure upon which federal programs expanded into the state during the New Deal. After 1935 her visibility as a key agent of state consolidation and expansion was neutralized, as her work became part of the larger national efforts of the Works Progress Administration to employ hundreds of female writers and teachers to implement national programs. Gray's work in the decades leading up to 1935 demonstrates the significance of her efforts before federal money and programs factored into the development of adult education. With federal money came new ways of financing and defining adult education. The advent of a compulsory attendance law in South Carolina in 1937, the use of adult education as a component of New Deal programs such as the Civilian Conservation Corps, and the emergence of new work opportunities for women brought about by the relief efforts diminished Gray's distinction and visibility as these transformations enveloped her work and rolled across the nation, radically altering the relationship between government and people in the process.[43]

Multiple factors constituted the environment that made Gray's work significant and viable in the interwar period. Like most upper-class southern women, Gray participated in the federated clubs and religious organizations and capitalized on these connections in her work, but her strength as an innovator and reformer stemmed from her position in state government. In 1919 she was one of only two supervisors of adult schools in the nation. As a state bureaucrat in a position few knew anything about, she had power uncommon to most women engaged in reform. She controlled the design and implementation of adult education curriculum—a new and unknown field of inquiry—and trained a cadre of black and white teachers to adopt her social vision and impart it to the semiliterate and illiterate masses. From within the structure of state government, she had access to powerful politicians and industrialists who controlled the revenue streams of tax money. Outside the walls of government, she participated in women's clubs and civic groups and garnered public support for her ideas through media exposure and publicity. With support from outside the walls of government and from within by state agencies such as the South Carolina Illiteracy Commission, she pressured the General Assembly to advance policies to develop educational options for adults that would ultimately improve the state. With the public behind her, Gray forced the General Assembly to take notice of her vision of social progress and recognize the value of adult education for all people regardless of race or caste.[44] Although statistically she failed to eradicate illiteracy in her early career, she created the infrastructure, concepts, and methods that shaped adult and vocational education as permanent parts of the public education system.[45] In so doing she blazed a trail for female leadership in state government, gained national recognition as a social scientist, published her ideas in annual reports and scholarly articles, and carved a unique place for herself in the social fabric of the state. Although she did not overtly use her position as a platform to speak out against racism and sexism in the state, she embodied protest in her existence and carried out controversial programs that challenged these issues while remaining in the good graces of the public.

Her efforts to combat illiteracy intersected with the reign of South Carolina demagogues Benjamin Ryan Tillman, Ellison DuRant Smith, and Coleman Livingston Blease, who preyed upon the ignorant by peddling racism, antiforeign sentiment, and states' rights to their constituents. To Gray adult education was the mechanism to combat demagoguery and promote effective political choice among poor, uneducated white males, one of the adult groups she targeted. How she managed the challenges associated with a career as a public agent with a progressive agenda in a region defined by demagoguery and traditional notions of race and gender make her personal politics central to the story.

The social context of early twentieth-century reform influenced the methods Gray used to navigate the complicated politics of her region.[46] Her career trajectory crossed three important thresholds of change in the South: the southern educational crusade that began at the start of the century, World War I, and the Depression. World War I was the turning point in her career, when she moved from local supervision of education to a state leadership position. The environment of change precipitated by the war effectively enabled Gray to carve a niche for herself in state government through which she carried out a vision that changed the state's educational system. Many reformers in South Carolina imagined that changes were possible in the immediate years prior to and after the war and used the energy of the era to work for economic and political progress in the state. Gray was unique among these reformers because despite white supremacy and the politics of regional custom that enveloped her work, she found alternative ways to get around obstacles as a state worker with national connections. Initially in her early work, she did not directly agitate against custom and worked cautiously to effect reform by tapping into the patriotic atmosphere of the times, making her case on economic and political grounds. But by the thirties Gray replaced the guarded approach with more aggressive methods that directly challenged regional perceptions about race, a change in approach linked in part to the Depression, her age, her solid reputation, and her sheer determination to force her state to recognize the need for reform.[47] She moved from cautious reform to protest and had the job, vision, and community organizing skills to effect results—and keep her job.

Gray navigated the politics of her region with determination, ingenuity, and a clear-cut vision of the educational tools South Carolinians needed to be competent and productive citizens of the nation. Her work was implicitly political. Conscious of the politics of progress, she created an adult-centered education program that benefited both the powerful in the state and the illiterate masses. As a woman in a leadership position in a state where women were outside the gates of government power, she constantly negotiated what she wanted for her state and the limitations the state imposed on what she wanted, a state that remained nationally at the bottom due to a plethora of social problems. She was an educator, but she used her supervisory position in a niche field to challenge regional practices that impeded state progress. I argue that central to her success and her politics was her image. To mask effectively the politically controversial nature of her work and status as a single, professional female, Gray nurtured a neutral public image that garnered on the one hand support from the state and private organizations and on the other admiration from the people she aimed to help.[48] Although Gray worked on behalf of the state, if all groups she engaged with perceived her work as beneficial, she was able to push boundaries and accomplish goals traditional, voluntary agencies and groups could not achieve without government assistance.

For Gray the personal was political. She challenged regional gender ideals as a wage-earning, single female in a high-ranking government job in a state that did not ratify the Nineteenth Amendment until 1969 or certify it until 1973.[49] She made a visible, public statement about the capacity of women to lead in a state that at present ranks fiftieth in the nation for the number of women in public office.[50] Her actions and ideas had complex meanings that underwent constant reformation as she fought to secure a place in the public domain as female mediator between the anointed and benighted. She forged a place for herself in a rigidly traditional culture by constructing a public home where from her state job she bolstered the power of the state and nurtured the less fortunate ultimately to uplift her state in the eyes of the nation. And she received a wage for her service.

It is critical to recognize that Gray was purposeful in her choice to focus on literacy as her primary cause, particularly since she used her job as a vehicle to effect reform. Literacy by World War I was a national security issue and had the attention of powerful politicians and male leaders across the nation. Aware of this, Gray, who already worked in the field of education, took up the cause, empowering herself by leading the literacy campaign as a scholar in the niche field of adult education few understood or even knew existed. In a state where approximately half the population was illiterate when she began her work, she carved out a spot for herself in state government and used it as a portal to dispense her vision. Her awareness of deeply ingrained gender mores informed her politics and shaped how she engaged with her work, peers, community, and family and with power brokers. With ease and skill, she moved freely between the voluntary world of clubwomen and civic activists and the professional world of government bureaucrats and industrialists. She kept one foot firmly planted in the voluntary culture of the times as a member of the South Carolina Federation of Women's Clubs, the Daughters of the American Revolution, and the Washington Street Methodist Church and the other fixed within the walls of state government as a waged supervisor shaping reform from the top down. This distinguished her work because she had a position of power and influence uncommon to most women in the state and region. Historian Alice Kessler-Harris states: "When the federal government linked wage work to tangible, publicly provided rewards, employment emerged as a boundary line demarcating different kinds of citizenship. . . . mothers and domestic servants all found themselves on one side of a barrier not of their own making."[51]

Although denied the vote in the early years of her career, Gray was on the right side of this barrier as a single woman and state employee. She was the propitiation of the clubwomen's efforts and had the means as a waged state agent to shape their ideas into public policy. She worked together with women's groups in a mutually beneficial relationship. Historians Penina Glazer and Miriam Slater argue it was the ability of women who worked in education and the social sciences to "forge a synthesis between the Progressive sense of burgeoning opportunities and the separate constricted world of female endeavor" that allowed them to "play new roles and exercise . . . social, moral, and intellectual concerns in new arenas."[52]

In the early twentieth century, Gray was among a select group of southern women who obtained higher education, worked for a living, and engaged in reform to improve her state. As one observer noted, "she labored incessantly to overcome ignorance and mental poverty so that South Carolina could grow in stature and wisdom."[53] Historian Glenda Gilmore argues that the New South was hypergendered, meaning that the accentuated roles of men and women functioned to define gender relations, class politics, and race control during a time of tremendous social change.[54] Men were honorable and chivalric and the defenders of southern womanhood, and women depended on the strength and protection of their male counterparts. Historian Anne Firor Scott argues that the South had "a more rigid definition of the role of women than any other part of the country and had elevated that definition to the position of myth," and as a consequence "southern women had to follow a more devious road to emancipation than those elsewhere."[55]

Gray's career achievements undoubtedly stemmed from her respect for and adherence to cultural ideas about women in her region. But as Scott suggests, she altered her behavior remarkably by making choices that were the exception rather than the rule. She worked for a living, never married, and devoted her career to the improvement of her state, alternative choices for a white, upper-class, southern women in the early twentieth century. By not making her exceptional status an issue and capitalizing on her role as a southern elite, Gray made gains for women, African Americans, and the laboring poor without direct political confrontation with traditional social practices. She believed it was necessary to recognize the shared humanity of people despite their skin color or station in life. This was the first step needed to democratize education and, in turn, society. "Regardless of wealth, prominence, age, station, or color, humanity is her passion and democracy is her creed," observed her sister and noted South Carolina poet Harriet Gray Blackwell.[56]

It is important to recognize that Gray was marginalized by virtue of her gender in a regional culture where women were outside power and expected to be mothers and grandmothers. Yet unlike the majority of women in her region, Gray engaged on a professional basis with men in power due to the nature of her work, an action feminist standpoint theorists call border crossing. Gray mediated the structural and social inequalities she encountered in her life and work as what feminist historian Patricia Hill Collins calls the outsider within, a term that describes "the location of people who no longer belong to a group" or "the social locations . . . occupied by groups of unequal power."[57] Collins perceives outsiders within as "able to gain access to the knowledge of the group/community which they inhabit (or visit), but [they] are unable to either authoritatively claim that knowledge or possess the full power given to members of that group."[58] As an outsider within, Gray was an autonomous, self-supporting woman in a high-profile, public position engaged with people across class and racial lines, mingling among the powerful and powerless, accessing knowledge of those in power, and working to empower the dispossessed.[59] Gray is unique because she overcame the source of her marginalization, her gender, by using her access to power—her job as a waged state worker—to empower the dispossessed, which ultimately empowered herself by making her viable in a region rigidly defined by tradition where she fell outside the normative roles of women of her background.

Scholar Judith Butler argues that "gender identity might be reconceived as a personal/cultural history of received meanings subject to a set of imitative practices which refer laterally to other imitations and which, jointly, construct the illusion of a primary and interior gendered self."[60] If gender identity is performance, as Butler suggests, it can be expressed in multiple and competing ways, a particularly useful conceptual model to consider the idea that Gray navigated numerous identities in her public and private life. Her capacity to shift personas when the moment demanded kept her in good esteem with those in power, with her family, and with her peers, but it demanded that she wear many hats. Her worldview constantly entangled with her multiple and often competing identities as southerner, American, woman, professional, humanitarian, daughter, activist, and cog in the state apparatus. As the moment demanded, she tapped into these multiple identities to mediate tensions between nation and region, professional and volunteer, state and individual, prescribed mores and reality, and, ultimately, the public and private economic, social, and political demands of her life. She navigated across these identities conscious that her work impacted the people, institutions, and organizations inside of her state and proffered a new perspective about her region to those outside of the South.

The life of Wil Lou Gray reveals transitions in women's public and private activism, participation in the public workforce, dependence on a living wage, and role in state government. Her career played out against the era's cultural shifts from benevolence to state control, volunteerism to professionalism, regional reconciliation to national reunion and reformism. Gray benefited from these transitions and actively engaged in this changing landscape. She participated in the wave of reform that swept across the South in the first decades of the twentieth century and implemented an adult education program that improved her state and made her an important leader in the history of the region. Her work reveals the significant role white women played in the decades leading up to modern civil rights movement in advancing equality of opportunity to all people and demonstrates that she successfully secured small but meaningful gains for black and white adults in South Carolina in the face of depressed economic conditions, white supremacy, and race violence.[61] Her efforts reveal a nuanced picture of the implementation and impact of southern educational reform between World War I and the New Deal.

CHAPTER 1

Ancestry and Heritage

At the heart of Wil Lou Gray's politics, professional practice, and social relations was her family. The traditions of her heritage anchored her belief system and defined her sense of place within the context of her community, state, and region.[1] "One of the finest services we can render our family founders is to perpetuate their traditions," wrote Gray.[2] But she challenged many of the traditions of her heritage. Nothing in her background prefigured her decisions to pursue and receive an advanced degree, work in a public, government position, and forgo marriage and family to devote her life to public service. Although she chose a path very different from the women in her family, her identity as a member of a respected Upcountry South Carolina family positioned her to succeed.[3] Throughout her career she used her family and class connections to access powerful politicians and industrialists in the state and to rally support from women and men of her class. The time and place into which Gray was born and raised and the social position and values of her deeply rooted South Carolina family grounded her identity and shaped her worldview. She never extricated herself from the web of social relations formed by her family and class connections.

Gray's ancestors came to South Carolina from England in the mid-eighteenth century. The Dial and Gray men served in both the Revolutionary War and the Civil War and owned slaves.[4] Her paternal great-great grandfather, John Gray, settled in 1785 on 325 acres along Duncan's Creek on the Enoree River, where he lived until 1802.[5] He served during the American Revolution as a private in the South Carolina militia and supplied provisions to those fighting against Great Britain.[6]

Gray's maternal great-great grandfather, Hastings Dial, settled on a 550-acre tract in the Ninety-Sixth District deeded to him by King George III, and he remained loyal to the king during the American Revolution.[7] Dial was one of the wealthiest men and largest landowners in the Upcountry at the time.[8] His wife, Rebecca Abercrombie, was the daughter of Sir James Alexander Abercrombie, attorney general of the Colony of South Carolina from 1733 to 1742.[9] Hastings's brother Martin Dial married Rebecca's sister, Chrystie, but Martin fought in the Revolutionary War as a patriot under Colonel Hayes' Regiment.[10] For his service in the war, Martin received a 327-acre tract of land in Laurens County and established Dial's Methodist Church there in 1808.[11] Although a Loyalist during the American Revolution, Hastings and his family remained in South Carolina after the war. His grandson Hastings married Mary Hudgens, who was the daughter of Revolutionary War patriot Capt. Ambrose Hudgens.[12]

Slavery was a part of Gray's ancestry. Hastings Dial accumulated more than twenty-five hundred acres of land and owned twenty-six slaves.[13] Her paternal great-grandfather, Zachariah Gray, amassed more than six hundred acres of land and owned eleven slaves. Upon the birth of his first child in 1809, his mother-in-law conferred a "small slave girl" named Fillis to mind the infant. Fillis "soon made herself indispensable minding the baby and succeeding children as the family increased."[14] Her maternal grandfather, Albert Dial, owned six slaves who remained on the family farm after emancipation.[15] Gray's paternal grandfather, Robert Adams Gray, owned two slaves.[16] His son, William Lafayette Gray, remembered when the family's slave Zeke Goodson was carried off by a band of Union soldiers while his father was fighting in Virginia for the Confederate army.[17]

Both of Gray's grandfathers supported the Confederacy during the Civil War. Robert Adams Gray served in Virginia as a private under Gen. Robert E. Lee and taught "dozens of Confederate soldiers to read and write around the campfires."[18] His son Robert Lee Gray was born in 1864 and named in honor of the Confederate general.[19] Albert Dial earned the title of captain while serving as head of a South Carolina company of militia in the antebellum years.[20] After the Civil War, he worked "courageously to rid South Carolina of the Carpet-Baggers and Scalawags" that appeared in the South during Reconstruction and "put forth every effort in order that South Carolinians could once again have a state of which to be proud."[21] Defective eyesight prevented him from actually fighting in the Civil War, but he contributed financially to the cause.[22] When the Confederacy lost, Dial lost everything, but "only by the utmost diligence was the Captain able to make a comeback."[23] He rebuilt his farm, diversified his interests, and became a model of the planter-industrialist in the region. He devoted his time to farming until 1870, when he became a merchant and built a commercial enterprise in the city.[24]

The Gray and Dial families managed to hold on to their social status and property after the Civil War. Traditions were sacrosanct to this generation of southerners and became more important after the Confederate loss in the war. In the wake of defeat, many southerners memorialized and mythologized the past in an effort to cope with the harsh realities of their surroundings. Many white southerners believed that life had actually been better prior to the conflict.[25] The key to perpetuating and preserving a sectional identity amid the dislocation and disorder that marked the postwar years was to maintain a sense of place, a community and environment that constantly reaffirmed one's identity, the phenomenon writer Eudora Welty believed balanced the southerner. "Sense of place gives equilibrium; extended, it is a sense of direction too," she wrote, "but it is the sense of place going with us still that is the ball of golden thread to carry us there and back and in every sense of the word to bring us home."[26]

To the Gray and Dial families, Laurens was that place. Gray was born in the decade after Reconstruction. It was a time of patent change in South Carolina, and the region struggled to establish some degree of economic, social, and political order in the wake of defeat, occupation, and redemption. Laurens did not escape the economic uncertainty, racial conflict, educational crises, and social confusion that plagued South Carolina in the postwar years. The town lies in the northwest portion of the Piedmont in a region known as the upcountry. It was described as a town where magnolias, elms, and crepe myrtle trees lined the streets and added to the town's "inimitable charm."[27] Most white residents stemmed from Welsh, Scotch-Irish, English, and German heritage, but an almost equal number of African Americans lived in the town as well. The men in the region were reputed to be fierce political independents. This trait often affected the relationship between the Upcountry and Lowcountry planters and insured a balance of political power between the two regions.[28]

At the time of Gray's birth in 1883, Laurens was an agrarian community. Local output of lumber, brick, stone, and cement was a portion of the economic base, but agricultural products were the backbone. The principal commodity and source of revenue was cotton.[29] The large cotton production enabled the county to maintain four cotton mills serviced on a regular basis by the Port Royal and Western Carolina Railroad. Although Laurens lies just thirty miles from the textile center of Greenville, industrialization came slowly to the town, and it remained predominantly rural.

As an agrarian community, the pace of life in Laurens was slow. Although it had a thriving merchant class, it served an agricultural region. The townspeople desired that the town remain small in an effort to control the political and economic development of the area.[30] They were successful in their aim. Property sold from five to twenty-five dollars per acre, and houses rented for about one hundred dollars per year. Horse and buggy served as the mode of transportation until the first horseless buggy—a car—appeared in 1905. The technological advancements in farming associated with industrial growth were threatening to small farm operations. To assist and protect the state's yeomanry, Gov. "Pitchfork" Ben Tillman established Clemson College in 1889, thirty miles north of Laurens, to disseminate new techniques in agricultural science to South Carolinians.[31]

Where farm technology found a home in Laurens, health reform did not. The medical illiteracy of the people of Laurens combined with unsanitary living conditions proved a double-edged sword to a community plagued by tuberculosis and hookworm. Even the most educated people in the community refused to recognize scientific progress and chose to remain blissfully ignorant. Gray's father cursed modern science when his sweet well water was diagnosed unfit to drink by Clemson College scientists.[32]

In 1883 the educational system in Laurens suffered the same problems that plagued schools across the South. The combination of poorly prepared teachers, uneducated parents, and poverty made teaching an exhausting and challenging task.[33] The conditions were harsh in the schools that did exist, and materials were scarce. A typical school had one room heated by a potbellied stove and depended upon the local community to supply equipment and books. The lack of phones, electricity, and indoor plumbing in the area until the 1890s added to the dismal physical learning environment in the schools. Laurens County had two private schools, the Laurens Female College and the Clinton Male High School, and each maintained a combined enrollment of less than 150 students. The average annual teaching salary was $300 for a male teacher and $275 for a female.[34] The lack of an enforced compulsory attendance law in South Carolina and delays in the enforcement of child labor laws facilitated illiteracy among poor families in the community where children were vital farmhands and the harvest took precedence over school.[35] Moreover the lack of health education in the region offered no preventive measures for health conditions such as hookworm and pellagra. Pellagra was epidemic in the South and in 1915 killed more than one thousand people in the state. In 1914 the first pellagra hospital in the nation opened in Spartanburg.[36]

Laurens bore the battle scars of the Civil War, and antebellum traditions did not die in the little town. The community numbered about 450 whites and 350 blacks after the war.[37] Although the black community in Laurens was almost equal in number to that of the white community, the civil rights of blacks went unrealized.[38] The community was largely illiterate, and most worked as domestics, farmers, and field hands.[39] During the last three decades of the nineteenth century, Jim Crow, the system of legal segregation, found a home in Laurens, and these policies relegated blacks to a social position that reinforced their political, social, and economic inferiority. The racial values of the community were evident in the established systems of lynching, tenant farming, and sharecropping.[40]

Laurens was a center of the disfranchisement movement in the state. The ruling white Democrats maintained their stronghold in the area by implementing policies and actions that kept the freedmen from exercising their newly gained civil rights. Laurens gained national attention for a race riot in 1870 and was known as a hub for racially motivated terrorist activity. The riot of 1870 occurred when fighting broke out between blacks and whites near the courthouse. Laurens was placed under martial law with eight other counties in 1871 as part of the second federal Enforcement Act.[41] Historian Allen Trelease explains that Red Shirts who disrupted the election in Laurens County orchestrated the race riot of 1870. He cites that three hundred blacks, with the help of white Republicans, faced up to one thousand white vigilantes. Democratic clubs, akin to the Ku Klux Klan, inspired racial terrorism and used intimidation and violence as political devices to control the black population. In Laurens County these methods worked. Less than half of eligible blacks cast their votes in the 1880s, and few if any did so by the end of the century.[42]

The Red Shirts exhibited the general race sentiment of the town and region at large, and the organization was instrumental in procuring white supremacy in the area. A white paramilitary club, the Red Shirts used intimidation to inspire votes for the Democratic Party. The men who participated wore red flannel shirts, rode on horseback, and openly disrupted black voting rights at polls. In his recollection of the Red Shirts, well-known South Carolina newspaper editor William Watts Ball recalled the impossibility of finding a red shirt in the stores in Laurens, a sign of the local support the community gave to this group.[43]

In Laurens the Red Shirts secured the election of Wade Hampton in 1876. They scattered the black voters who had been rounded up and locked in the jail by the local Radical Republicans to secure votes for Hampton's opponent, Daniel Chamberlain.[44] Gray's stepmother, Mary Dunklin Gray, proudly recorded this election-day spectacle in her biography, referring to the Red Shirts as "patriotic men on horseback, wearing shirts of crimson flannel." She recalled "the color and thrill, the sound and drama" of the day as women and children in horse-drawn buggies and men on horses listened to bands play "The Bonnie Blue Flag" endlessly. Mary claimed that her regional passions first stirred at this event when "her heart swelled with something she could not name.... She knew intuitively that she would live or die for this nameless thing, this thing of the spirit for which the Red Shirts rode."[45]

This thing of the spirit underscored the racial violence and segregation that defined regional race relations in the decades following the Confederate loss in the Civil War. A local farmer declared the two most important developments in South Carolina history as "the Red Shirt movement and the entire elimination of the Negro as a factor in South Carolina politics."[46] The state's notorious Election Law of 1882 required separate ballots and boxes for each office challenged. Historian Hugh Bailey suggests that the law "imposed enough limitations on aiding illiterate voters to effectively neutralize the political power" of blacks in the democratic process.[47] The years after Democratic redemption of the South were some of the darkest for African Americans in South Carolina. Violence, disenfranchisement, and segregation defined race relations. Race-baiting demagogue politicians emerged, such as Benjamin Tillman and later Coleman Blease and Ellison DuRant Smith, who dominated South Carolina politics well into the twentieth century. These leaders played upon white working-class fears of economic competition from free black labor.[48] Historian Dan Carter claims these men rose to power by attacking their conservative opponents as rich, self-interested men. But once elected, the demagogues "made their peace with powerful interest groups and offered their working-class supporters little more than a heavy-dose" of race-baiting rhetoric.[49] Gray's male family members opposed Tillman and his followers. Conservative "Bourbon" Democrats, they represented the men Tillman accused of wearing "boiled shirts."[50]

Wil Lou Gray's male family members participated in the Red Shirt movement in Laurens. Her grandfather Albert Dial, a local merchant and farmer, exclaimed during the election of 1876, "Give us Good Government and we give you our suffrage be we called what we may."[51] His son, Nathaniel Dial, practiced law in the firm of John Haskell, whose brother was a Red Shirt and son-in-law of Wade Hampton. After graduation from Wofford College in 1876, Gray's father, William Lafayette Gray, returned to Laurens and studied law with Col. Beaufort Watts Ball, the father of the *Charleston News and Courier* editor William Watts Ball. The young Ball, born in Laurens in 1868, was only eight in 1876 but later wrote a recollection of his experience in the events of that year. He held Wade Hampton's hat on Election Day 1876 during the Red Shirts' successful disruption of black Republican votes.[52] Wil Lou Gray's father and grandfather, and presumably most of the male members of her family, participated in this event.

Historian W. Scott Poole argues that as late as 1932, South Carolina politicians invoked the Red Shirt campaign of 1876 to remind the public of the power of Democratic political unity. He further argues that white men used a gendered rhetoric of resistance to fight against the occupation of the region, black political rights, and the social instability of the postwar era. Poole writes, "Both a South Carolina gendered as feminine and the actual wives, sisters and mothers who inhabited the domestic sphere faced 'violation' if yeoman did not resist an intrusive central government. The only options were 'manly resistance' or effeminate submission."[53] Mary Dunklin Gray's account of the Red Shirt rally in Laurens reinforces this idea. She referred to the men as patriots who resisted the intrusion of Republican occupation by fighting to restore their honor and political viability in the 1876 election. Her passions for her region were stirred by the manly show of force displayed by the Red Shirts that day. These beliefs undoubtedly shaped Gray's understanding of her region's history and her view of womanhood, family, and masculinity.

The generation of children raised during Reconstruction was vital to both regional progress and retention of the old order social status and economic power in the New South. Gray's parents, William and Sarah Gray, were part of this group and bore the responsibility of learning how to live in this new place without abandoning the values and traditions of their heritage. William would pass on to his children the importance of heritage and the narrative of the Civil War known as the "Lost Cause."[54]

William Lafayette Gray received a common school education in Laurens and attended Wofford College from 1872 to 1876. At Wofford he was a member of the Kappa Alpha fraternity, a group that promoted the chivalric protection of "Dieu et les dames" (God and the ladies) and honored the life and work of Robert E. Lee.[55] Upon graduation at the age of twenty, he taught at Chestnut Ridge in Laurens County for two years then served as principal of the Laurensville Male Academy and prepared for a career in law under the tutelage of Col. Beaufort Watts Ball. He was admitted to the South Carolina bar in 1878 and briefly practiced in the firm of J. L. Irby.[56] Like William, Sarah went to college, receiving her degree in 1878 from Spartanburg Woman's College, a Methodist sister institution to Wofford.[57] She married William in 1879.

William's law career lasted just three years and ended soon after a case he successfully defended in 1881. The case involved a black man named Henry Whittimore, who was accused of killing his wife and subsequently setting fire to their home. With his Red Shirt background, it is unclear why William chose to defend Whittimore, but it is plausible he represented the man for the sole purpose of criminal trial experience. The jury returned a sentence of not guilty after thirty minutes of deliberation. The following day Whittimore brought "a pumpkin, some apples and hickory nuts" as a token of thanks to William and expressed his intention to marry a woman named Magnolia Bowers that afternoon. William asked if it were not too soon after the trial for such an event, and according to William's wife, Mary Dunklin Gray, who recounted the event in her biography, Whittimore confessed, "Mr. Gray, don't you never tell nobody, but I did kill Annie. I was half-drunk and we got to quarrelin' and I hit her in the head with an ax and poured kerosene around the house and set it a-fire."[58]

This story elicits numerous questions about William Gray's racial ideology, his view of justice, and his character, issues that shaped his worldview and undoubtedly influenced that of his daughter. The Whittimore case took place a few short years after the Red Shirt riot at the Laurens courthouse that played a role in restoring home rule to the region, a rally in which William took part.[59] It is unlikely that William used his newly acquired law degree to challenge regional race interactions by way of this one case. It is more plausible that William took the case on as a test to try his hand at his new legal skills. Because Whittimore was black, whether or not justice was served may not have been important. In the wake of the confession by his client, however, justice was apparently important enough to William that it prompted his decision to quit practicing law. There is no proof that he retired as a consequence of this event, but it is recorded in his second wife's biography as if it was a catalyst for his choice. In 1881 his court win coupled with his client's confession must have been bewildering. It is not known what happened to Henry Whittimore after the trial, but it is clear that William Gray was disillusioned with law and became a merchant and farmer.[60]

After his brief legal career, Gray emerged a privileged and prominent member of the thriving commercial sector of Laurens. In 1883, at the time of his daughter's birth, he was a shareholder in the People's Loan and Exchange, the Oil and Fertilizer Company of Laurens, the Laurens Building and Loan Association, and the Port Royal and Western Carolina Railway and an active member of the Methodist Episcopal Church. He owned interest in the Ware Shoals Water Power of Laurens County and a hardware store and served as a member of the Wofford College Board of Advisors.[61] He owned valuable farmland in the area and also worked as a cotton buyer.[62] In 1887 his father-in-law, Albert Dial, became the president of the People's Loan and Exchange, a position he held until his death. As a shareholder in the bank controlled by his father-in-law, Gray was privy to special considerations granted to "good depositors with a good balance," such as reduced interest rates.[63]

In his classic book *Origins of the New South*, historian C. Vann Woodward argued that a new elite emerged in the New South that marked a break from prewar leadership. Often called the "Old Whig" thesis, Woodward's interpretation created what historian James Tice Moore calls the "Woodward wars" by the 1970s, a feud defined by those who supported Woodward's view of change in the New South versus those who disagreed. Moore argues that the Woodward interpretation can be almost completely discounted in South Carolina, where the Redeemers, many of whom were part of the planter elite prior to the war, resumed power at the end of Reconstruction.[64] The Gray and Dial men were Bourbon Democrats, also known as Redeemers, who had prestige and power before and after the war. Moreover these men modified their economic interests to meet the postwar needs of the area. They remained rooted in Laurens, and although the two families faced adversity during the Reconstruction years, their diversified business interests placed them among the leaders in South Carolina and the New South.[65]

Historian Lacy Ford has shown that the real power in the New South was in the hands of those who controlled the extension of credit.[66] The economy relied upon sharecropping, tenancy, and crop lien, and merchants and institutions with lending power determined who received preferential treatment. William Gray's choice to marry the daughter of Albert Dial inextricably bound his access to credit to his personal web of close family relations. His brother Robert Lee Gray married Emma Dial, a sister of William's wife, Sarah. Thus the two Gray brothers married into the Dial clan, lived beside each other in Laurens, and enjoyed, by virtue of marriage, privileged banking status.[67] There is no doubt that in this unique, financially powerful, extended family relation, knowledge of finance and economic development schemes in the town were exchanged over Sunday dinners and relaxing afternoons on the porch and at family gatherings.

William Gray was among a group of men who Ford suggests had a "sense of collective purpose, the air of self-confidence, that transformed the Upcountry mercantile community, and some of the large landholders as well, into a cohesive bourgeoisie" anxious to leave their imprint on the state.[68] Reared during the Civil War and Reconstruction, he grew up in a time when the nation pushed for sectional uniformity and racial, social, and economic transformation of the South. He reconciled his heritage and personal history to coexist with the changing landscape.[69] As a result he retained prestige in the community, participated in local politics, directed the economic progress of Laurens, and maintained a position of influence in the area.

Another very important family connection was William Gray's relationship with his brother-in-law Nathaniel Dial, a lawyer and a successful politician. Both Gray and Dial were Bourbon Democrats who favored conservative progress rather than the fiery, race-baiting rhetoric and strategies of their opponents, known by the 1890s as Tillmanites.[70] The agrarian protest of the 1890s was a rebellion against the success of conservative Democrats such as Gray and Dial. Historian Jerry Slaunwhite claims that Dial was "one of the most constructive architects of the New South" but that his "arrogance cost him votes among constituents and his wealth prompted many people to regard his political ambition with suspicion."[71] Dial served as mayor of Laurens from 1887 to 1891 and again in 1895, declined to serve as Grover Cleveland's nominee in 1893 as the consul to Zurich, Switzerland, and during his political career challenged for office three of America's best-known demagogues: Benjamin Ryan Tillman in 1912 and in 1918 for state senator, Coleman Livingston Blease in 1918 and 1924 for state senator, and Ellison DuRant Smith in 1926 in the Democratic primary.[72] Dial practiced law at the firm Haskell and Dial and later Dial and

Todd. His political and business affiliation with Alexander C. Haskell, Tillman's opponent in the gubernatorial elections of 1890, labeled him a "Haskellite" and anti-Tillman for the duration of his career. Blease supporters used this against him in 1918 and 1924.[73] His greatest political win came in 1918 when he defeated the legendary Blease in the race for the Democratic seat in the United States Senate. He served from 1919 to 1925.[74]

Both Dial and Gray served as state politicians in the 1920s. As a senator from 1919 to 1925, Dial voted against many measures that challenged his conservative politics and arguably caused his subsequent failed attempts to stay in office. He voted against child labor legislation that prohibited children under age eighteen from working. He argued that federal legislation interfered with the state's right to regulate age in the workplace, and the bill failed to be ratified by South Carolina. He voted against the Soldier's Bonus and Compensation Bill that paid bonuses to veterans of World War I in the form of cash or life insurance. He decried the spending habits of Congress, often in the form of pensions for veterans of American wars and subsidies to northern companies. He also voted against the Nineteenth Amendment that gave women the vote and helped derail ratification of the amendment in South Carolina.[75] Dial further attacked the rights of women when in 1921 the state passed a secondary law that prohibited women from serving on a jury, a law that remained intact until 1966.[76] Gray served as a Laurens County representative to the South Carolina General Assembly from 1922 to 1924.[77] Their political success undoubtedly influenced the politics and skills of Wil Lou Gray during her early career.

William and Sarah Gray had three children: Albert Dial in 1881, Wil Lou on August 29, 1883, and Robert Coke in 1888. Although they had a small family in contrast to those of their parents and siblings, who had nine or more children, William and Sarah's close contact with relatives made for a large extended household. These kinship bonds forged lifelong friendships between Wil Lou Gray and her relatives. In her final years, she recalled that her "family was a close knit group.... We all Grays and Dials lived in Laurens."[78]

Gray was described as an "enchanting child, plump as a cupid, with very fair skin and red curls."[79] She loved to talk, ride about town in her goat-pulled wagon, and listen to her mother read stories.[80] People considered her a tomboy, and she was often scolded for sitting on the gatepost of her home and talking to everyone who passed by. Gray recalled that her mammy scolded her and said, "Missy, you know it ain't ladylike." Gray replied, "But, mammy, people are a lot more interesting than being ladylike."[81] Affectionately known as Mammy, Addie Byrd was the black woman to whom Gray referred. Gray's half-sister, Harriet Gray, described Byrd in the following way: "Mammy was a medium-brown woman with deep-set dark eyes, pleasant features and deft hands. She braided her hair close to her well-shaped head, and her skin stretched softly over high cheekbones. Her mouth was quick with sparkling words spoken in a durable-sounding voice, and she was not stingy with smiles that grew into throaty laughs. While she was ample she was neatly put together, with no surplus material to create an effect of untidiness. Invariably the general impression Addie Byrd made was one of competence and honesty, the overall lavishly spread with her own inimitable charm."[82]

Gray enjoyed a sheltered childhood devoid of the poverty and destitution commonplace to many in her hometown. Her household included a black woman who cared for her, fine linens and sterling silver tableware, cooks, housemaids, lovely clothes, a large, loving extended family, and a sense of belonging to the community's affluent class. She socialized and attended church and school with people like her. Her family lived in a modest home that was a wedding gift to her parents from her grandfather Albert Dial. The house lacked electricity and running water until 1896 and relied upon a privy for waste disposal and a well for water. Fireplaces warmed her home, and kerosene lamps brought light to the dark country nights. There were many jobs done by paid labor in the Gray household. Miss Mollie Bonham cleaned and cared for the children; the laundry was sent out each week; each meal was prepared by the cook and served formally in the dining room; ice was delivered twice a week; and canning was done each summer at Gray Court. The tenant farmers on the farms provided fresh meat and produce year round. "My first memory of Christmas," recalled Gray, "was a happy one.... Everything had to be done at home... storing, preparing, cooking, decorating... all this in preparation for the family dinners."[83]

A series of events shocked Gray between the ages of seven and twelve and seared within her a deep commitment to her family and an eternal spirit of optimism she manifested throughout her life. The death of her mother, her subsequent relocation to live with relatives, and her father's remarriage were critical events that defined Gray's adolescence. The trauma of her mother's death in 1893 was complicated by her father's decision to send his children to live with relatives for three years. In the interim he married Mary Dunklin, who the Gray family knew as a babysitter, neighbor, and friend. In these critical years of emotional and physical development, Gray's life was turned upside down. She would never outgrow the pains of her childhood.

In 1890, when Gray was seven, her mother, Sarah, became ill with tuberculosis. The disease settled in her lungs and had the side effects of chest pain, fatigue, night sweats, coughing, and weight loss.[84] The lack of modern plumbing contributed to the unsanitary conditions in rural areas such as Laurens, and the well from which Gray's family drew their drinking water stood in close proximity to the privy. The water was found in later years to be "teeming with bacteria."[85]

Sarah suffered for two years under the strains of the sickness, and throughout the ordeal William and the children went to great lengths to ensure her comfort. The tension created by her mother's illness made Gray eager to please and finish well the simple, practiced tasks of her young life. William Gray followed his daughter's example and did what he felt necessary to help his wife improve. Although an ardent teetotaler, he purchased whiskey to allay Sarah's cough and kept a decanter on the fireplace mantle in her bedroom. Young Wil Lou, though instructed to stay away from the caramel-colored liquid, once took a swig while her parents were out. It burned so ferociously that she spit it into the fire, causing a great flame to leap out into the room. She believed the fires of hell had come to consume her, and she never touched a drop of alcohol again her entire life.[86]

Gray first encountered death when she was six years old and observed a wake behind her house held for a "dead baby wearing a white lace dress and bonnet" in a "beautiful white casket." When she asked her mother about the event, Sarah told her that the little baby had gone to live with the angels in heaven, a peaceful place where everyone lived happily after they died.[87] Years later, when death came to the Gray home, Sarah's explanation of heaven may have instilled in her child a sense of peace about dying.

Sarah died in January 1893, whispering "I see the angels coming" in her last breath.[88] Sarah's sister Emma Dial Gray wrote a recollection of the event and recalled, "She was content to die young. Although called upon to bear months of suffering... her trust in God never wavered and death was met without fear. One wondered at the grace that enabled her to accept with resignation the inevitable."[89] Gray remembered that "her most marked characteristic[s] were her self sacrificing, unselfish disposition, and her loving, sympathetic nature never too busy or tired to give her time to those who needed her care.... Her helpfulness only heaven can repay."[90]

Gray claimed never to have wept in the open after her mother's death because she felt the need to be strong for her brothers and father.[91] Years later in 1918, on her thirty-fifth birthday, Gray received a letter from her father that explained his emotional state at the time of Sarah's death. William Gray told her that as a little girl she had been a "supreme source of comfort" during the traumatic time. He wrote: "When it seemed more than I could bear, it was then that you threw your little arms around my neck and so affectionately appealed to me to be resigned—Ever since when the way seems rough and the sky became clouded with despondency—it seems to have been your mission in life to come in with your optimistic disposition and dispel gloom with sunshine. I pray that you may live as long as I do and I may long have the joy of your companionship through life."[92]

Sarah Louise Dial Gray.
Author's collection.

Although he remembered his daughter as a great comfort in his moment of grief, he was little comfort to his grieving children. In the wake of the tragedy, William coped with his sorrow by sending them away to live with his sister Laura and her husband, Dr. Jerome Christopher, in nearby Gray Court.[93] Laura had a large cotton farm but no children, and his siblings Dora, Lula, and Robert lived within a few miles of Laura and agreed to take responsibility for the children. William came to visit once a week, and this was the state of the Gray family for three years.[94] The children had no choice but to accept their circumstances and patiently wait to see their father each Sunday afternoon. Six days of the week they turned to each other for comfort.

Gray and her brothers, Dial and Coke, developed a close bond during this period. In 1904 Coke delivered Gray to her first teaching job at rural Jones School, and later, in 1921, Dial christened her first summer opportunity school at Tamassee, South Carolina, with a barrel of flour.[95] It is cruel irony that in 1946 both brothers died within twelve hours of each other and left Gray with "man's only real possession . . . a memory."[96] On her eighty-first birthday, Gray reflected, "I had such a quiet peaceful day with the music of the rain on the tin roof and somehow I felt Dial and Coke were with me during the day. . . . Loved ones who have gone away without too much sense of separation are all to me very much alive only in another sphere."[97]

During those years apart from his children, William bought an extra farm, taught Sunday school, and courted his neighbor Mary Dunklin, who was just ten years older than his daughter.[98] Despite the seventeen-year age difference between William and Mary, she was a longtime family friend. Having lost her father when she was eight, she looked upon William as a father figure.[99] Mary often babysat the children during Sarah Gray's illness.[100] William managed to share his time, money, and problems with Mary in the years preceding his wife's death.[101] Like a father he was instrumental in every step of her academic and professional development. He made sure she received a suitable education and career. When she turned seventeen, Mary received a scholarship to study at Columbia College in the state capital as a result of William's encouragement. He even drove her to the depot the day she left for college. Upon her graduation from Columbia College, William secured her a teaching position in Laurens due in part to his influence on the school board.[102] Mary was present the day the children were sent to live in Gray Court with their aunt, and she remembered how they clung to her moments before they were taken away.[103]

William and Mary married on December 18, 1895.[104] The children attended the nuptials, and Mary recalled how they stood "near the window, looking after their father whom they could no longer see" as he rode off on his honeymoon to New York City. They reunited with the newlyweds on Christmas Day.[105] With the marriage the Gray family was restored and made whole again on the eve of a new year. However the adjustment to the new family was not simple. Mary came from a small household that consisted of her mother and her brother, Jim. According to her biographer, she never imagined mothering three children that were not her own, especially the Gray children for whom she had babysat while a teenager. Furthermore the vast number of relatives and family get-togethers that were customary to the Gray clan were now a part of her life, and she found the constant engagement with relatives not only exhausting but also inconvenient and time-consuming.[106]

Like Mary the Gray children struggled to accept the new situation. Having lost his mother and in essence his father, the eldest Gray child, Albert Dial, did not like the dramatic change that took place in the life of his family. The fourteen-year-old was eight years Mary's junior and left for Spartanburg Finishing School at Wofford College within a few weeks of the family's reunion.[107] He stayed on at Wofford to attend college and married Lillian Caine of Laurens when he graduated. They moved next door to Mary and William in Laurens, and he bought a farm and worked as a traveling salesman for Red Baron flour, traveling between Laurens and Hopkinsville, Kentucky.[108] He fathered three daughters, Rosa, Marigene, and Toccoa, and one son, Albert Dial Jr., and required that his children visit Mary Dunklin, even though his daughter claimed that he considered Mary "bossy, too talkative," and "someone who never looked at you."[109] Albert Dial paid respect to Mary out of a sense of duty even though his dislike of her "turned [his children] against her."[110] Albert Dial eventually became a cotton broker and retired after accumulating what his family claims to be approximately one thousand acres of land in Laurens County.[111] His only son named his first granddaughter Wil Lou Gray II in honor of his sister.

Coke's adjustment to the new family was easier. He was only seven when the family reunited, and he was partially blind. He had a hard time in school and did not attend beyond the fifth grade. Mary felt compassion for the child and took his education upon herself and became his tutor.[112] She read to him on a regular basis and helped him learn what he could not see to study. His visual impairment kept him from attending college but did not limit his life. He married Virginia Agnew of Due West, South Carolina, and soon after moved to Gastonia, North Carolina, to sell Honey Boy Ice Cream. He did extremely well in this business and moved to Columbia in 1930 to retire. Here he played the stock market and served as a silent partner in a prominent car dealership. He remained connected to Laurens through the cotton and peach production on the land he owned with Albert Dial. Since he had no children, his estate went to his only sister after Virginia's death.[113]

It is unknown whether Wil Lou Gray struggled with the new marriage, but she did struggle with the exodus of her older brother from the household in early 1896. Mary recalled in her biography that the first night after Albert left for school in January 1896, Coke and her new stepdaughter were "dawdling and dallying" at bedtime, nervous "about sleeping upstairs without Dial."[114]

At this point female guidance and influence in Wil Lou Gray's life resumed. For the first time in years, Gray had a mother, someone to answer her questions, doubts, and fears and to serve as an example of what a woman was expected to be. This no doubt required a period of adjustment. Although Gray lived with family members who were women during her stay in Gray Court, she identified with her brothers, and people considered her to be a tomboy.[115] One tribute to Gray claimed that "as a child in school, Wil Lou was always most interested in the active subjects and people.... She was forever organizing her friends into games, though her brothers tried to put her in her place by telling her girls had no sense and could not compete with them in school."[116] She proved their chauvinism wrong with academic and professional success during her remarkable career. Whether the men in her family were the real source of motivation in Gray's life is a question that cannot be answered.

The lack of intimate female guidance at a critical time in her development may have instilled in Gray a spirit of liberation. Without the constant reinforcement that a woman's place was in the home, she experienced a degree of autonomy as a child that may account for her independent spirit and choice to live a life of public rather than domestic servitude. One of the main reasons Gray claimed to have never married was because she feared "a man would hold her back."[117] And it may also account for her ability to love her family, her students, her work, and her state. Historian Blanche Wiesen Cook argues that "until recently, historians . . . have preferred to see our great women writers and activists as asexual spinsters, odd gentlewomen who sublimated their lust in their various good works. But as we consider their true natures, we see that it was frequently their ability to express love . . . that enabled them to achieve all that they did achieve."[118] Although she received "two or three" marriage proposals, including one from Isaac Gray of Woodruff, South Carolina, Gray refused to marry because the men who asked "were not smart enough" and "would limit her."[119] She said in her old age that "she did not miss anything by not getting married."[120] This view of marriage as an impediment to freedom of choice illustrates an independence that Gray plausibly formed and fortified in her youth.

In relation to identity formation, this is very important. How Gray managed to acquire such emotional fortitude is a perplexing question that can best be answered by examining her within the context of adolescent development. Psychologists define separation-individuation as a developmental phase in adolescence when the adolescent becomes less dependent on the family and takes an increasing responsibility for his or her own behavior and identity. The disruption of Gray's home environment may have caused this process to occur prematurely. Her strength and self-identity formed in part from the trauma of her mother's illness and death.[121] In *Endings: A Sociology of Death and Dying,* Michael Kearl argues that death can impact children by causing depression and withdrawal or it can inspire individuals to achieve new levels in their performances.[122] Instead of acting out her grief in a negative way, Gray channeled her energy and anxiety into activities and pleasing behaviors that won approval.[123]

Education was an important part of Gray's development. In the aftermath of her mother's death, she was one grade level behind her peers in school, a sign of the impact of death and displacement in her formative years.[124] She completed the tenth grade in 1899 at the Laurensville Female College, a private school established in 1829 by Dorothy Teague and Isabella Mason Young. The institution was reputed to be one of the finest in the Upcountry and required studies in "Latin, Greek, ancient geography, algebra, philosophy, chemistry, geometry, trigonometry, English literature, composition, the essentials of Christianity, analogy, and astronomy."[125]

Wil Lou Gray, 1896.
Author's collection.

It was built and maintained by the Presbyterian Synod of South Carolina and gained wide support from many denominations. It served only females until 1887, when boys were allowed admission into the primary department. The school perpetuated the tenets of progress and southern heritage. Laurensville Female Academy advertised that its textbooks were "the most modern" and proudly announced a "preference to Southern authors."[126]

Gray prepared for college at this preparatory school until the age of sixteen. The glaring gap in South Carolina education at the time was the lack of tax-supported secondary schools to prepare students adequately to enter college. Just four years after her high school graduation, the superintendent of education in South Carolina, O. B. Martin, calculated that there were just 606 pupils in the private schools and a scant 253 in the public common schools prepared to enter college.[127] Whether his estimation included women is unknown, but in a total state population of approximately 1.5 million people, of which half were black, this was an extremely small, privileged group.[128]

Upon graduation in the fall of 1899, Gray enrolled at the all-female Columbia College in the state capital. When she left Laurens, she was among the 2.8

percent of American women who attended college at the turn of the century.[129] A decade later fewer than fifty thousand women held a college degree, and Gray would be among this elite group.[130] Historian Joan Marie Johnson states that "colleges fostered self-confidence and intellectual curiosity and encouraged their graduates to go beyond the traditional domestic role expected of women at the time."[131] Although Johnson suggests that there were very few legitimate southern women's colleges and that the primary function of these schools was to bolster traditional gender roles, Gray's pursuit of higher education inspired her toward self-reliance and professional autonomy and away from the domestic ideal.[132] By 1900 women's clubs and associations, higher education, and new occupations enlarged the traditional boundaries for American women, and during this period women moved toward achieving a greater degree of participation in public life. Gray was among these women. Historian Linda Rosenzweig argues that the period from 1880 to 1920 disrupted the generational continuity between the world of daughters and the world of their mothers and grandmothers.[133] Gray, motherless at age nine, was liberated from the generational restraint of the traditional mother-daughter relationship, and that may explain in part her willingness to embrace new opportunities for women to engage in public life. She declared that "my college opportunity changed me and inspired me."[134]

CHAPTER 2

Awakening

From 1899 to 1912, Wil Lou Gray attended college, worked as a teacher in rural South Carolina, taught at Martha Washington College in Abingdon, Virginia, and earned a master of arts in political science at Columbia University. Her education and early work experience intersected with southern reform campaigns for suffrage, education, prison reform, prohibition, and child labor legislation. It is in this period that advanced education, exposure to regions outside of the South, and participation in reform awakened her interest in rural education reform. From this period of intellectual growth, Gray emerged as a "new woman" of the New South who engaged in reform through women's clubs and associations and through her occupation as a teacher.[1] In a region defined by traditional ideas about women and race, Gray pursued advanced training beyond her college degree in search of not only methods and ideas about how to improve social conditions in rural South Carolina, but also her place within the larger landscape of work and reform in the South.[2]

When Gray arrived at Columbia College in 1899, her schoolmates numbered "about 100 … it was a lovely group," and each paid $225 dollars for room, board, and instruction.[3] She described herself as "not so much a student as a person who liked to read, liked to do things."[4] Organized in 1854 by the Washington Street Methodist Church, the college was located on Plain (now Hampton) Street two blocks east of the church in the heart of the city. Church attendance was mandatory each week, and every Sunday while the college was in session, Gray and her classmates graced the pews en masse.[5] Here people of her same class and faith surrounded her, and many of the women in the congregation actively participated in the social reform efforts of the day.

Gray's ties to the Methodist Church provided the basis for her social work and philosophy of social justice.[6] The denomination promoted the tenet of the Social Gospel, a belief that the Kingdom of God could be built on earth through reform of the social order.[7] Historian Archie Vernon Huff states that "of all the sects in the South, the Methodists were deeply influenced by the Social Gospel."[8] Historian John Eighmy argues that the Methodists were the most receptive to the Social Gospel and "churchmen of the New South became more receptive to outside ideas, more responsive to social ills and more involved in the Protestant search for secular relevance" during the Progressive Era. He adds that social Christianity was a national movement and the South, although aware of its sectional distinction, was very much a part of the national experience.[9] Gray stated that she "was a quiet promoter of social justice" and had always felt the difference between what she had in contrast to those in need.[10] Influenced by social Christianity, she addressed "the needs of humanity with the gospel of love" and believed in the "unbounded potential of the human spirit."[11]

While Gray was a student, the charitable work under way at the Washington Street Methodist Church exposed her to progressive ideas about social reforms that aimed to improve the lives of her fellow citizens. The Woman's Christian Temperance Union (WCTU), the Women's Missionary Society, and the Woman's Society of Christian Service were organizations within her church that motivated the women members to participate in social reform. Many of the women in the congregation served in civic clubs such as the South Carolina Federation of Women's Clubs and assisted Gray throughout her career as a force of unpaid but dedicated voluntary workers. In addition to a reform impulse among the women of the church, preservation of heritage was an equally strong message advocated by the congregation at large. Many churchwomen participated in the United Daughters of the Confederacy (UDC), and the organization served to bond together the young girls and many prominent older women of the church with a common history and the desire to memorialize those who sacrificed and served in the Civil War. The UDC, founded in Nashville by Caroline Meriwether Goodlett and Anna Davenport Raines in 1894, was a unifying force among southern women and soon superseded all other female patriotic societies.[12] As a visible sign of its commitment to heritage, the Washington Street Methodist Church erected a Confederate monument that presently stands before the State House in Columbia.[13]

Not only did the Washington Street Methodist Church nourish Gray's spirit of Christian service, but it also served as a backdoor into a circle of powerful men. Prominent South Carolinians graced the pews of the church during

Wil Lou Gray in white dress. Courtesy of South Carolina Department
of Archives and History, Opportunity School Records, Columbia.

Gray's decades as a member, including Coleman Blease, South Carolina senator
(1904–8), governor (1911–15), and United States senator (1925–31); Thomas B.
Stackhouse, president of National Loan and Exchange, whose wife, Eunice, was
a lifelong friend and comrade of Gray; John W. Lillard, the developer of Fort
Jackson; and John J. Cain, architect of many of the skyscrapers built in Columbia during the 1920s.[14]
    At Columbia College Gray studied basic liberal arts and took classes in
"world history, English, geography, elocution, science, Latin, French, German,
and civics." She excelled in English and history, and civics was her favorite

class.[15] Gray was an average student and known to have a penchant for mischief. She "wasn't a shining light when it came to grades," by her own admission, but she did "try to be a good model of the student body."[16] When the school burned to the ground in 1903, Gray recalled her joy that the records of her grades were lost. "I remember when it was burned. I was so distressed about it and of course took a big cry," she said. "Then, all at once it flashed through my mind that my grades were burned up, and I thought that's good."[17]

During her senior year, she served as president of the Wightman Literary Society, an organization named in honor of the wife of William M. Wightman, a well-known South Carolina Methodist bishop. In 1883 his wife and Frances Willard formed the state's first WCTU chapter at Washington Street Methodist Church.[18] The WCTU endorsed prohibition but expanded its scope to include child labor and women's rights soon after the turn of the twentieth century. Gray's stepmother belonged to the literary circle the Wednesday Club of Laurens, a charter club of the South Carolina Federation of Women's Clubs, which may have inspired her to participate in the literary society. As a senior Gray also served as the editor in chief and business manager of the school magazine, the *Criterion;* vice president of her class; and vice president of the Young Women's Christian Association.[19] Her unusual executive ability was evidenced when Gray took the deeply in debt college journal and turned it over to the school "in the clear" and "with money in the treasury," she recalled.[20] Her participation in school and community organizations taught her the necessary leadership and organizational skills to manage a workforce of women, two skills she called upon later as an educator and state supervisor.[21]

During Gray's college years, women began to organize into clubs to connect with public reform. These efforts were a response to discrimination in the male public sphere and the attraction of bonds established in the "female world of close, personal relationships."[22] The intent of female organization was to provide women with an outlet for fellowship and social activity. However, by the turn of the century, the need to address social problems such as poverty, child labor, suffrage, and disease stimulated reform efforts that served to politicize these same women. It was the era of separate female institution and organization building, where women addressed public ills by extending their private nurturing instincts to public reform through women's clubs, church groups, and numerous voluntary agencies. Historian Estelle Freedman argues that the separate institution building of the late nineteenth century grew out of the commercial and industrial growth of the period and stemmed from the belief that women shared unique life experiences, values, and traditions as women. The homosocial networks that were built through friendships and family ties in the early nineteenth century helped women transcend the "alienation of domestic life" and served as the springboard for the development of separate female organizations. These organizations enabled women to organize within their designated sphere and redefined womanhood by extension of a prescribed place rather than rejection of it.[23]

Southern women came to realize their power and value as political entities through club culture.[24] With education, public and child welfare, and suffrage as key reform platforms, grassroots-level club activity served to politicize southern women and teach them to define themselves as citizens, not just ladies.[25] Club work was a springboard into the larger culture outside the confines of home, school, and church. Women saw such work as an extension of their natural roles as mothers and caregivers. The South Carolina State Federation of Women's Clubs claimed that "home is the basic rock of government where respect for law and order begins, where the child learns to govern by being governed."[26] Club philosophies and projects evolved with the times, and Gray joined the movement at a moment when important changes were under way in South Carolina. Historian Sarah Wilkerson Freeman states that the relatively exclusive and racially segregated women's clubs in the South mirrored mainstream values and attitudes in the shape and design of reforms. The club movement was socially and racially exclusive and directed by elite white women who focused on uplift of the disadvantaged—typically mill women and children. Clubs assured women their authority to determine the needs of women and to give voice to social issues that concerned women and the home. Poor rural and working-class white women who struggled for survival in mill villages and tenant farms had little opportunity for club activity and were rarely asked to join.[27] Shut out by racism, discrimination, and segregation, elite black women also participated in club culture and organized to implement similar reforms in the black community.[28]

Club culture connected Gray to a network of active women and gave her a platform to promote her belief in the Social Gospel through reform. During college she participated in the Young Women's Christian Association and in subsequent years joined the South Carolina Federation of Women's Clubs, the Daughters of the American Revolution, UDC, and the Methodist WCTU.[29] The single-sex infrastructure of these groups taught Gray that women were powerful when bound together and could shape the direction of public reform. Club culture introduced her to the mechanics of social reform and the organs through which information was disseminated, discussed, and acted on by groups of women.

When Gray graduated in 1903, teaching was considered "the only genteel way by which a cultivated young woman could earn a living," and Gray secured a teaching job in Greenwood County.[30] In the first decade of the twentieth century, 70 percent of all college-educated women worked, but less than 3 percent of American women held college diplomas.[31] Teaching was a feminized occupation, and women held eight of ten teaching positions.[32] Gray was not expected to work, and her father asked that she allow him to take care of her, a request she denied.[33] She was representative of an exceptional group of young women who opted for economic and social independence. The professionalization of women was under way and had dramatically increased by the time Gray entered college. Professional degrees held by women increased 226 percent between 1890 and 1920.[34]

Education was what historian Dewey Grantham calls "the epitome of the South's problem."[35] Progressive reformers saw education as a redemptive tool. It could be used to ameliorate the economic and social problems in the South if properly designed to reflect the needs of the region. In many rural areas of the South, there existed no system of public education, and the powerful textile interests and political conservatism in the South Carolina legislature limited education reform aims in the state. Compulsory education was shunned by these powers for fear that mandated education would require state funds to improve black education and disrupt the labor needs of the textile industry.[36] The first bill to address child labor and school attendance passed in 1915 but went unenforced.[37]

Gray entered the teaching force when a sentiment was growing among northern philanthropists and southern educators in favor of more adequate support of public education. At a New York gala to inspire interest in southern education, Dr. Francis Peabody asked a crowd at the Waldorf Astoria, "If the common school is the basis of our civilization, what can be said of conditions where . . . school teachers are paid on an average of $25 a month, and the average child of the South gets 5 cents worth of education per day for a term of only eighty-seven days in the year? Now this is a situation which the South simply cannot and certainly ought not to attempt to meet alone."[38] A northern observer, upon return from a tour of the southern region, declared that the system of raising taxes for public schools was little known or understood in the South. Aside from the lack of adequate funds for public education, he claimed that two additional problems explained the high illiteracy in the region: "One is the extreme difficulty of founding country schools in sections that are poor and ignorant, and the other is the striking and general want of trained teachers."[39]

The southern states had the highest illiteracy rates in the nation. South Carolina was at the bottom in the first half of the twentieth century. South Carolina and Mississippi contained the highest population of black people and in turn had high rates of black and white illiteracy combined.[40] In most southern states, primary schools in rural areas met for only three to four months during the year, and few secondary schools existed.[41] In 1903 there were 4,877 white and black schools in South Carolina that maintained 288,713 students for an average of ninety-three days per year.[42] The average state expenditure per student annually was $1.61 per black student and $6.10 per white, and the average annual teacher salary was $83.04 for blacks and $210.30 for whites. Prior to 1904 the public school system was primarily supported by the poll tax of $1 per male, levies imposed on property, and profits from the State Whiskey Dispensary system. In 1904 the first state appropriation for public education allotted $5000 dollars for the establishment of public school libraries.[43] Only in 1920 did the state require teacher certification, and by then it had established five public school laws to improve the dismal system: the Term Extension Act (1910); the Act to Establish and Maintain High Schools (1916); the Rural Graded School Act (1917); the Equalizing Act to Guarantee a Seven Months' Term (1917), and the Law to Relieve Overcrowding in the Elementary Grades of Approved High Schools.[44]

The most ardent activists against black and white illiteracy were educators and philanthropists. In response to the stagnant environment and the insidious problems in the region, the rural South became a laboratory for intellectuals and reformers with progressive ideas and practices in education.[45] The first experiment came after the Civil War, when northern aid in the form of teachers and missionaries came to educate millions of freedmen as part of the Freedmen's Bureau. The approximately four million freedmen were generally poor, illiterate, and unprepared to participate as new citizens. Between 1865 and 1870, the Freedmen's Bureau supported several hundred elementary schools for blacks. After 1870, however, most of the common schools were absorbed into the new public education system in the South, and missionary societies and northern philanthropists focused their resources on providing aid to black schools. The teachers at these schools were predominantly white, but a shift to black teachers occurred after 1915.[46] Educators of the freedmen believed that the economic and political progress of blacks in the region depended upon literacy, hard work, and goodwill toward whites.[47]

The Blair Education Bill, introduced by Sen. Henry W. Blair of New Hampshire in the mid-1880s, proposed a system of "free common schools for all children without distinction of race or color, either in raising or distributing of school revenues." The bill appropriated $105 million to southern states over a ten-year period, with two-thirds of this sum "without provisions for federal interference along racial lines."[48] The states with the highest illiteracy rates—those in the former Confederacy—stood to benefit the most from the bill, yet southerners were extremely critical of the bill and debated it on the grounds of constitutionality and the taxes that would have to be raised to fund it.[49] It was defeated four times in Congress between 1883 and 1890. Blair was denounced as an "educational crank" who presumed southern states would be willing to "muddy the waters" of education by using predominantly white tax dollars to help fund black education with "the most dangerous bill possible."[50]

With the defeat of the Blair Bill emerged a national movement to aid and improve southern education. In 1898 a group of ministers held the Conference for Christian Education in Capon Springs, West Virginia, to discuss church-related instruction primarily for black people in the region. The following year northern philanthropists Robert C. Ogden, George Peabody, and Albert Shaw and southern leader J. L. M. Curry attended the meeting. The organization was renamed the Conference for Education, and Curry became chairman. The group declared white southern education and public schools its primary concern, which was a dramatic change of philosophy from that established at the first meeting in 1898.[51] In 1900 Ogden replaced Curry as president, a post he held until 1913, and an executive committee named the Southern Education Board was chosen to direct the "southern crusade for education" with a yearly budget of forty thousand dollars.[52] In 1901 when John D. Rockefeller attended the Conference for Education in the South, he was converted to the cause of southern education, and at his request a General Education Board was formed in 1902. Under the direction of Rockefeller, Ogden, and other leaders from the Southern Board, the new organization proposed to raise and disburse money for general education needs. In 1905 Rockefeller granted the General Board ten million dollars to establish a "comprehensive system of education in the United States," and millions of dollars were donated to the Southern Board for teacher training, farm demonstrations, and school development.

Many individuals who served on the two boards also administered the Peabody Fund and Slater Fund and assisted in the creation of the Jeanes Board, formed in 1907 by Quaker Anna Jeanes to improve black instruction by subsidizing model teachers.[53] George Peabody of Massachusetts created the Peabody Fund in 1867 with an endowment of two million dollars. It was the only national effort to improve southern education until the creation of the Slater Fund in 1882. The Slater Fund, established with an endowment of one million dollars to aid black schools, was first directed by Atticus Haygood and later J. L. M. Curry. Until his death in 1903, Curry, a former Confederate leader who believed in education for all, was the head of the Peabody Fund from 1881 and the Slater Fund from 1891. At the helm of these funds, he promoted the southern educational renaissance.[54] His efforts were inadequate because they favored industrial rather than academic training for blacks, an approach that became the standard in the region.[55] Jeanes named her fund "The Fund for Rudimentary Schools for Southern Negroes" and endowed it with one million dollars to aid rural communities in the South.[56] The two boards worked closely together to create something akin to a national board of directors to steer the course of educational developments in the South. The establishment of these funds reflected northern interest in southern educational progress, but white southerners in general remained apathetic about the educational needs of both blacks and poor whites.

Northern philanthropic funds assisted in promoting school improvement, curriculum reform, health education, and vocational training in the South. Under the guidance of the Southern Education Board, northern philanthropists shaped southern education and, as historian Dewey Grantham states, "touched the lives of more of the region's inhabitants."[57] With appropriations from the Southern Education Board and the Jeanes, Slater, and Peabody funds, southerners could no longer defend illiteracy and the racial division of taxation because of the benevolence demonstrated by leaders such as Ogden, Curry, and Rockefeller.[58] The Southern Board had no formal charter, no constitution, and no bylaws and was a voluntary association of men who historian Charles Dabney called "a band of brothers who found a bond of union."[59]

It was at this historic moment of transition in southern education that Wil Lou Gray started her teaching career in two rural communities near her home in Laurens County.[60] In 1903 she taught at a crossroads community named Jones in honor of the local medical doctor Walter Jones. She earned thirty-five dollars per month and lived with a local family in a three-room cottage. The school was seventeen miles from her home in Laurens, and the trip took seven hours by horse. The classroom environment was primitive—a one-room schoolhouse without electricity, students from grades one to ten, no privy, and no clock. Homemade benches and a blackboard were the only furniture in the room, and hogs used the cellar to cool off in the summer. Gray described the conditions as "a pretty bleak experience."[61] The next year she taught at Wallace Lodge, a school located between Gray Court and Woodruff. Gray taught only nine students the first three months but sixty-three by the end of the harvest when children were no longer needed in the field to help collect the crop. Of the experience she recalled, "I was not prepared to meet the needs of those children, so I felt like I was cheating the pupils. I learned that in South Carolina we were not giving all children the proper opportunity."[62]

In the fall of 1905 Gray enrolled at Vanderbilt University in pursuit of additional training.[63] Dr. James Kirkland, chancellor of Vanderbilt, had attended Wofford College and was a close friend of Gray's father.[64] He agreed to take Gray as a boarding student, and she lived with Dr. William Vaughn, a professor of mathematics; his wife, the daughter of Bishop Holland McTyeire of the Methodist Episcopal Church, South, who was the president of the board of trustees; and three other young women. A self-taught speaker of the Russian language, Vaughn believed "only a fool needs a teacher" and instilled in Gray the belief that no matter the level of schooling or circumstance, a person could learn if given a chance. While at Vanderbilt she took a literature course titled

Wil Lou Gray in black graduation gown. Courtesy of South Carolina Department of Archives and History, Opportunity School Records, Columbia.

"The Fatherhood of God and the Brotherhood of Man," and she claimed it inspired her work to eradicate illiteracy. In the class her professor asked what she planned to do for her community when she left Vanderbilt, and she responded by telling him there were no poor in Laurens "even though I knew there were children working fifty-five hours a week in the mills," she recalled.[65] From that point her awareness drove her desire to help improve opportunities for people in South Carolina.

In the first decade of her work as a teacher and graduate student, Gray was highly influenced by three prominent men involved in the southern education movement: James Kirkland, chancellor of Vanderbilt; Dr. David Bancroft Johnson, founder and first president of Winthrop Normal College in Rock Hill,

Male and female friends at Vanderbilt. Courtesy of Margaret Gray Choate.

Female classmates at
Vanderbilt, 1905. Courtesy
of Margaret Gray Choate.

Wil Lou Gray and Vander-
bilt classmates. Courtesy of
Margaret Gray Choate.

Wil Lou Gray and more Vanderbilt students. Courtesy of Margaret Gray Choate.

South Carolina; and William Tate, supervisor of rural schools in South Carolina from 1906 to 1914 and head of Peabody Teachers College from 1914 to 1917.[66] All three men were leaders in the southern education movement and brought to their respective work the Southern Education Board's vision of how to remedy the South's pitiful educational system.[67] Training teachers and establishing community schools in the South were two fundamental goals of the board, and Gray, as a rural teacher in the trenches, worked to put their ideas into action. Her connection to these men linked her with the larger southern education movement and inspired the organizational and training methods she used in her work.

James Kirkland served on the Southern Education Board from 1910 to 1914.[68] He claimed "a spell" had come over him when he heard Walter Hines Page, a North Carolina–born journalist and advocate of the Southern Education Board, speak at the 1904 Conference for Education in Birmingham. Page made a plea in favor of black education and urged the South to assume a leadership role in the nation through regional educational reform.[69] To meet the call, Kirkland helped organize the George Peabody College for Teachers in 1909 that opened in 1914 on land adjacent to Vanderbilt. The school's purpose was to provide a regional institution to educate southern teachers and educational leaders "on their own soil and in intimate touch with Southern life and in direct response to Southern educational conditions and needs."[70] It is important to note that Kirkland established in 1895 the Southern Association of Colleges and Secondary Schools. He facilitated the standardization of college admission and graduation requirements to "elevate the standards of scholarship and to effect uniformity in entrance examinations."[71]

Likewise Dr. David Bancroft Johnson was very involved in aiding the work of the board in the South and was responsible for transforming Winthrop into a center for teacher preparation. He participated in the Summer School of the South in 1902 held in Knoxville, Tennessee, by the Southern Education Board and brought to Rock Hill modern ideas about how to implement rural education and to prepare teachers for the work. He was known to encourage his students at Winthrop to go out into South Carolina communities and serve others.[72] In 1903 Gray attended a summer session at Winthrop because she "did not know how to teach." Annie Bonham, a progressive southern educator, was one of her teachers and influenced Gray to know the families of her students, establish a book club among local adults, and get acquainted with the community where she taught.[73] Of the summer session, Gray claimed that she "never had a more rewarding experience."[74]

Like Kirkland and Johnson, William Knox Tate, the superintendent of education in South Carolina from 1910 to 1914, pursued the same type of standardization in the rural areas of the state. Tate supervised Gray from 1912 to 1914 when she was supervisor of rural schools in Laurens County, and together they transformed Laurens County into an organized, consolidated district by connecting the community to the teachers, the teachers to national organizations, and the district to state and national philanthropic agendas for education. In 1912 Tate established at Winthrop an experimental school to study rural academic courses and relate them to rural work. His classes were on such topics as training a county school, county school administration and supervision, social and economic phases of rural life, and the school problem in the South. The General Education Board paid Tate's salary in South Carolina, and his office was associated with the University of South Carolina, where he was appointed a professor of elementary instruction.[75] In 1914, when he joined the faculty at Peabody Teachers College in Nashville, he wrote to Gray, "Laurens County has passed into proverb at Peabody College. I mentioned your work so often that they even brought it into the faculty stunt last week."[76] High school entrance exams, parent-teacher associations, and vocational education were hot topics floating around in the South, and Gray tested them out in her job as a rural teacher.

Along with the influence of these three important leaders in the southern education movement, Gray was also inspired by the philosophy of Booker T. Washington, who she first heard speak when she was a student at Vanderbilt. Washington embraced industrial training as the most pragmatic and effective way to advance race progress in the South. In 1906 the renowned black educator spoke in Nashville, and Gray attended. Unable to get a seat, she stood for the duration of the lecture.[77] Washington's speech, "How Can the Young Southern Man Help in the Lifting up of the Negro Race?," was given at the McKendree Methodist Church in January 1906 before a large crowd. More than five hundred people were turned away. He spoke for more than an hour, and his speech promoted vocational education and experiential learning as alternative methods of teaching.[78] Washington argued that education had to meet the practical needs of people, and this approach was "something more than the abstract cube root and verb conjugation" taught in conventional school lessons. Experiential learning was a way to "bring to life" the learning process.[79] In the weeks after the Nashville speech, Washington wrote to a friend, "The more I get about among the people, the more I am convinced that a large element of Southern white people are sick of the slavery in which they have been held by the radical newspapers and political demagogues. Of course this class is far from being the majority . . . but I do believe it is growing in number."[80] He observed that his white audience recognized the consequences of black illiteracy and the shortcomings of race-baiting politicians, and he was hopeful that white southerners would move beyond the racial practices of the past and embrace regional reform.

Gray was among this growing number of southerners who celebrated Washington's ideas. He urged blacks to work within the limitations of discrimination and race oppression to develop skilled trades as a solution to black economic woes, the antithesis of the approach to race advancement held by W. E. B. Du Bois. At the Tuskegee Institute, Washington's vocational training center in Alabama, he worked to dovetail his academic curriculum to fit the needs of the people in his region.[81] Gray was deeply influenced by his ideas and developed an adult education program in the twenties that mirrored his concept of practical education. She advocated the experiential learning model in her adult education curriculum and used pilgrimages to important state and national historic sites to educate her students about American citizenship and civics. As a vocal proponent of black education, she consistently urged the General Assembly to support black adult schools to eradicate the high level of illiteracy in the black community.[82] Vocational education was at the core of her educational philosophy, a possible result of the "indelible impression" Washington's speech made upon her.[83]

After a year of graduate study at Vanderbilt, Gray returned to South Carolina and taught at Wallace Lodge in the fall of 1906.[84] She bought an organ for her school with funds obtained from selling brick from a building her father demolished and won the School Improvement Association's one-hundred-dollar regional prize. But Gray found the position limiting. In 1907 she accepted a position as a professor of English literature at Martha Washington College in Abingdon, Virginia.[85]

It was both an honor and a responsibility to accept an invitation from the prominent female college. To acquire a professorship at a well-respected woman's college was an accomplishment for the young educator. Opened in 1860, Martha Washington College was named in honor of the First Lady, who was "a woman of wide culture, a magnetic personality, a refined and noble bearing, a gentle spirit, and a woman of pure heart and high purpose."[86] The college sought to "perpetuate her name . . . also her virtues by reproducing them in the lives of the pupils."[87] The college catalog extolled the achievements and virtues of the great women who attended the school: "Here was the home of the daughters, who afterwards became the wives of Gen. Wade Hampton, General Robert J. Breckenridge . . . and Col. John M. Preston. Thus not only does the name of Martha Washington, but also the names of those who had their home here in the antebellum days, suggest that gentleness of manner, that culture of mind, that love of home, and that purity of life so necessary to high and holy womanhood."[88] One of the most recognized graduates of the school was suffragist Nellie Nugent Somerville. The catalog also advertised the health benefits of the campus, claiming Martha Washington College was "free from all malaria" and full of "invigorating air of the mountains."[89]

Gray was one of the approximately eighty-five thousand women with advanced degrees who worked for a wage in the first decade of the twentieth century.[90] Women were what Grantham calls "marginal benefactors" of higher education in the South and were categorically denied access to placement in state universities and professional schools.[91] Gray's annual salary was $450, and aside from one preparatory student, she was the only South Carolinian on campus.[92] Most of the student body came from Virginia and Tennessee. William Shakespeare, Charles Dickens, Geoffrey Chaucer, John Milton, Alfred Lord Tennyson, and Henry Wadsworth Longfellow were a few of the authors on the reading list for Gray's course. She described the rationale of her course:

"knowledge of the world's best literature, an acquaintance with the biography of the great producers of literature, and the times in which they lived, is essential for the highest culture."[93] The objective was for the student to gain "knowledge of one's own language, both in its technical construction and the history of its art," which was "essential to a good education."[94]

Although an all-female institution was fertile ground for discussions about issues such as suffrage and equal rights, Gray promoted male-centric themes. Her semester topic, "The Fatherhood of God and the Brotherhood of Man," did not drip with feminist sentiment and contained lectures not of her design but those of a former male English professor at Vanderbilt.[95] With a paternalistic semester topic and a classical reading list, Gray did not impart a feminist worldview to her students through her curriculum. The all-female environment in the isolated, rural mountains of Virginia may have been stifling to her, whose professional experience as a rural teacher and graduate training at Winthrop and Vanderbilt had exposed her to cutting-edge ideas and methods with respect to rural education. Even though she did not preach feminist doctrine, she was ambitious and likely found the constraints of a woman's college that perpetuated values such as the "love of home" and "high and holy womanhood" much too confining.[96] While in residence she managed to paint a set of china and "exert an uplifting and Christian influence," but she lasted just one year. Biographer Mabel Montgomery claims that "her teaching was rewarding . . . but she desired more preparation as well as close contact with the rural people whom she wanted to reach."[97] Gray wanted to make change not from a lectern but in the field. She left Martha Washington College and returned to Youngs (Wallace Lodge) for a two-year teaching stint before entering the graduate political science program at Columbia University in the fall of 1910.[98]

At Columbia University she was surrounded by leading intellectuals of the day. Her primary adviser and teacher was William Archibald Dunning, a historian whose interpretation of Reconstruction defined the historiography on the topic until the 1950s. Her course of study included "The Social Evolution of the English and American Political Philosophy," taught by Dunning, and "The Protestant Revolt" and "The French Revolution," taught by James Harvey Robinson.[99] Gray's thesis research mirrored the pro-southern sentiment of Dunning.[100]

At the turn of the century, the standard version of Reconstruction held that after the Civil War a new nationalism unified the nation and replaced the old sectional and state loyalties common in the antebellum period. Dunning was sympathetic to the plight of the South during the Reconstruction era and claimed that "never have American public men in responsible positions, directing the destiny of the nation been so brutal, hypocritical, and corrupt. . . . The southern people were literally put through torture."[101] Dunning argued that the South should have been restored to the nation without enduring years of Republican-mandated Reconstruction because southerners were willing to pledge allegiance to the Union. He also believed that the responsibility for the freedmen should have been entrusted to southerners and not northern Republicans. Republicans did not care about the freedmen's future, he argued, only about using the black man as a tool in the further punishment of the South for its transgressions of secession and war.[102] In 1901 Dunning attacked Republicans by pointing out that no "new crusade in favor of Negro equality" was initiated after the turn of the century, proof positive of his view that Republicans abandoned blacks and never intended to enforce black social and political equality.[103] Dunning's view gained widespread support, and a school of thought emerged within the historical profession known as the Dunning School of Reconstruction, which prevailed in the first half of the twentieth century.[104]

Dunning's pro-southern view was evidenced in his support of Gray's master's thesis. Gray defended secession as just by examining the prewar meaning of sovereignty and states' rights and the postwar transformations of how these concepts were understood as a consequence of southern loss. In "The Political Philosophy of John Codman Hurd," Gray examined the legal definitions of states' rights and sovereignty as presented in two books written by Hurd, *The Theory of Our National Existence as Shown by the Action of the Government of the United States since 1861*, published in 1881, and *The Union-State: A Letter to Our States-Rights Friend*, published in 1890.[105] Hurd, a Boston lawyer, wrote extensively on the issue of sovereignty and its historic, legal meaning. Using Hurd's theory of sovereignty as the framework of her analysis, Gray claimed that the nation's view of sovereignty before 1861 changed as a consequence of the Civil War. Her purpose was to reveal the ahistorical foundation of postwar American nationalism by explaining the prewar understanding of sovereignty that was erased with the outcome of the war. She argued that a new nationalism came with the Union victory that redefined and expunged the prewar, historical understanding of states' rights, the nation, the Constitution, and the concept of sovereign power as it existed in the federal system. To Gray postwar nationalism was an invention of the victor and an idea designed and perpetuated with ahistorical facts. Gray wrote: "They took the political events which occurred since 1861 . . . as indicating that sovereignty was held by the people as a whole represented by a 'National' government but that this sovereignty had so existed since 1789 and was now only coming to the front. . . . This law of Nationalism . . . cannot be supported by historic fact. . . . The change from structural separatism to a structural nationalism has come about through the action of some distinct political organization employing fraud, force, marriage, etc."[106]

The starting point of her analysis was Hurd's claim "that the struggle for power is not a struggle of right but one of might" and that the "confused idea concerning this question [of sovereignty] was the cause of the Civil War."[107] Hurd set forth a theory of national existence that she believed was true to history because his writings favored a position neither for or against the war and transcended the petty politics of the times. "Hurd is not a Union man, neither a States Right's advocate, he is not an apologist for or against slavery and he speaks only for himself . . . to find a theory of political existence which is true to history," wrote Gray.[108] Although the controversial political and moral debates about secession and slavery were absent in her paper, Hurd's work provided a legal framework for her to argue a legal position that the North violated the Constitution by usurping the power of the southern states. Gray explained: "In supporting this general policy the people of the North not only violated the Constitution but also consented to a usurpation on the part of these persons constituting the General government. This power usurped was not only over the ten Southern states but that of the political people of the States remaining in the Union. The recognitions of a revolution should end controversies and also exclude from future acts any support of past history. Acts which had previously been unconstitutional may no longer be spoken of as usurpatica."[109]

The idea that different regional views about the meaning of sovereignty caused the war and a new nationalism was born from the ashes of the conflict was a common belief held by many southerners between 1865 and World War I. It is important to consider the interpretation Gray advances in her thesis because it provides a glimpse of her views about the history of her region and its narrative of the past in relation to that of the nation. Her graduate education and early career played out at a historic moment when a shift occurred in the nation away from sectional differences toward national reunion and reconciliation that was clearly evident by World War I. Historian David Blight argues that this shift was important in the way that it shaped how the nation remembered the Civil War. Blight claims the memory of slavery as part of the conflict was sacrificed on the altar of national reunion and basically extracted from the national remembrance of the event. Blight argues the emancipation narrative of the event survived in the black community but that remembrance of the war became a memory of a conflict fought over honor rather than race.[110]

Gray's thesis is a provocative, intellectual critique of the new nationalism that took shape in the postwar era and reveals her twin identities as a southerner grappling with her region's narrative of the past and as an American in graduate school in Progressive Era New York. This particular sort of tension is best illuminated in the life and work of North Carolina journalist Walter Hines Page. Page scholar John Milton Cooper Jr. argues: "That phrase, 'the Southerner as American,' and the evocation of Page as a figure caught in the classic dilemma of the post-Reconstruction South suggest both his historical significance and the great theme that he illuminated. . . . As an editor of national magazines in New

Health Habits. Courtesy Wil Lou Gray Opportunity School,
West Columbia, South Carolina.

York and Boston until 1913, he wrote and reflected constantly on the meanings
of the twin identities of southerner and American. At the same time, he was
advocating—as a philanthropist, social reformer, and amateur politician—and
promoting reconciliation between those identities."[111]

A contemporary of Page, Gray negotiated between her identities as a southerner and American in her graduate thesis and later the curriculum she imparted in her work with the underprivileged in the state of South Carolina.[112]

Upon graduation from Columbia University in 1911, Gray returned to Laurens with a masters of arts in political science. She received two job offers: one
to teach history at Louisiana College and the other to serve as a rural supervisor
in Laurens County. These jobs placed her atop the ladder of women professionals. Women held only one in sixty-three supervisory positions in the field of
education.[113] She accepted the position as supervisor of rural schools.[114] Her
choice to forgo Louisiana in favor of her hometown of Laurens planted her back
home in South Carolina, where, with the exception of one year, she would work
for the remainder of her life.

CHAPTER 3

The Making of a Professional

Between 1912 and 1918, Wil Lou Gray climbed the professional ladder and connected her teaching and extensive educational training to rural fieldwork. For the first four years, she served as the supervisor of rural schools in Laurens County. During the last two, she left the state to pursue an additional year of graduate study at Columbia University and to take a job as the supervisor of rural schools in Montgomery County, Maryland. She returned to the state in 1918 to assume the job of field secretary for the South Carolina Illiteracy Commission, a wartime agency formed during World War I to address the high level of illiteracy in the state. During these years Gray forged a reputation as an innovative rural reformer and found a niche open for leadership and experimentation in the fledgling field of adult education. This chapter examines her efforts during these years of professional growth to prepare a force of committed teachers to teach in a state where one in four adults lacked an elementary education and compulsory education went unenforced. Additionally it identifies the moment when Gray recognized the extent of adult illiteracy in South Carolina and took steps to address the problem—first locally with a night school experiment and then at the state level as the field secretary for the South Carolina Illiteracy Commission (SCIC). Here it is argued that in 1918 Gray wrested the disparate statewide literacy campaigns from the hands of voluntary agencies such as women's clubs, defense groups such as the Women's Council of Defense, and civic associations that were responsible for the work prior to the war and centralized the work under the control of the SCIC and state auspices in its immediate aftermath. World War I was the turning point in her career and provided the atmosphere of patriotism, fear, reform, and possibility that legitimized her work and shaped the future course of career.[1]

In 1912, as supervisor for rural schools for Laurens County, Gray earned an annual salary of $600, $250 of which came from the Peabody Education Fund. She traveled Monday through Friday to various communities in her district to oversee 71 schools and supervise 125 teachers.[2] She traveled to schools across the district each day visiting classrooms, training teachers, meeting parents, and holding community meetings where she encouraged citizens to attend school.[3] A fourteen-hour workday was common for Gray. The average annual salary for a white female teacher in the district was $367 and for a black female teacher just $82. The average annual salary of a white male teacher was $769, and his black counterpart earned a mere $93. Average expenditure per white pupil was $4.15 and per black student $1.26 annually. Approximately 25.7 percent of the state's 1,515,400 inhabitants were illiterate, of whom roughly 90,000 were males over the age of twenty-one, with black men accounting for nearly two-thirds.[4] These statistics indicate that Gray as a supervisor made more than white female teachers but considerably less than a white male teacher in her district. They also reveal the huge disparity in the distribution of public funds for black versus white school instruction, an illustration of how racism, white supremacy, and the politics of segregation played out in the structure of the state educational system.

At the start of her duty as rural supervisor, Gray found that Laurens County lacked uniformity. Each school in the district operated autonomously of the other. Her first goal was to unite the schools and teachers through monthly in-training workshops she called institutes. This approach was common. In 1902 the Southern Education Board established summer institutes in the South to provide training in new ideas, methods, and material to southern educators. From 1902 to 1907, the Summer School of the South in Knoxville, Tennessee, trained 11,016 men and women from forty-six states.[5] Of the program historian Charles Dabney declared that "attention was directed to the improvement of the teachers and their enlistment in the movement. They were to be the real builders of the future."[6] Dr. David Johnson, the president of Winthrop, attended these summer schools and used the modern ideas and methods to prepare teachers at the college. By 1920 Gray as the supervisor of adult schools required that white teachers involved in adult instruction attend training institutes at Winthrop.[7]

Like the regional Summer School of the South, Gray's institutes in Laurens County aimed to facilitate communication between local teachers and her and provide additional training to teachers. One Friday a month, teachers from across the district met to set goals and discuss local issues and concerns. At these meetings Gray introduced the staff to current topics in the field of education and encouraged the teachers to participate in national and state professional organizations. Gray was successful in stimulating their interest and carried a group of seventy-five teachers to the National Education Association's national meeting in Washington, D.C., in 1913.[8] She set a further example by serving as the vice president of the South Carolina Teachers' Association in 1913.[9] Gray also served on the executive board of the South Carolina Improvement Association from 1912 to 1916.[10] These efforts aimed to professionalize her teachers and to educate them about new ideas and trends in the field by connecting the local district to national and state-level organizations. Additionally it was a concerted attempt by Gray to create a system of organization and management that did not exist in the county prior to her arrival and, in turn, legitimize it within the larger context of the southern educational reform movement.

To establish legitimacy of the schools in her district and to create a uniform curriculum, Gray worked to establish a high school entrance examination. This was important in relation to the general attitude that southern high schools did not effectively prepare students for college. Publicly supported high schools in the South were scarce and poorly funded, and the teachers were often unprepared to teach at the secondary level. As a consequence there existed a general sentiment that those southerners who did attend college were ill prepared. By implementing a high school entrance examination, Gray set a standard at the local level that would impact the quality and success of the secondary education in her district and improve college readiness among her district graduates. Gray's efforts preceded those of the state. To fill the gap between common public schools and higher education, the state passed a High School Act in 1916 and improved upon it in 1919.[11]

In addition to establishing a high school entrance examination, Gray promoted universal school enrollment, encouraged community participation in the educational process, advocated for tax-funded public education, held forums where leaders in the educational field spoke to her teachers, and instituted plans to construct outhouses at every school.[12] On the district level, Gray carried out the objectives of William Knox Tate, who was the state supervisor of rural schools.[13] In the early twentieth century, Tate was one of the most successful rural supervisors in the South, and he greatly influenced Gray. He promoted school supervision, parent teacher associations, agricultural and industrial programs, and community financial support of local schools, all goals Gray aimed to attain as a county supervisor.[14]

The methods Gray used to organize her district included direct leadership and initiative and referendum.[15] She developed a network of school personnel to stimulate school-community relations and to inspire interest in educational reform. Under her guidance her teachers, peers, and community transformed into an integrated, organized county system with a clear agenda. Across Laurens County she found a willingness and enthusiasm on the part of local educators to improve school conditions.[16] Gray established a School Improvement Association in her district to raise funds for area schools.[17] The SIA was an independent organization made up of charitable and voluntary groups in the community that worked to fill the gap where taxes fell short of public school needs. Gray so enjoyed her work that during a tour of Europe in the summer of 1913, she wrote State Superintendent of Education John Swearingen, "I have thought often of my work at home. If I shall be able to take back to it a better informed mind and a greater desire for service, I shall be grateful for this wonderful opportunity."[18]

In four years Gray successfully organized the rural schools of Laurens County into institutions supported by the local communities on one side and effectively supervised by the state on the other. Her work in Laurens coincided with educational reform gains made across the South in the years prior to World War I. In the first two decades of the twentieth century, southern school revenues increased, the school day lengthened, teacher salaries increased, and schools were consolidated and constructed.[19] Through ambitious restructuring she prepared teachers and enlisted charitable groups in the community to raise money for school materials and supplies.[20] As a native of Laurens, her family connections surely factored in to the positive reception of her work.[21]

During these years her landmark achievement was the creation of a night school program for adults in 1915. Adult education was under experimentation in the state, and she immediately developed an interest in the field. In the 1890s the first attempts to provide night schools in the state for working-class people failed because of questions concerning who should attend, student matrimony, change of work, and movement from the area. But by 1903 a mill school to teach adult men was established in Union County. By 1913, when the need for literate voters became a national issue tied to the Americanization efforts of progressives, an intensive campaign for the development of adult night schools was waged by Julia Selden of Spartanburg, a wealthy educator.[22] Gray followed the lead of Selden, who developed the first successful night school program in the mills of Spartanburg County in 1913.[23] Selden seems to have modeled her program on the moonlight schools developed in 1911 by Cora Wilson Stewart, a Rowan County, Kentucky, educator. Designed for adult illiterates, these schools were held at night when men were not working and the moon cast enough light to guide the students to the schoolhouse.

Both Selden and Gray communicated with Stewart, and Gray built upon the night school model advanced by these two women. Stewart described the educational hunger of students as they came to the first night school: "They came singly or hurrying in groups, they came walking for miles, they came

carrying babes in arms, they came bent with age and leaning on canes."[24] Like
Stewart, Gray described her first night school in a similar fashion: "I remember
the first night as if it were yesterday.... We waited at the school for our adults
to come. Nobody came, and we waited and waited, I was almost ready to give
up. And then, through the darkness we saw lanterns coming from everywhere.
They were coming to learn how to read and write."[25] Historian Hugh Bailey
argues that South Carolina was a breeding ground for alternative educational
programs aimed at poor whites because these programs could be developed and
financed without tax dollars or benefit to blacks.[26] The mill school was one
such example where the welfare capitalism of the mill owners included funding mill village schools for their white workforce. The night school proved to be
another.

In 1915 when Gray conducted her first rural night schools, the staggering
illiteracy rate in South Carolina placed it sixth highest in the nation for white
illiteracy and third for blacks. Of the estimated 4,500 voters in Laurens County,
608 had to make a mark because they were unable to sign their name, a problem
Gray discovered while examining the Democratic registration roll at the county
courthouse.[27] The discovery inspired her to start the night school program.[28]
Aside from the obvious limitations of illiteracy symbolized by the mark, Gray
was aware that the community would support work that improved the efficiency
and productivity of farmers and male workers.

Gray developed the night school experiment with the help of James Sullivan, the county superintendent of education. She promoted her idea at agricultural, civic, and political clubs and succeeded in organizing seven night
schools in January 1915. She documented the formation and development of
these schools in a pamphlet that the State Department of Education published
that year. True to her background in social science, Gray called her night school
program an experiment. The opening page of her pamphlet set forth an explanation for why her state was among the most illiterate in the Union. She
claimed the chaos of the Civil War, its impact on the region, and poverty as the
primary causes of the high rate of illiteracy in the state. She also blamed the lack
of a compulsory attendance law, an explanation she consistently used in the
illiteracy campaigns of the 1920s.[29] Black illiteracy was absent in her study, an
indication that she did not find it necessary to address the issue at this point in
her career or was wary of tying it to adult education for fear that it would render
her night school experiment dead on arrival.[30]

In 1915 the bulk of students who attended the experimental night program were white farmers. Gray engaged the state agricultural extension agency
to send a home demonstration agent to the community night school meetings
and wrote to her local congressman for farm bulletins that contained information about agricultural products.[31] When he could only provide ten bulletins

because he had sent "one to every person on a rural route," Gray appealed for him to stop the mail-outs, since most people on rural routes could not read the material. "He [congressman] didn't believe me when I said that one out of every four persons on those rural routes couldn't read or write," she recalled.[32] Gray found that relating classwork to the work lives of students greatly enhanced the chances of success. Reading material at the night schools used information "about 8-4-4 fertilizer and tomatoes and potatoes" to teach the men how to apply what they learned in class to their work outside of class, a pragmatic approach similar to that advanced by Booker T. Washington.

Gray's night school program was popular in Laurens. Adults from all walks of life were interested in her night schools. One well-to-do but uneducated farmer who attended one of the night school sessions claimed that the class was "like going to new ground without tools," but he, like others, gained the "tools of the mind through Miss Gray's direction."[33] The positive results of the night school experiment led State Superintendent of Education John Swearingen to hail her program as "the way for practical removal of illiteracy by 1920."[34] Though the state was reluctant to fund the program, it allotted five thousand dollars in 1915 at the insistence of progressive governor Richard I. Manning to develop adult schools.[35] In Gray's opinion the government's support was "merely a token effort to combat the problem of adult illiteracy in South Carolina."[36] She believed the issue to be far more serious and persisted in her efforts to raise awareness and money despite the lackluster support she received in the form of meager appropriations from the state.

The State Department of Education published her night school experiment and distributed it across the state with the help of Swearingen. By conducting an experiment, publishing it, and distributing it through a state department, Gray validated her theory that adult education was effective and useful in her district and, in turn, could universally benefit the state. This experiment demonstrated her ability to use the scientific method and social science as a way to authenticate and test an idea. Moreover, by printing and distributing the results, she created a scientific precedent for the development of public policy to address the issue. Most important, her publication provided an algorithm for how to initiate, organize, staff, and conduct a night program for adult illiterates in a rural community, a useful tool for educators interested in the idea. She couched the program and its success in economic and political terms for state political leaders to read and understand better the long-term impact of adult night programs on their political base and state progress. "The appropriation ought to be increased," she stated. "An appropriation of $10,000 for Night Schools is ... a step in the right direction, and let us hope that all agencies in the State which can render a service in the work of eradication of illiteracy will lend a hand. Night Schools have proved one of the most effective means of reducing the percentage of illiteracy."[37] A news article captured the initial energy by highlighting the "state appropriation of $5,000 in 1915" to carry "the work to more than five thousand beneficiaries."[38] But the interest in the program fizzled just two years later because the total amount of the appropriation allotted went unspent; thus the appropriation for the night schools was reduced to $2,500 in 1917.

Aggravated and disillusioned by the state's flat support for adult schools, Gray submitted her resignation and returned to Teachers College, Columbia University, in the fall of 1916. State Superintendent of Education Swearingen expressed "deep regret" that the "lack of money prevents South Carolina from holding you within her borders."[39] Gray believed the answer to "public and legislative indifference" that was "holding literally thousands of South Carolinians in bondage" was somewhere beyond the borders of her state and possibly within the walls of academia.[40] After a year of graduate study in education at Teachers College, Gray accepted a position as assistant superintendent of elementary school supervision in Montgomery County, Maryland.[41]

She began her work in the fall of 1917. Her salary was $1,200 per year, a sum "higher than what the best teachers of the city get paid" and double what she was paid as supervisor in Laurens.[42] Despite her reputation and the glowing recommendations from Columbia University and her former boss William Knox Tate, the Montgomery County school board claimed "that the teachers will welcome a supervisor heartily if her salary is not too out of proportion to the salaries of the city."[43]

Gray set about restructuring Maryland's rural schools in the same energetic way she had organized Laurens County. She corresponded with fellow educators to learn about regional school organization, curriculum, conditions, and trustees. Most of the teachers shared the philosophy that a clean, organized school created the environment for sound education. Not all of the schools in the region met this philosophical ideal, and Gray observed this firsthand in her daily trips across the county. In need of advice, she wrote to a friend about the deplorable conditions in one school: "I visited today a rancher teacher. He stood with his cap on the back of his head picking his teeth till school began and sat until recess. I took a picture of his toilet with a panel out of the door, his library room that looked like a dump heap. It violated every principle learned in ED 410-411."[44]

Headquartered in Rockville, Maryland, Gray spent four days a week in the field visiting schools. She would visit each of the forty-one schools for half a day, an assessment process that took about five weeks. Gray evaluated each school with the same questions: "Is this school system preparing the boys and girls for a broader, more intelligent life, is it training them to think, is it giving them ideas as well as ideals?"[45] Although bad weather complicated her ambitious visitation schedule, Gray dedicated herself to the establishment of a library in each school. Twenty-five of the forty-one schools developed libraries with a twenty-dollar appropriation from the Maryland State Library Law. Gray pursued the same goals she had achieved in Laurens. She asked the county newspaper for a section devoted to educational news, encouraged teacher professional development through reading circles, held monthly teacher conferences in each section of the county, promoted teacher-community relations, and established school improvement associations.[46]

Gray worked with the seven fledgling school improvement associations to stimulate community participation in the schools and joined the Montgomery County Federation of Women's Clubs in February 1918.[47] This organization was especially fond of Gray and admired her work. Gertrude Stevens, the director, expressed this affection in a letter to the new member. "Let me be just personal enough to say how gratifying it is that your experience, training, and broad vision are to be at our disposal so generously this year," wrote Stevens. "It seems almost too good to be true! Miss Magruder and I are holding our breaths for fear you'll be snatched away from us by some masterful fairy!"[48]

Maryland was an interesting transition and different from Laurens County. The schools in the area were reported to be some of the most progressive in the nation, but Gray was disappointed that many patrons were uncooperative and resistant to change. At a board of trustees meeting, Gray praised a teacher for her use of materials such as cans and cartons to help her students learn elementary arithmetic lessons. The chairman of the board was not as impressed by the activity and warned Gray that "children go to school not to play but to learn," a red flag that indicated the interests of trustees trumped the creative license of the teachers.[49]

When the United States entered World War I, Gray made her schools "centers from which information could be disseminated in regard to the war aims of the nation."[50] As a sign of patriotism and support for the war effort, she encouraged students to purchase Liberty Bonds and formed a Junior Red Cross in each of the county schools. The schools planned programs to raise funds to purchase material for bandages and garments for the armed forces. Her work as rural supervisor in Maryland contributed to her professional growth, but it did not solve the illiteracy crisis in South Carolina. World War I created an environment of opportunity that led Gray back to South Carolina in the fall of 1918 to serve as a member of the South Carolina Illiteracy Commission.

In the months preceding Gray's return, a series of communications between Prof. Patterson Wardlaw, who chaired the fledgling commission starting in late December 1917, and Julia Selden of Spartanburg, a well-known volunteer, educator, and member of the South Carolina Federation of Women's Clubs and the state Women's Council of Defense, reveals the shifting role of volunteers in state-managed work and the part Gray played in removing volunteers from the teaching profession.[51] The South Carolina Illiteracy Commission's express task was to locate illiterates and design steps to eradicate illiteracy.[52] In 1917 Selden volunteered her services to Wardlaw as a liaison between the Illiteracy Commission and disparate grassroots civic organizations across the state engaged in literacy work to organize a statewide campaign to stamp out illiteracy.[53] Between December 1917 and October 1918, Wardlaw used Selden to craft and implement a literacy campaign over which the state would assume control under the leadership of Gray and the South Carolina Illiteracy Commission.[54] The overlapping and transforming relationship between volunteer women and wage-earning, professional women who participated in wartime literacy work in South Carolina is revealed in this event. During World War I, these two elite, white, unmarried, educated South Carolina women experienced two very different encounters with state power. At the end of the war, only Gray, the woman with a waged, state-sponsored job, advanced in her work to eradicate illiteracy, while the volunteer, Selden, moved to the margins of state-controlled literacy work.

When the nation entered World War I, women's housekeeping became a matter of national defense, and clubwomen extended their housekeeping duties beyond the home and into the community through voluntary work. George E. Chamberlain, the chairman of the Senate Committee on Military Affairs, argued that the war allowed women to feel "more at liberty to act." "In my opinion," he wrote, "she will win this war, as she has done in the past wars, make the slacker impossible and drive the coward to his duty at the front."[55] She was the heroine of the home front and an inspiration to a nation at war.[56] The metaphor of domesticity was commonly used to prompt women into civic action. "The mother is the heart of the home just as the home is the heart of the community," wrote Mrs. Grant Beebe, chairwoman of the General Federation of Women's Clubs.[57] On southern club activities, Mrs. A. O. Granger claimed that "women's clubs in the South have brought women into partnership with their husbands and brothers in the civic responsibility . . . of raising the standard of thought and action about all other national housekeeping problems. . . . The conscientious club woman makes her decision calmly for club work is also God's work for home—for our land, for all who need us."[58]

In South Carolina the issue of illiteracy brought clubwomen and the state together during World War I, because the war politicized illiteracy. Illiteracy work prior to the war was directed and financed primarily through voluntary networks because the state did not see the necessity in using tax money to educate its large population of illiterates, who mainly worked as mill hands and farmers. This changed when the war broke out, because World War I transformed illiteracy from social problem to a matter of national defense. At the outset of the war, state governors met and proposed to spread the values and ideals of America within their respective states to combat antidemocratic ideologies from taking root on the home front. To the nation at war, Americanization was an effort to establish philosophic continuity across the nation about what it meant to be an American citizen. Americanization was "a matter of self defense and self preservation," and citizenship education was key to imparting the values defined as uniquely American.[59]

In South Carolina and other Deep South states, illiteracy was the chief obstacle to this process. South Carolina ranked second only to Louisiana in the percentage of illiterates, with 18.1 percent of whites and approximately 38.7 percent of blacks in a population of 1,683,724 unable to read and write.[60] The effort to Americanize the white citizenry with pamphlets and texts on American citizenship was ineffective when approximately one-fifth of the white population and an even higher percentage of the black community could not read or write. In response to the illiteracy problem, the South Carolina Federation of Women Clubs in conjunction with civic and religious institutions across the state urged the governor to appoint an illiteracy commission to wipe out the "foe of Americanization."[61]

As early as 1914, the South Carolina Federation of Women's Clubs had asked the state to establish a commission, but it took two years to find anyone willing to lead the group.[62] In 1916 Governor Manning appointed a six-person illiteracy commission that included Gray, but "the Commission never met as a body," she wrote.[63] In a second attempt, on January 10, 1917, "a number of prominent educators" "met with the Federation Board and agreed to ask the Governor of the State to appoint a State Illiteracy Commission."[64]Although the first attempt to establish a commission had failed, the second one did not. The South Carolina Illiteracy Commission was formed on December 24, 1917. The members included Patterson Wardlaw of the University of South Carolina (chairman); Mrs. James Coker and Mabel Montgomery of the South Carolina Federation of Women's Clubs; Dr. Samuel Henry Edmunds, superintendent of the Sumter Schools; Dr. Charles E. Burts, pastor of the First Baptist Church of Columbia; John Swearingen, state superintendent of education; and Augustus Shealy, state supervisor of mill schools. The express goal of the commission was to eradicate the high internal levels of illiteracy and to advance the values of the Americanization movement.[65] The SCIC worked under the leadership of the State Department of Education, and its aim was "to cooperate with, encourage, and aid all persons, organizations, and other agencies that are striving for the eradication of illiteracy for the State."[66]

The SCIC "had no funds at its command," and all expenses incurred were the responsibility of the individual members. The members began their work with money from donations and a belief that if a successful beginning could be made, the General Assembly would appropriate money for permanent continuation of its work.[67] It commenced a campaign to arouse the public to the need for literacy in the state and to raise funds to employ a full-time field worker. "Never has a Commission so quietly or so faithfully fulfilled its purpose," wrote Gray.[68]

The SCIC believed literate citizens were the "antidote to the brutalizing effects of war" and the first line of defense against the "pernicious principles" of German nationalism. It advocated education that produced "a sound body, a broad gauged mind and a generous soul"; compulsory attendance; publicly funded schools; and universal education. The commission's most zealous aim was to "remove within the next 18 months as far as possible all adult illiteracy from the borders of the state."[69] Like the State Council of Defense, a wartime body known as the citizen army, the SCIC relied upon civic mobilization to accomplish its aims and illustrated the necessity and effectiveness of the interdependence of public and private associations during the war. Historian Terry Helsly suggests that what has been attributed to Governor Manning as progressive reform during the war, such as the establishment of the SCIC, was actually not progressive at all. Helsly argues that Manning used extreme patriotism to achieve defense aims and to excuse antidemocratic acts in wartime South Carolina. The SCIC's promotion of literacy as the weapon to fight antidemocratic ideology illustrated its role as an arm of the state during the war and its use of patriotism to advance its goals.[70]

In South Carolina the extent of illiteracy among draft-aged men exposed the severity of the crisis to the volunteers registering men for the Selective Service Act of 1917, the first nationally mandated military service act since the Civil War.[71] Mabel Montgomery of the SCIC observed that "World War I had focused attention on the number of soldiers who could neither write nor read letters. Anglo-Saxons of fine lineage, the soldiers were often too proud to admit their limitations."[72] Included among Montgomery's draftees were poor blacks as well as white men, and it was believed that their illiteracy posed a threat to state and national security.[73] Fellow clubwoman and night school founder Julia Selden claimed that "Russia's fall was caused by German propaganda among the ignorant classes . . . a great effort must be made to mobilize our illiterates and near illiterates into night schools where they will be taught not only reading and writing but farm industry and patriotism."[74] Ignorant people were internal enemies susceptible to the sway of undemocratic forces. A history of successful demagoguery in South Carolina no doubt fed this fear among the educated, apparent in Wil Lou Gray's question "Can demagogues (again) sway men and women too ignorant to form their own opinion?"[75]

The South Carolina Federation of Women's Clubs, a state division of the General Federation of Women's Clubs, endorsed a platform that promoted "adult civic education, education for democracy and an effort to adjust democracy for human welfare."[76] The web of data the organization collected on state poverty, health, illiteracy, and the plight of the lower classes served as a road map for government agencies such as the SCIC.[77] Many SCFWC members also volunteered time to wartime agencies such as the state Women's Council of Defense.[78] The Women's Committee of the Council of Defense was a temporary wartime body comprising numerous women's organization from across the country.[79] The Women's Committee was a subordinate body within the Council of Defense and was "frequently reminded by its superior body" that it should not "initiate but should only advise" on matters of defense.[80] One member described its creation in biblical terms: "When the Government created its war body... it followed the precedent set by the Creator of the universe, in that it created its man body first and made woman a side issue, extracting or subtracting nothing whatever from the man body in the process—not even a rib or a piece of governmental backbone.... It was a consummation devoutly to be wished that the Government, having created the woman body of its war machine, should have breathed into it the breath of life."[81]

The SCWCD was an extension of the National Woman's Council of Defense formed by an act of Congress in April 1917. The first meeting of the SCWCD "organized the state by calling together representatives of all state organizations of women at Rock Hill, July 12th, 1917." The executive board contained "all state presidents of women's organizations" and thus politicized state club work by transforming it into a patriotic arm of national defense. With the aim to "eliminate waste of all kinds" within the state, the activities of the SCWCD involved the registration of the thirty-five thousand women, the signing of twenty thousand "Hoover Cards," and the sale of Liberty Bonds.[82] Selden was a member of both the SCFWC and the SCWCD, and she served as the education chairman of the SCWCD in 1918. When illiteracy intersected with national defense, Selden in the months before the arrival of Gray volunteered to help the SCIC connect with existing literacy work and offered her assistance for free.

Family background and education shaped Selden's civic leadership. Born to Joseph Selden and Emma Julia Lucas Selden of Spartanburg on November 5, 1880, she had one brother, Joseph, who died in 1885 eight months after his birth.[83] During the Civil War, her father served the Confederacy as a captain in the Alabama Light Artillery Unit. He was a native of Virginia and a widower whose first wife and two children died during the war. He moved from Perrysville, Alabama, to Spartanburg in 1880 to live in proximity to the family of his second wife, Emma. She belonged to a prestigious Charleston family that moved to the Upcountry town of Spartanburg during the Civil War. She was twenty years younger than her husband and died in 1898 when Julia was eighteen. Selden attended the Livingston Female Academy and State Normal School (now the University of West Alabama), Converse College in 1901, Winthrop College, and George Washington University.[84] When her father burned to death in a house fire in 1905, Selden apparently moved to the home of her mother's widowed sister-in-law, Hettie Lucas, in Spartanburg.[85] Hettie, her five adult children, Julia, and Julia's maternal, unmarried Aunt Ella lived in a large home on Main Street known locally as the Lucas House.[86]

A hub of the South Carolina textile industry, Spartanburg had many mills and mill villages. In 1912 Selden initiated the first intensive state campaign against adult illiteracy in the state in those Spartanburg villages. Her solution to illiteracy was the adult night school, a worksite school that operated after mill hours to provide educational opportunities to individuals who otherwise would not have the chance to learn. Selden petitioned local mill owners to consider her program, and in December 1912 night schools for boys and girls aged fourteen to twenty-one opened.[87] Selden did not receive compensation for her work, and the county supervisors refused to fund the schools. Local industrialists promised financial support if her adult education concept proved successful, and it did. The next year fifteen local mill owners donated one dollar per night to pay for Selden's mill village night schools. The fifteen schools operated for thirty nights, and Selden received twenty-five dollars from the state superintendent of education and thirty dollars from each mill owner to run the schools. A total of 1,100 students, including 331 adults and 272 illiterates, attended the schools. "I felt like a young politician hearing the returns after his first election," exclaimed Selden of her success. "In Mrs. [Cora Wilson] Stewart's schools there were 1200 pupils, so my schools were the second largest in the South."[88] The success of her program led the city delegation of Spartanburg to appropriate funds for a full-time supervisor of mill and night schools in 1915.[89]

Selden considered herself the founder of the adult education movement in South Carolina and wrote in 1918 to Gray that for her "it started back in the dim dark ages when the world was asleep on the subject."[90] In 1915 Gray's seven night schools in Laurens County were similar to Selden's adult night school model used in the mills.[91] Gray praised Selden as "a public spirited young woman of wealth who realized the need for literate voters and who gave her services without compensation."[92] She described Selden as "a lady by birth and by training" who "because of her democracy . . . coveted for all people the culture which had been hers. . . . She willingly gave her time and money that South Carolina might be a more intelligent and democratic state."[93] "I looked upon her as a co worker," reflected Gray; "in fact, before I accepted my present position [supervisor of adult schools for the State Department of Education] I suggested that she be offered the position."[94]

Selden's absence in the historic record is interesting in light of her importance to state educational history. Although a teacher by trade, she is listed in
the census of 1920 as unemployed.[95] Modern records regarding her life are
scant, but Gray claimed that she "was one of South Carolina's great pioneers"
and an "outstanding" volunteer.[96] Like Gray, others in the state recognized her
important work. In 1927, the year Selden died, the alumni director of Converse
College suggested that April 19 be deemed Julia Selden Day across the state "in
appreciation of Miss Selden's work for adult education in the early days."[97] In
the 1930s, to honor her contribution to state history, a Japanese magnolia was
planted across from the State House in Gonzales Square. Her tree was one of
four planted to honor the memory of those who supported adult education in
the early years of the literacy campaigns, the other honorees being Wardlaw,
Ambrose Gonzales, and Alex Long.[98] Today no marker exists at the square to
commemorate Selden's work.[99]

From the beginning the SCIC relied upon volunteers and civic networks to
raise money and public awareness about illiteracy. Selden was the ideal volunteer to help because she was "lined up with so many organizations" and hailed
from Spartanburg, a town that claimed to have the most school buildings,
teachers, and pupils in South Carolina.[100] "I think I can do it [coordinate the
illiteracy campaign] better than anyone else," declared Selden to Wardlaw.[101]
Her network included the Farmers Union, the Patriotic League, the Southern
Sociological Association, the School Improvement Association, the YWCA, the
Tomato and Corn Club, the South Carolina Sunday School Association, the
South Carolina Federation of Women's Clubs, and the South Carolina Women's
Council of Defense.[102]

As the SCIC organized an initial meeting to get a program in place, Selden
voluntarily began to organize and carry out the statewide literacy campaign.
Immediately she began to campaign aggressively against illiteracy, as she had
done since 1912, and call upon her connections to get the word out about the
devastating impact of illiteracy on the state. When she became the education
chairman of the SCWCD in May 1918, she came armed with experience, materials, and connections. Wardlaw wrote to Selden, "You have the great advantage
of being able to act on your own individual initiative," an indication that he was
aware of her active work.[103]

Unbeknownst to Selden, Wardlaw chaired a commission that for the most
part existed only in name during the war. The SCIC did not hold a formal meeting until June 1918, five months before the end of the war. "I have been unable
to get a meeting of the Commission," Wardlaw wrote to Selden. "Date after date
has ... prevented a quorum. ... I am helpless. ... I am much interested in your
plans for work. ... If ever we can get our Commission to work I hope that we
can combine forces."[104] From the outset tension mounted between the virtual

SCIC and Selden. The SCIC had no agenda because it had not yet met. Selden did not know this and viewed Wardlaw's letters as indicating unwillingness to share with her the SCIC's agenda. "Some time ago I wrote to you but you did not answer my letter," wrote Selden. "I hope the Commission can meet soon and plan out a line of work.... Wouldn't it be wise for the Commission to follow up my work by letters to the same organizations and others?"[105] She further suggested that Wardlaw tell the female members of the SCIC to get busy: "If Mrs. Coker will write to the heads of all the Federated Clubs it will help very much."[106] Wardlaw responded, "You are doing splendidly, and I hope you are blazing the way for the Commission to follow if ever it can get together." In the note he asked to keep the material she had mailed him to critique "unless you wish me to return it."[107] Selden responded, "Will you please tell me what the Illiteracy Commission has been able to accomplish for we must work together or our work will overlap."[108] An express goal of the SCIC was to cooperate with other agencies and groups working to eradicate illiteracy. Yet with no program in place and no formal meeting, there was no concern on the part of Wardlaw about overlapping the work of other state agencies.

On the contrary Selden was a member of the SCWCD, an organization with the "avowed" purpose to undertake community service with a "spirit of enthusiasm and patriotism" and to "restrict overlapping of activities and to eliminate waste of energy" with other organizations in the state.[109] Selden's correspondence with Wardlaw was an effort to coordinate the fieldwork of the SCIC with that of the SCWCD, and as a pioneer in adult education, Selden knew how to rouse the public, raise money, and create programs to promote literacy. She had a plan.

In early April 1918, as a token of mutual cooperation (or philanthropy), Selden sent a small donation to the SCIC. Wardlaw thanked her and explained, "One of our sorest need has been for money to work with; and this is the first to come into our hands."[110] Wardlaw suggested that she contact the South Carolina Sunday School Association, a powerful organization in the state, to promote the "similar resolutions" of the SCIC and Selden. "The Commission believes that one of the most fruitful lines of work will be thru the rural churches and Sunday Schools," wrote Wardlaw, "and of course they can be more effectively reach[ed] if the movement has the endorsement of the State Association."[111]

The politicization of illiteracy transcended the modern concept of the separation of church and state. In South Carolina churches, like schools, were instruments used to disseminate American values. Literacy was considered both a civic and a Christian responsibility. Church leadership considered civic benevolence an expression of faith and patriotism. Wardlaw believed that the SCIC's resolutions would be well received by the state meeting of Sunday school superintendents. "Write to members of the executive committee and others who will attend the meeting" he wrote Selden, "and make haste as the meeting is to begin the first day of May."[112]

Encouraged by Wardlaw's directive, Selden contacted the South Carolina Sunday School Association. The churches in both the black and white communities were important allies in her campaign against illiteracy. She wrote to Wardlaw in May that she planned "to speak at a Negro man meeting in which I hope all are ministers."[113] This letter is elicits numerous questions about race and gender mores in South Carolina during World War I.

Although blacks in South Carolina were excluded from the ballot box, they served in the war. One-seventh of all adult African American males, 27,000 of the 865,000 blacks in the state, served in the war.[114] In 1910, 38.7 percent of the black population in the state was illiterate, a total of 226,242 people. By 1920 the rate decreased to 29.3 percent with a total 181,422 black illiterates in the state.[115] Selden may have viewed black ministers as a portal into the black community, where she could inspire community uplift and encourage literacy among those with power and the means to fulfill her goals.[116] For Selden the ministers' Christianity may have compensated for the fact that they were black men. Her use of the word *hope* implies a concern that if they were not ministers, they were simply black men, a group defined by negative racial stereotypes familiar to a white southern woman. Lynching and race violence were realities in wartime South Carolina, and Selden's decision to speak to a group of black ministers not only challenged gender and race conventions but also illustrates her determination.[117] She was unmarried, in her late thirties, white, and from the upper class, which made her choice to speak to a group of black men a radical departure from conventional practice. She may have hoped for a crowd of ministers because if the black men to whom she spoke were not literate or politically effective, a meeting was a waste of her time. The border between church and state was elastic in wartime South Carolina, and apparently, in Selden's case, race and gender parameters were flexible as well.[118]

Somewhat of a spectacle with "the greatest array of talent ever secured for a Sunday School Convention," the South Carolina Sunday School Association meeting was held in Greenwood the first weekend in May 1918.[119] Selden took it upon herself to attend the convention and to ask church leaders personally to adopt resolutions to eradicate illiteracy in the state. The meeting did not go as she planned. Days after the convention, she wrote to Wardlaw that she "hung around for three days" waiting to speak to the representatives, and "finally after nearly all of the delegates had gone," she was given "five minutes of the last meeting of the last day" to promote the literacy campaign.[120]

Selden had no reason, other than her social position as a lady, to expect any type of special treatment or recognition from the delegates at Greenwood.

Despite the slight she experienced at the convention, Selden assured Wardlaw that "at present I am trying to get a letter which I will send to all of the Sunday school workers and others."[121] What may have been compromised at the convention was her sense of importance. "After a time one learns to judge men by the smell of their cigars," wrote Selden. "The man who knows a good cigar knows to put it by and offer a chair.... The two-for five man sits still and continues to puff."[122] Apparently Selden's "two-for-five" men outnumbered the other at the Greenwood gathering.

R. D. Webb, the director of the Greenwood event, wrote to Wardlaw a few days after the convention and made no mention of Selden or her speech. He did, however, enthusiastically share that the South Carolina Sunday School Association adopted the SCIC resolutions to eradicate illiteracy from the state.[123] At the Greenwood meeting, illiteracy was declared "a great obstacle to Christian truth."[124] A flurry of public service announcements followed. The media campaign urged "every Sunday school . . . to provide at least 1 class in which illiterates shall be taught to read the Bible."[125] "Endorse Education" appeared in the headlines, and in the *State* attorney J. W. W. Boyd declared, "Be it resolved by the Bar Association of South Carolina that the present efforts throughout the state to overcome illiteracy are commended and the work of the Illiteracy Commission is in this respect approved."[126] Amid the public rally, no account was made of Selden's speech at the convention or her pioneering work in adult education. All of the credit went to the SCIC, a body that had not yet met.

As Selden continued to work and send regular reports to Wardlaw, he explained that "I am obliged to report that the Commission has done little as of yet" but assured Selden that a meeting was imminent. He asked to have Selden's "plan of cooperation by that time."[127] Preempting any confusion or conflict with Selden, Wardlaw wrote: "I think it very desirable that your work and that of the Illiteracy Commission be combined and correlated. I hope it may be worthwhile for us to work together as parts of one system. I should be glad if you would write out your ideas as to the best ways of bringing about this union of effort."[128]

The only "system" at work in June 1918 was Julia Selden's literacy campaign. After his plea to combine and correlate campaigns, Wardlaw wrote, "You have the great advantage of being able to act on your own individual initiative," an indication that it was difficult to coordinate a meeting of the SCIC.[129]

On June 22, 1918, six months after Manning appointed the commission, the SCIC held its first meeting. In that six-month period, Selden had commenced the campaign through her voluntary networks, but she was not invited to attend the SCIC meeting. Exhausted by Wardlaw's poor communication about the SCIC's agenda, Selden contacted Mabel Montgomery, an SCIC member and fellow clubwoman, to find out from a female insider what happened at the first meeting. What she learned caused her to fire off an angry letter to Wardlaw. "Miss Montgomery told me you plan to get money for the Illiteracy Commission," she wrote; "she also told me your plan would use this money to take a census of each county. . . . Please do not do this. The School Improvement Association . . . has promised to do this and it will only mean overlapping work."[130]

A subsequent letter attacked his plans "to do nothing but get money and take a census" and warned that "there will be a great waste of time, money and energy" if the SCIC failed to "pull together" its work with her own.[131] She reminded Wardlaw of his past promise to handle paying for public speakers while her organization, the SCWCD, with the assistance of the private, community-based School Improvement Association, would carry out the state census of illiterates. One reason why Wardlaw did not support the School Improvement Association's taking the census of illiterates was that the SCIC had no oversight of the private group; to legitimize the census, the state had to be in control of collecting the data.

Wardlaw sent Selden's angry note of July 10 to David Coker, chairman of the State Council of Defense and state food administrator. Coker was a pioneer cottonseed broker and president of Pedigreed Seed Company of Hartsville, South Carolina, and he served on the South Carolina Land Commission chaired by Richard I. Manning. He was also an original member of the Federal Reserve Bank of Richmond.[132] As chairman of the State Council of Defense, Coker had ultimate authority over the work of the SCWCD, as it was the female appendage of the Council of Defense. Upon receipt of Wardlaw's letter, Coker sent a stern but polite reprimand to Selden that effectively squashed her plans to take the census. "It seems to me that it will be beyond your powers to organize and put on an effective campaign of this kind in all counties," he wrote. "The State Council of Defense has no organization particularly fitted for carrying out this type of work. It occurs to me that the work should be carried on under the direction of Professor Patterson Wardlaw who is a member of the National Illiteracy Commission for South Carolina."[133]

In this condescending directive, Coker exposed both his distance from the actual work of his appendage organization and his ignorance of Selden's trail-blazing fieldwork in the state literacy campaign that was quickly being appropriated by the SCIC. Coker explained to Selden that "a well worked out campaign in a few counties might furnish a demonstration which would make it easier to put through a campaign in the whole state."[134] He suggested she "get to work locally" and effectively put her in her place.[135] However Coker also understood the value of developing a campaign in a few counties.

In his resolve Coker did not reveal that he knew Selden was a pioneer educator who had crafted the first campaigns against adult illiteracy in the state. While Wardlaw had spent the greater part of the war trying to get the SCIC to hold a meeting, Selden had attended civic meetings, sent mailings, and formulated resolutions to promote the literacy campaign. In this one letter, Coker, the chairman of the organization for which Selden volunteered her time and energies, eclipsed her power, clipped her wings, transferred ownership and control of state illiteracy work to the SCIC, and silenced her voice in the state-run campaign.

Taken aback by the reprimand, Selden wrote to Wardlaw that Coker had "practically asked for her resignation." "If the Illiteracy Commission is better able to carry on the work than I, I will be happy to resign," wrote Selden. "I have only the good of the state at heart and am quite ready to go into some other line of work."[136] He responded, "I did not understand Mr. Coker's letter as asking for your resignation of your chairmanship, in fact the copy sent to me makes no mention of that. . . . I should sincerely regret if you resign or slacken your efforts."[137] Likewise Coker also wrote a second conciliatory but still firm letter to Selden and asked her not to quit but to cooperate with the work of Wardlaw. "It is the duty of the State Council of Defense not only to supervise all work of the kind you outline, but to see that different organizations do not work of the same nature which will overlap or conflict," he wrote. "Consequently, it is our duty to see that the Illiteracy work done in South Carolina is done with one purpose and under one head. . . . Prof. Wardlaw is most anxious to cooperate with you and coordinate his work with yours."[138]

It is hard to imagine the frustration, anger, fear, and anxiety that Selden must have experienced when two powerful state leaders appropriated her work. She was an unmarried, ambitious, and professional volunteer. To add insult to injury, Coker instructed Selden to coordinate her work with the nonexistent work of the SCIC. This meant that the SCIC was given the power to assume control of her work. She was effectively removed from her position and soon replaced by Gray. Did Selden invite her own removal? It is probable that her strong personality and ambition tainted her efforts to advance her agenda during the war.

With her work wrested from her control, Selden had her lawyer draw up a legal document that described her campaign against illiteracy. It was a futile attempt to patent her work. The attorney's inability to capture in a legal document the spirit and magnitude of her work sent Selden into a sick spell. "I am going to the mountains for a very short time," she wrote. "My attack was really a nervous breakdown."[139] Wardlaw sent a telegram to encourage a speedy recovery.[140] Meanwhile the SCIC asked Gray to join as the field secretary, the job

Selden had voluntarily performed for months. Gray had more education and a broader work experience than did Selden, and she was known for her ability to work with others. Four years earlier in 1914 at the Conference for Education in the South, Gray gave a lecture on how to supervise teachers and explained that her participation in the conference was at the behest of her boss, William Tate. She declared that she "unhesitatingly obeyed the head man," a form of work-related deference that surely factored into her subsequent professional success.[141]

In July 1918 Wardlaw urged Gray to return home to South Carolina and join the SCIC as a full-time, salaried field worker. "Please say what salary would bring you," he wrote. "We need you and we want you."[142] A second letter reiterated his request: "For this field worker, we want you. Provided we can raise the money, will it be possible to obtain your services? I earnestly urge that you give this question very favorable consideration. Your state needs you and the Commission wants you."[143] A third letter laid out what the SCIC could offer Gray in terms of a salary. Reliant on charity as the source of its funds, the SCIC proposed "to pay 150 dollars a month to the end of 1918, and promise the remainder of 1600 dollars and expenses for a full year" if it could be raised. The salary was not as attractive as Gray desired, but Wardlaw pitched the job as a chance to make a difference in South Carolina. "I know this does not seem as attractive as could be desired," he wrote, "but think of the splendid opportunity if we can carry it thru and I think we can!"[144]

Gray did not initially accept his offer and began the fall school term in Maryland. She was under consideration for a salary raise of two thousand dollars per year, more than double the amount paid to a teacher.[145] The job in South Carolina offered a salary cut and no long-term job stability. She did not agree to the salary and expense package offered by Wardlaw and chose to hold on to her job as leverage as she negotiated a higher wage. In a telegram the following month, Wardlaw wrote: "Proposition enthusiastically accepted. Salary 1800 dollars and expenses with hope of early increase. Come immediately." He continued excitedly, "I cannot tell you how eager we are that you come. Now is the opportunity to do the greatest thing for South Carolina that has been done in years."[146] Years later Swearingen looked back on the moment and wrote to Gray, "One thing I can look back on with pride. That is the fact that I was one of the group that induced you to come back to South Carolina. The more I think of the wonderful work that you have done, the more proud I am of my connection with it."[147]

In October 1918 Gray accepted the post of field secretary for the SCIC and returned home to South Carolina. Maryland released her from her contract, although State Superintendent of Education William Holloway lamented, "I feel as if we are losing our best supervisor," a cry echoed by others in the state.[148]

Wil Lou Gray, 1920. Courtesy of Wil Lou
Gray Opportunity School, West Columbia,
South Carolina.

Gray began her job in the final month of World War I.[149] She immediately
initiated ways to identify the number of illiterates and arouse public interest in
the fight to remove illiteracy from the state. Soon after her arrival, Wardlaw enlisted Gray's help to deal with Selden and informed her of the stressful relationship that had developed. He shared with Gray a manuscript on illiteracy sent to
him by Selden and explained, "As you know, our relation to Ms. Selden must be
handled with great tact. Dealt with successfully, she can be of great help to us,
but if we turn her the wrong way, much harm may follow."[150] Eager for Gray's
response, Wardlaw asked, "That is fine, isn't it?"[151]

Interestingly Selden was one of Gray's biggest fans. Although close in age
to Gray, Selden wrote that "by the paper I see that the Illiteracy Commission
has you as a field worker. If I were not so old and dignified, I would have thrown
up my hat and shouted for joy when I read it. You are the one and only person
in the state that I feel has their heart in this work as much as I have. We could
ill afford to be without you."[152] A few days later, Wardlaw received an excited
note from Selden. "The morning paper tells me you have Miss Gray. . . . She is
perfectly splendid," she wrote. "There is no one in the state who I had rather
have in the position or who could do so well."[153]

Selden seemed as relieved as Wardlaw that she now had a comrade on the
inside of the SCIC. In the first few weeks of her new position, Gray engaged
Selden in the SCIC work. "Wil Lou Gray and I are going over our work together
to see how we can help each other," wrote Selden to Wardlaw. Despite her new
inclusion and Gray's consideration, Selden ended the note with her typical

apprehensions, asking, "Did you send a copy of the Sunday School Resolutions to each of the County Sunday School Associations? If not, I will. I do not want to duplicate your work."[154] As the field worker, Gray was responsible for communication with community organizations, and Selden should have sent her directive to Gray instead of Wardlaw.

Gray's job for the SCIC was to coalesce all statewide illiteracy work under the banner of the SCIC. She relied on "the help of many club-women" as she traveled "throughout the state convincing mill presidents to employ teachers."[155] She worked with Selden not only as a gesture of respect for the woman who pioneered adult education in the state but also to heed Wardlaw's warning to handle Selden with great tact. By including her in the early months of her job, Gray eased Selden out of official state literacy work without completely offending her and took the pressure off of Wardlaw by assuming responsibility for communication with her. This move on the part of Gray speaks to the deference female professionals paid to male leadership in the workforce and her willingness to use Selden's support to benefit the state and advance her agenda.

Three weeks after Gray started as field worker, Selden resigned as education chairwoman of the SCWCD. "I do not feel that I am particularly needed," wrote Selden.[156] With Gray at the helm of the SCIC's fieldwork, the distance grew between the SCIC and voluntary groups who just a year earlier had served as essential citizen armies of the literacy movement. Selden realized this shift and expressed to Gray her feeling of exclusion: "Mr. Swearingen writes me polite nothings and refuses to give me any information as to whether I am doing the right thing or not, he will make no comment. If someone else were in my place, he might condescend to advise. It is not that I want to get out of work, I do not want to work ineffectually."[157]

She was outside the system by late 1918 but not fully aware of her irrelevance. Gray encouraged her to stay involved. "Really though," wrote Selden, "with all the backing you have you could get on without me, but if you want me I will stay. But what is there for me to do?"[158] After months of urging Wardlaw to define the course of the SCIC to avoid overlap with her campaign, Selden asked what she could do for the SCIC rather than dictate the terms of engagement. This strategy forced Gray to tell Selden what the SCIC was actually doing and what she could do as a volunteer to help. Within a month the war ended, and by 1919 the SCWCD disbanded.

Tragically Selden emerged from the war years a captain with no ship. She and a large force of volunteers who had served in the SCWCD offered their assistance to the SCIC. The SCIC did not respond to the offer. With the state firmly in control of domains that before the war had welcomed volunteerism, a new and limited landscape for voluntary service emerged after the war. The wartime aim to eradicate illiteracy became a permanent goal of the State

Department of Education and manifest in the postwar position, supervisor of adult schools, created for Gray on January 1, 1919, a position she held until 1947. The purpose of her job was to continue the work she did as field secretary of the SCIC but as a waged, state-level supervisor.[159] The SCIC remained an important arm of Gray's new position and continued to assist her efforts to promote adult education as the means to eradicate illiteracy from South Carolina. As the supervisor of adult schools, she traveled around the state to assess night school teachers and their learning environments. In Spartanburg Selden's night school received one of the most critical assessments. Gray claimed the classroom was dark and instruction boring, a harsh critique and a final blow to the woman who pioneered adult education in the state.[160] The correspondence between Selden and members of the SCIC ended in 1919. In the years after World War I, she spent winters in Washington, D.C., and took graduate classes at George Washington University, a possible sign that she recognized the changing professional standards for women leaders in education. She died in 1927 at the age of forty-six in Georgia.[161]

During the war the interdependence of public and private agencies was essential to reform culture in South Carolina. The SCIC relied upon voluntary organizations such as the South Carolina Sunday School Association, the Women's Council of Defense, and the South Carolina Federation of Women's Clubs to dispense its resolutions, raise funds, solicit volunteers, interest the public, and help coordinate literacy campaigns.[162] Likewise the scope and effectiveness of voluntary civic work was limited without legislative and state agency support. When Gray joined the SCIC, she took charge of centralizing literacy reform under the guidance of the state. Her participation in both the professional and voluntary worlds enabled her to bridge disparate work as the line blurred between state-controlled and voluntary reform.[163]

Julia Selden and Wil Lou Gray shared class, education, and career experience but did not reap the same benefits doing similar work. The Wardlaw-Selden-Gray correspondence sheds light on the different experiences of women as they engaged with state leadership and negotiated the shift from volunteerism to professionalism during World War I. As Gray's career advanced during the war, Selden's amateur rank placed her outside the realm of official literacy work. Once the state intervened to remove illiteracy, it took control of the work engineered by Selden, eclipsed her contribution, and erased her from the story. At this critical moment in national history when conceptions of American democracy were undergoing constant reformation, government took the reins of reform from private sector volunteers, and professionalism became a prerequisite for female involvement in official work. Professional license coupled with deference to authority enabled women such as Gray to advance to the top professional ranks in southern education as amateur volunteers such as

Selden, once a central force in literacy work, moved to the margins and disappeared from state history.

World War I dramatically impacted gender relationships and economic strategies in American households, particularly in the New South. Recent scholarship in women's and southern history focuses on the impact of economic restructuring on gender relations within households and how these inform the construction of public power.[164] The war was a catalyst for new definitions of gender and power, not only in the workplace but also within the home, where households of unmarried, wage-earning women and those comprising only females fell outside the boundaries of traditional definitions of southern domestic life. Gray and Selden illustrate how the work of volunteer women intersected and overlapped with the waged work of professional women during World War I. After the war the wage, coupled with emerging professional standards in the fields of social work and education, established a boundary between women active in these fields. World War I fueled this transition and bolstered the presence of wage-earning women in the southern public sector. The war served as a catalyst for the postwar removal of volunteer leadership in state-run educational programs.

By 1920 Gray established training sessions and degree requirements for teachers of adult students. Credentialing teachers for this type of instruction was novel, since adult education was still in its infancy. Gray had the power and liberty to develop credentialing requisites, as there existed no national standards or precedents to follow.[165] The war gave her the opportunity to take the lead in an unknown field of education and craft it into a unique division in the State Department of Education. When the war ended, "Wil Lou Gray became the state's voice for remedying adult illiteracy," observes historian Janet Hudson.[166]

Gray was optimistic that she could eradicate illiteracy from the state. She wrote that "the need for the schools for illiterates should pass in a few years provided that County Superintendents realize the necessity of promoting the work, the sufficient financial support be given, and the Compulsory Law be strengthened." Gov. Robert Archer Cooper, a fellow Laurens County native, showed his support of her campaign to stamp out illiteracy by declaring July 4 "Illiteracy Sunday." "The message of the Governor was a clarion call to everyone in the State for Real Christian Service," wrote Gray in her annual report.[167] Her goal was to eradicate illiteracy by way of adult schools. These institutions were the site where civic ideology could be dispensed, illiteracy wiped out, and the ignorant transformed under the control of the state. Bright Williamson of Darlington, a member of the State Council of Defense and president of the Bank of Darlington, wrote to Gray that "after your drive there will be but few white people in South Carolina who can not read and write." He urged every church and churchgoer, every school and schoolteacher, every child in the state and "various fraternities—the Rotary Club—the Kiwanis Club—and the Units of the Tobacco and Cotton Growers Association" to get involved in her fight. He considered the agriculture clubs essential, because "they reach the country folk directly."[168]

In December 1919, at the end of her first year as supervisor, Gray organized the first Southern Conference on Adult Education. Of the event she recalled: "The total attendance was seven people—two from North Carolina, one from Arkansas, one from Tennessee, and three from South Carolina." There is no mention of Selden's participation. Cora Wilson Stewart of Kentucky, Elizabeth Kelly of North Carolina, Sarah Luther of Arkansas, and a few representatives from other southern states attended.[169] Six years later at a National Education Association meeting, Stewart praised Gray's teacher training methods in South Carolina and noted the transition from volunteerism to professionalism Gray marshaled. "The state has now passed through the period of volunteer teachers without whose aid the work could never have been established," wrote Stewart.[170]

With many supporters and a clear vision of what she aimed to accomplish, Gray set out to develop adult schools, implement literacy campaigns, produce teaching materials, and create training requirements for teachers of adult students. Her career took off in 1919, and over the next four decades, she would shape and define the field of adult education in South Carolina and the nation.

CHAPTER 4

Commodifying Literacy

A commodity is an article of commerce. To commodify something is to say that it is valued primarily for its commercial value. Commodification is "the process by which technologies and resources are given value, often for the purpose of making them interchangeable."[1] Legal scholar Peter D'Ericco states, "The essence of commodification is the transformation of unique individuality into generic form."[2] In the post–World War I decade, literacy was commodified in South Carolina by Wil Lou Gray, who marketed it as a product critical to the economic progress of South Carolina. To powerful state leaders, Gray sold literacy as the key to economic growth, discerning consumers, and smart political constituents. To illiterate adults she promoted literacy as the source for increased wages and elevated social status. Economic prosperity was common ground between the powerful and powerless, and by linking it to adult education, Gray, as the purveyor of literacy for the states, brought both sides to the table.

The pressing problem she faced was how to get the illiterate interested in literacy and the powerful to finance it. "When the Supervisor began her work in 1918 the public, both literate and illiterate, had to be convinced of the value of attempting to teach adults," wrote Gray. "The illiterate had to be inspired with a new ambition and had to be taught a new faith in himself while the literate had to be shown his obligation to society and his less fortunate neighbor."[3] By assigning economic, political, and moral value to literacy, Gray effectively commodified literacy as a product valuable to all citizens of the state.

Mothers Training Class. Courtesy of Margaret Gray Choate.

Literacy appealed to different groups for very different reasons. On one side were those with the power to control the means of production and on the other were those whose job was to produce. To elite white professional, political, and industrial leaders, Gray claimed the value of literacy was in its use as a tool to indoctrinate the masses to their ideals and to advance their economic interests. On the other end of the spectrum, to a hodgepodge of the economically dispossessed—the mill worker, the poor farmer, and the black laborer—Gray defined the value of literacy in terms of better pay, the increased capacity to buy things, and improved self-worth. To the dispossessed the value of literacy was as complex as earning more money to buy a car and as simple as the ability to write one's name in place of a mark. Gray was in the middle of these two extremes, fashioning literacy to appeal to both sides.

Gray began her work as a state supervisor at a historic moment when literacy was considered essential to national progress. World War I was the catalyst for this transformation. During the war literacy shifted from a local reform issue to an issue of national defense. By the war's end, literacy was hailed as the antidote to poverty, crime, lethargy, and other social blights and illiteracy as the enemy of democracy. If effectively packaged and dispensed from the top down and assigned economic, political, and social value, literacy was the tool to create a hegemonic idea of correct political, social, and economic expectations of American citizens. The wartime focus on literacy magnified the internal illiteracy crisis in South Carolina, where the illiterate population remained among the highest in the nation.

The war ended one month after Gray began her job as the field secretary for the South Carolina Illiteracy Commission. Although most wartime organizations disbanded at the end of the war, the Illiteracy Commission continued its work to eradicate illiteracy.[4] The Illiteracy Commission was Gray's ally between World War I and World War II in the fight against illiteracy. She declared that "no record of the development of the movement for a literate state can justly be written without including the work of the Illiteracy Commission."[5] The Illiteracy Commission often supplemented the General Assembly appropriations for Gray's work with funds and material. In 1922 it donated money, provided four months of stenographic assistance, published some literature about literacy, purchased office equipment, paid for perfect attendance buttons given at the adult schools, assisted with expenses of state contests for adult pupils, paid for the entertainment at the State Teachers Association meeting, and offered seven scholarships to the 1922 Lander Opportunity School.[6] That same year Gray noted in her report to the General Assembly that the Illiteracy Commission donated to her state work $719.25 of the $812.95 contributed to the organization by women's clubs and interested parties.[7] Because of her connection with the Illiteracy Commission, Gray found a wide range of support for her work. In 1923 she wrote:

> The people of the State are thoroughly aroused to the need for popular education.... The State Press Association ... pledged its support. ... Many editors offered to send their papers for a limited time to pupils enrolled in the night schools.... The State Bankers Association ... passed a resolution pledging its active and moral support ... and recommended ... that a deposit of one dollar be given to every person who learned to write his name.... The Governor, at the request of the Illiteracy Commission, recently invited one hundred and fifty prominent men and women to meet in Columbia to make plans for the elimination of the cross marks.[8]

Gray used a two-pronged strategy to eradicate illiteracy. First, from her position inside state government, she created training standards for teachers and curriculum to use in adult schools across the state. Since adult education was a fledgling field with limited academic representation, Gray was at liberty to design and implement material she believed could best meet the needs of South Carolina adult students. Second, she used the media and the postwar atmosphere of superpatriotism as instruments to market her work to men of means who had the capacity to fund her work, to lure potential students into adult schools, and to rally the public behind her cause.

One of Gray's greatest challenges was the lack of skilled teachers who knew how and what to teach adult students.[9] "It has been hard to find capable, tactful teachers," wrote Gray in 1921.[10] As Supervisor of Adult Schools, Gray allowed only teachers with a first or second grade certificate to teach in adult schools.[11] Teachers were expected to have a "vivid personality and organizing ability," to board in the community where the adult school was located, and to attend a Winthrop training course. "Teachers must not only have a desire to serve but they must know how to teach and what to teach," explained Gray. Married women were not eligible to teach in adult schools, she continued, "for there would be danger of having divided interests, local prejudices, lack of training."[12] It can be assumed that she meant that married teachers—who would be assigned to teach primarily adult males (at least in the first five years of the Gray's campaign)—might raise eyebrows because of the innuendo and impropriety that the public might assign to the situation. Her choice to exclude married women averted public scrutiny of adult education at a moment when she needed public support for her work. Moreover she needed General Assembly support because her job was funded annually by the state. One bit of bad publicity could handicap her work and put her out of a job. Her choice to omit married teachers might also reflect that she wanted to make sure her teachers were committed completely to her project instead of a husband and family.

"It is expedient for every school official to see that only the best prepared and most skillful teachers are employed in order to enable the school to keep pace with the progressive movements in education," declared Gray.[13] Her work to credential adult teachers garnered national attention from well-known innovator Cora Wilson Stewart of the Kentucky Moonlight Schools. In 1925 she noted the credential process at work in South Carolina: "The actual teaching is today being done by those trained for the work. A complete report is filed at the end of each session and the teachers who do this work are paid at the rate of $1 per hour, provided at least twelve students are enrolled.... South Carolina's motto 'Let South Carolina secede from illiteracy' is becoming a reality."[14]

By creating adult teacher certification standards, Gray bolstered the power of the state by giving it, and her by proxy, the power to shape literacy material and determine who could teach adults and what they were taught. "Education was once the exclusive function of the family and church; today it is a function of the State which also looks after the health of the individual, inspects food and throws safeguards around his life and property," she wrote.[15]

Once she established training standards, Gray set about designing curriculum that was then used by the teachers in adult schools across the state. The material she developed included a text titled *The Lay-By School Messenger* and plays written for adults. "The High Cost of Spitting," "Pop Goes the Money" and "Good Bye, Hard Times" contained specific value lessons used to inspire the adult student to view literacy as the agent of self-improvement.[16] The underlying message of "The High Cost of Spitting" was that spitting produced disease, and Gray firmly believed that with this knowledge, the student would quit spitting. Acting out the plays was part of the learning process, and in 1920 at the Town Theater, adult students performed *SAND*, a play written by Gray's first cousin Rebecca Dial. It portrayed illiteracy as a prison that confined a person in a life of ignorance.[17]

Once she established state-mandated standards for adult education, Gray used the media to market literacy to potential students and investors and raise awareness among reform-minded citizens. The literate public was her target audience. Through the media she effectively built a groundswell of support for her cause in the first decade of her work. Her message was clear: investment in literacy produced economic, political, and social returns for the state and its citizens. She asked the public to think about literacy as the tool to combat the forces that stagnated the state: "If ignorance and superstition, these twin pillars of demagorgism, stalk in the life of a State we will perish from our own limitations. Well may we ask 'How long?'"[18] "The literate public has not generally awakened to its responsibility for making the [adult] schools a success," lamented Gray.[19] She appealed to the political and economic sensibilities of the powerful captains of industry and politicians and asked, "Does the State not owe a like obligation to those belated learners … and to those children who were forced out of school to aid in earning their own and the family's bread?"[20] Although she received mixed responses, state leaders typically supported adult education when the political and economic outcomes worked in their favor. Historian A. V. Huff stated that the point of adult education was "to teach the mill worker how to be a good mill worker, not a CEO."[21]

Inspiring public action to eradicate illiteracy was the chief objective of Gray as the supervisor of adult schools in the decade after the war. Broadsides about adult night schools and the deleterious effects of illiteracy appeared in newspapers across the state to prompt public support for adult education. One headline read, "Let South Carolina Secede from Illiteracy by having a X-LESS CLUB ROLL in 1924!" Beneath the slogan Gray wrote, "Wanted: 32,988 men unwilling to register with a mark" and "Remuneration: Your proud and glorious state cleansed of a blot and removed from the sneers of alien statisticians; the poignant gratitude of free men who are no longer 'made to feel ashamed when asked to sign name.' WILL YOU BE ONE?"[22] Gray listed the causes of statewide illiteracy as poverty, ignorance, isolation, superstitions, devastation from the Civil War, and inadequate compulsory attendance and child labor laws. To her illiteracy produced immorality, economic loss, poor citizenship, demagogues, inefficient workers, ignorance, and poverty.[23] Gray believed the only way to eliminate illiteracy was to establish a compulsory education law and adequate adult school facilities. "The stigma of a cross after the name of any Democratic voter should make him resolve to learn to write his signature before 1920," wrote State Superintendent John Swearingen in 1919.[24] By casting responsibility for illiteracy and its offspring on the state through media slogans and broadsides, Gray forced the public to reflect upon its role in the stagnation of the state.

The newspaper connected the public to the state campaign to eradicate illiteracy led by Gray and the Illiteracy Commission. "Stamp Out Illiteracy," "Blot of Illiteracy Must Be Removed," "Illiteracy Must Be Removed," and "Are You Proud of This Record of Your State?" graced the headlines of the press and presented to the public staggering figures on state illiteracy. Ambrose Gonzales, editor of the *State* newspaper, was among Gray's chief advocates.[25] As a sign of his support for the literacy movement, Gonzales published material for Gray's adult schools and donated space in the *State* for advertisements about adult schools. In 1919 he published ten thousand copies of *The Lay-By School Messenger*, an eight-page newspaper specially designed for beginning adult readers. "The progress of the work has been materially advanced by the . . . South Carolina Federation of Women's Clubs, the Extension Department of South Carolina University, Mr. A. E. Gonzales of *The State*, and the press generally," wrote Gray in her annual report of 1919.[26] Bright Williamson, president of the Bank of Darlington, wrote to Gray, "I had had some correspondence with Mr. Gonzales about the best method of offering five thousand prizes of $1.00 each for those who make the best progress in your campaign."[27] Until Gonzales's death in 1926, Gray recognized his generosity and support in her annual report each year.[28]

Across South Carolina local papers were as important to Gray's campaign as the *State* was. The country newspaper in the New South was a reflection of what historian Thomas Clark calls "the common man's thinking and changing opinion."[29] Between 1868 and 1929, the number of weekly publications in the South grew from 499 to 2,201.[30] Many newspapers in the state donated space to print ads about night schools and literacy work. "For a period of six weeks the columns of the newspapers were free for the use of the night schools," wrote Patterson Wardlaw of the Illiteracy Commission.[31] Many editors allotted free classified space for the state work, and Gray published advertisements to entice pupils into the classroom. In 1922 Horry County in the southern coastal region of South Carolina organized a night school drive. "Horry's Great Campaign" appeared in the headlines of the local paper, which "generously gave of their space to prepared articles having the night school as their theme." As a result of the media coverage, "public interest was rapidly ... crystallized."[32]

In her media announcements, Gray connected literacy to democracy and the emerging market of commodities and economic opportunity. One ad read, "Our State Needs Educated Men and Women" above a picture of an old man wearing a patriotic hat with "old man opportunity" written on the brim. Beside him sat a human head as tall as the old man. The top of the skull was opened like a hood of a car and exposed the contents of the brain. The head was filled with a ticker tape of numbers. Beneath the ad was an explanation for the state's rampant illiteracy. It claimed that the devastation of the Civil War prevented many from receiving an education and the lack of a compulsory attendance law created a state marred by poverty and ignorance caused by illiteracy. Although somewhat hard to decipher, the ad conveyed to the public the message that "old man opportunity" was an expression of democracy and that it was the state's duty to fill up the minds of people with worthy information.[33] Another broadside advertised a summer opportunity school at Erskine and asked, "Oh Boy! Oh Girl! How's Your Engine? Want to Grease Up? Men to go to Erskine and Women to Anderson College—Tuition $12.50 for one month in August." Courses offered were home economics, sanitation, spending and investing, beautifying the home, studies in the Bible, and educational moving pictures.[34] How the public received the ads is unknown, but perspective students no doubt anticipated a month away from tedious twelve-hour work days six days a week to watch movies and learn health habits.[35]

Gray's early literacy campaign assigned political value to literacy and tapped into the patriotism of the postwar era. She wrote, "Individual illiteracy may not be a menace but collective illiteracy may jeopardize the welfare of a State and democracy itself."[36] The rhetoric of her early literacy campaigns mirrored the language used to inspire patriotism during World War I. She appropriated the wartime nationalist language to inspire participation and support of adult education and literacy after the war. Words such as *Bolshevism, Americanization, Americanism,* and *patriotism* appeared in the literacy literature. "We rejoice that the word AMERICANIZATION has been changed to AMERICANISM, for the former seemed as foreign to us in the South as our aliens themselves. We are lucky to have so little Americanizing to do, and lucky, in a way to have so much Americanism to pass on, to foster, to inculcate, and to strengthen," declared Gray in a passionate and patriotic statement.[37]

The aliens she mentioned made up a small fraction of the population in South Carolina. Historian Rowland Berthoff suggests that "the appeal to foreign laborers and settlers was but a minor and futile phase of the New South." Berthoff illustrates that in South Carolina the appeal to foreign-born labor between the end of the Civil War and World War I intersected with the political careers of Benjamin Tillman, Coleman Blease, and Ellison Smith. The immigrants desired in South Carolina were those of Saxon origin, because the state feared mongrelization if undesirable aliens from southern Europe were dumped on the region in the wake of the social devastation the South experienced after the war.[38] One press release read "Learn English to be American—Be American in Thought and Heart." With a population of less than 1 percent foreign-born illiterates in the state, this ad was propaganda. It revealed the implicit Americanization efforts tied to literacy campaigns and probably caused many in the state to support the need for literacy, fearing that immigrants were the seedbed of anarchy and undemocratic ideas.[39] One county superintendent wrote to Gray, "Self preservation demands the riddance of such conditions [illiteracy]. Seeds of Bolshevism have their foundation in the harts [sic] of the unlearned."[40]

Appeals to the public tapped into public fear of antidemocratic forces. If the illiterate were not enlightened, they were a security threat, and in South Carolina, where before the war 18.1 percent of the white population and 38.9 percent of the black population were illiterate, this was a crisis.[41] In the Union only Louisiana contained more illiterates than South Carolina. Wardlaw wrote, "What we need is not information but waking up. South Carolinians, are you willing that your state should be everlastingly sneered at as the most ignorant in the Union?"[42] Strides were made during the war, and in 1920 white illiteracy was reduced to 10.3 percent and black to 29.3 percent, but these strides were only the beginning of a battle that would continue for decades.[43] When State Superintendent of Education John Swearingen asked, "Should not these men [illiterates] be taught? The dangers to the State and to society which lurk in their groping blindness are clearly seen in the shipwreck . . . of Russia," Gray answered his question.[44] "The old theory in ignorance is obedience has long been exploded. Russia is now suffering from an ignorant class gone mad," she cautioned.[45] By linking illiteracy to Russia and the Bolshevik Revolution, Gray used nationalist rhetoric and patriotism to convey to the public the political value of literacy and adult education.[46]

Many of her peers on the state level tapped into the same energy to inspire public action. In 1919 the chairman of the Illiteracy Commission, Patterson Wardlaw, argued that illiteracy was an issue of national security that threatened the state.[47] He claimed the public apathy and the high illiteracy rate in South Carolina produced "ideal soil for Bolshevism" and left many citizens unarmed with the "weapons of efficiency—that they must fight machine guns with flint rocks!" He urged the state to look at illiteracy "as a matter of humanity" and appealed to the Christian sentiments of his fellow statesmen, asking, "You who call yourselves Christians can you really believe that the truth will make them free, yet lift no finger to hand them the key to the truth?"[48]

Gray used the patriotic rhetoric familiar to the public to attack local resistance to state reform efforts. She declared that a literate population dealt a blow to localism: "The campaigns have dealt staggering blows to the old barrier of suspicion between people of the country and people of the town."[49] Gray argued that the rural population was not as inspired to learn as their city counterparts because of a "prevalent laissez faire policy and emphasis on individualism which makes a cooperative venture difficult."[50] To her city-dwelling men were willing to give of their time and money to the literacy campaigns because "the establishment of night schools gave proof of the fact that all of the benefits of government do not go to the wealthy and to the dwellers of the cities," and their willingness to finance adult education testified to the bridge literacy built between town and country.[51] Gray believed literacy healed the historic fissures between the city and the countryside, and she ended her appeal on a patriotic note: "The inevitable result . . . has been an increased reverence and respect for the State in the minds where that attitude has heretofore been lacking."[52]

Historically local resistance was a complicated problem and impediment to social progress. It was also the power source of local demagogues who ran state politics from the late nineteenth century through the post–World War I era. Gray's efforts to create learning opportunities for adults intersected with the political reign of South Carolina demagogues Tillman, Smith, and Blease, who preyed upon the "emotions and prejudices of the ignorant voter" by promoting racism, antiforeign sentiment, and states' rights among poor white men. Political Scientist G. M. Gilbert described the demagogue as "a person who seeks notoriety and power by exploiting the fears and desires of the people, . . . His behavior is guided more by its potential effect in beguiling public opinion than by any scrupulous regard for the truth."[53]

Although considered shiftless, ignorant, and degraded, the poor white man was the support base of the demagogue and the target of Gray's early campaign. In 1925 D. R. Hundley labeled the group "the laziest two-legged creatures on the face of the earth" and offered the following assessment of this class: "Even their motions are slow, and their speech is a sickening drawl . . . while their thoughts and ideas seem likewise to creep along at a snail's pace. All they seem to care for is to live from hand to mouth; to get drunk . . . to attend gander pullings; to vote at elections; to eat and sleep; to lounge in the sunshine of a bright summer's day."[54] Reformers believed the uplift of this group relied on political and economic reform coupled with medical science because their laziness and ignorance was attributed to hookworm.[55] "It is the hookworm and not the rise of industry nor the concentration of wealth that has been responsible for the existence of this class of economically helpless people in the South," wrote historian Emory Hawk in 1934.[56]

Gray believed adult education could remedy the political and economic behavior of this group that did not advance the state. To her adult education could combat demagoguery and promote effective political choice and foster economic growth. This was clear in literacy material written by Gray, in which she asked, "Can demagogues (again) sway men and women too ignorant to form their own opinion?"[57]

Historian William Link argues that the paradox of reform in the South lay in the cultural chasm between the reformers and those that they aimed to reform. Localism was a chief obstacle. Link claims that reformers were agents of democracy but also of coercion and control.[58] Two fundamental value systems clashed in their efforts transform the rural regions of the state—the paternalism of reformers and the localism of the country people.[59] Like Link historian Joseph Kett argues that reformers such as Gray faced a daunting task in a landscape characterized by a dispersed population, a devoutly conservative legislature, social and economic backwardness, and fierce opposition by rural individuals to mandates issued from city folk.[60]

Both Kett and Link agree that localism was a central and distinct feature in the South, particularly evident in the method by which public education, "perhaps their first and greatest cause," was administered.[61] The consolidated school was a tool of socialization that aimed to assuage rural individualism and establish cooperation among the rural people.[62] The school was a portal through which progressive values were dispensed to the rural population. Gray created adult education in South Carolina but not nationally. She trained the teachers, wrote the curriculum, and mandated the requirements for literacy work from a top-level state position. Kett claims that even into the 1920s, the lack of professionalized education and social work provided a lasting arena for reform-minded women.[63] Gray illustrates his point. Historian Leon Fink considers intellectuals such as Gray the stewards of a democratic mass citizenry, and they attempted to connect to the masses by struggling with the questions of how to advance the ideal of democratic culture and yet act as a cultured democrat. He states that democratic ideology, nationalism, and faith led many well-educated people to identify with the problems of the masses; yet in their efforts to reform, they often produced the results of "misunderstanding, condescension and disappointment."[64] Progressive intellectuals usually combined "individual forms of expression with specific institutional strategies and political projects of redress." They had a "missionary sense of public service," and "their degree of effort—if not success—was greater than most of their later-day counterparts."[65]

Gray fit the description of Fink's southern intellectual and approached illiteracy with an institutional strategy and a media blitz to mass-market literacy. An equally compelling example of Gray's knowledge of public fear and opinion was in the gendered nature of her early literacy campaign. The word *he* was used instead of *she* in the literacy literature, although both men and women enrolled in night schools across the state. In a circular titled "State Wide Campaign Aimed at Wiping Out Stamp of Illiteracy," Gray asked, "Does it matter to you that one-fourth of South Carolina's population can neither read nor write, that in 1916, 19,878 men signed the Democratic club role with a mark, that South Carolina sent to the army the largest percentage of any state of boys who could not stand the Alpha test for intelligence?"[66] She compiled her illiteracy statistics from draft enlistment sheets and Democratic Club rolls, where she counted the number of men who made a mark in place of writing their name. Both gendered documents, they revealed only the number of illiterate male registered voters and draftees. Here she asked the public to ponder the literacy of the men who represented the state as soldiers during the war. It was her effort to force her fellow statesmen to recognize two things: first that illiterate men represented South Carolina in the national army and second that these illiterate soldiers were threats to the nation and a poor reflection on the state. She excluded black illiteracy from this specific appeal. By doing so she decreased the percentage of state illiteracy, an indication that her early campaign either aimed to decrease white illiteracy only or that she feared an appeal for black literacy would alienate some whose money and support she needed.

The initially male-centric reports and circulars were likely due to the politics of the time and region. Although illiteracy crossed class and racial lines, the illiterate poor white was the initial population Gray aimed to reform, and public opinion did not favor the poor white laborer. In South Carolina poor white men were depicted as shiftless and indolent and, because of their ignorance, the victims of demagogues who preyed upon their fears and prejudices as they exploited their vote.

An appeal for male literacy in the immediate aftermath of war had more weight in the economic and political logic of the public audience than did an appeal on behalf of literate men and women. The 1919 labor unrest across the nation and the state made reform of this caste a social, economic, and political imperative understood by her public audience. Gray argued that male literacy produced more effective workers, healthier families, and smart voters. "Patent medicine remedies in education sweep over the country as do epidemics. What is needed most . . . is that the fundamentals in education be given to them. . . . If we fail to prepare we prepare to fail," she declared.[67] Historian Bryant Simon argues that by this period male mill workers in South Carolina were a viable political class with the power to shape state politics.[68]

The emphasis on male rather than female literacy in the state-run campaigns before, during, and immediately after World War I may explain why Gray funded female-only summer opportunity schools, four-week camps in late

August for adult illiterates, in 1921 and 1922. The first two opportunity schools, at Tamassee in 1921 and Lander College in 1922, were for women only.[69] Seventeen of the thirty-six pupils at Tamassee were women (nineteen men attended a community night school that was separate from the summer program), and eighty-seven women enrolled the following year at Lander.[70] These camps provide an interesting contrast to the large-scale, statewide efforts Gray oversaw at the same time that promoted the value of male literacy. She likely chose to devote her first two opportunity schools to women because they were excluded from the initial state literacy campaigns. Too, she may have realized the value of household politics. Scholarship in the history of southern women reveals the intimate connection between the household and public power.[71] Gray may have considered female mill hands and rural women as keys to the successful indoctrination of their male counterparts. These women could apply what they learned in a short summer session in their homes and, in turn, effectively convert their husbands, children, and relatives to new ideas about hygiene, science, etiquette, and citizenship. If both men and women among the lower class were taught the correct values and customs through adult education, the state would benefit. And the greater the numbers enrolled in the adult schools, the better the outcome. If enrollment doubled each year, a number that increased if both men and women enrolled in adult schools, it added pressure to the legislature to pay attention to the work and vote money to support the cause.[72]

The gendered nature of early literacy work is most striking when placed within the context of the times. It is ironic that Gray couched the political value of literacy in patriotic terms when she was outside politics and lacked the right to vote in the first year of her work. The Nineteenth Amendment was not ratified when she started her job in 1919. It is remarkable that at the war's end and in the subsequent decade, Gray was the best qualified, most experienced, and most recognized person in the state in regard to adult education and as state supervisor of adult schools held a leadership position to oversee state-sanctioned adult education work but was denied the ballot. As a woman who knew the most about a field few knew anything about, she promoted nationalism in a nation where she could not fully participate in politics for the first two decades of her professional career. Historian Harvey Neufeldt states, "My guess is that once adult education became a major part of the education funding, males would be more inclined to take over the lead role. I know some wanted Gray to become the chief education officer in the state gov't but Gray did not pursue it. Probably she realized that such a position went to a male."[73]

In South Carolina just how powerful Gray's position was in terms of shaping and dispensing ideology flew under the radar both politically and publicly because she was a woman in a fledgling field that by 1920 had state government representation in only two states, New York and South Carolina.[74] Adult education was a field unfamiliar to politicians and foreign to the public at large. Gray had power to shape the field through a job that in any other discipline would have typically gone to a man. With no national model to emulate, she was at liberty to craft the teaching material, hire and prepare the teachers, and dispense her version of democracy to the people she aimed to help—despite the fact she lacked the franchise. Through a job few knew anything about, she wielded a type of political power uncommon to most women in her state.

In 1921, 240 adult schools for whites and 181 for blacks operated across the state.[75] The New York Times reported that 2,715 adult illiterates in South Carolina were taught to write during the year and that 8,338 pupils, of which 4,815 were white, attended the summer adult programs. Classes met three times a week from 8 to 10 P.M., and 451 teachers were employed at a cost of $21,976. "The oldest pupil was a Negro aged 88, and the oldest white pupil was 72," declared the report.[76] By the mid-1920s Gray supervised four types of adult schools in the state—lay-by schools, continuation schools, mill schools ("all-time" schools), and opportunity schools for adults.[77] Held at various sites across the state, at different lengths of time, and at different times of year, these schools provided an array of options for illiterate and semiliterate adults to attend school.[78] Vocational in form, they required cooperation from factory owners and farm schedules in the development of a work-compatible educational program.

The first of what became known as "lay-by" schools was conducted by Gray in 1919 and was a short-term, four-week session held when the crop was laid by. The September report of the first lay-by session of 1919 reported 250 schools, 294 teachers, 4,943 students with an average age of thirty-one, and a 70 percent attendance rate.[79] Five years later Gray reported on the growth of the lay-by program: "240 of the best teachers in the State went to isolated districts for the purpose of giving to the unlettered their belated chance."[80] Approximately 6,380 students registered in 226 schools, and 1,297 did not miss a day. Gray contacted counties and urged them to employ an organizer to plan the teaching strategy, hire the teachers, and solicit community support for the program. Organizers took a census of illiterates in each school district by visiting every home. They were to invite illiterates to school and contact missionary societies and Sunday school classes to provide refreshments.[81] Teachers were paid one dollar per ten students, and they were required by Gray to attend a one-week training session at Winthrop College to receive specific instructions on teaching adult students. "This enabled them to go to their schools with some technical training and a group consciousness which made success inevitable," she wrote.[82]

A second type of school was called the continuation school. Continuation schools were organized in mill villages and taught by day-school teachers during the winter months for two hours per night, two to three days per week for four to six months. Semiliterate students were encouraged to attend these schools because it was "impossible for teachers to teach when classes included semi-illiterates, advanced students, near illiterate and illiterates." Teachers encouraged the advanced students to attend continuation schools, and Greenville, Cherokee, and Rock Hill had advanced programs in continuation schools.[83] In October 1924 Gray held a fall institute for continuation teachers who worked in textile centers. The event took place on the campus of Greenville Women's College, where a banquet brought mill executives and the teachers together to exchange ideas about the best methods to educate the adults in these mill villages. Gray exclaimed, "For the first time in the history of the work, mill executives were asked to meet with the teachers and discuss ... the needs of the work and the means of interesting the employer and employee." More than one hundred executives and teachers registered, and Gray claimed the exchange improved classroom organization and instruction.[84] It is likely she used the institute to allow the mill owner to tell the teacher what he expected his employees to learn in the classes that he was funding. Gray provided the forum where numerous mill owners could also swap ideas and information about how to utilize the schools most advantageously and glean social and economic progress in return.

The all-time school was the third type of school administered by Gray. All-time schools were located in a mill village, and the school hours were set around the workday so that learning could commence without economic loss to the student or employer. All-time schools existed at a number of local mills in the Upstate. Aragon–Blue Buckle, Arcade Victoria (Rock Hill), Clinton Mill, Brandon Mill (Greenville), Gaffney Manufacturing Company, Baldwin Mill (Chester), Clover, Mollohon, and Riverside-Toxaway (Anderson) employed all-time teachers.[85] These teachers were engaged for a year and paid $1200, and the state and the mill owner shared the cost of the teacher, $750 paid by the mill and $450 by the state. Teachers lived in the mill village and devoted all of their time to adult students. During the day they visited homes and gave instruction to illiterate mothers and at night provided organized classes for those who worked in the mill during the day. They also offered instruction at any hour or location convenient to the pupils.[86] "In Clinton mill the teacher gave instructions at the loom," wrote Gray in her report to the General Assembly to indicate the resourcefulness and dedication of the teachers involved in the work.[87] The all-time teacher is an example of what historian Lizabeth Cohen calls the welfare capitalism of the mill owners. She argues that by the 1920s factory owners in a paternalistic turn instituted policies to improve the living condition of their workers. Examples of welfare capitalism included wage incentives and the creation of self-sustaining mill villages equipped with a school, housing, and a mercantile store. The idea was for the industrialist to provide incentives to keep the workers happy and productive and in turn benefit from their satisfaction. Only after the Depression did the state replace the industrialist as the source of worker protections and incentives.[88]

Many mill owners supported all-time teachers. L. G. Potter of the Gaffney Manufacturing Company wrote to Gray, "The adult school has been successful. ... We will be glad to contribute 750 dollars in order to put the work on a 12 month basis and in addition to this if we can possibly do so, we will be very glad to place a house at a teachers disposal."[89] Mrs. Aug. C. Smith of the Brandon Mills, Greenville, wrote to Gray, "I certainly think the schools for adults have done our people good. Coming in contact with such characters as the teachers is elevating and will help to make the people less suspicious as these people usually are. I do not think that the state can do a more worthy act than to continue to do this work. ... I know that this work will make the people appreciate their work and make them more efficient to their employers."[90] In 1929 J. P. Gossett, the president of Gossett Mill in Anderson, wrote, "Having been left an orphan boy and thrown on my own resources in my early youth I soon realized that if I ever amounted to anything in life it would be through my own efforts ... to work, to save and to study. The carrying out of this resolution has brought me safely to my present position. ... The same resolution if properly applied will make you and your associates ... successful and honorable citizens."[91]

Gray argued that the only way to end illiteracy in the state was through the establishment of an enforced compulsory education law. Although many mill owners endorsed adult education, they did not favor compulsory education because of the possible removal of children from the workforce and the impact that law might have on the relationship between the state and the individual. Gray argued for a compulsory attendance law in every report to the General Assembly between 1919 and 1935. Her argument was both moral and economic. She believed if children were made to attend school, in two generations illiteracy would be removed from the state. Also public education costs did not match school attendance. When the state paid for one hundred children and only seventy-five attended, the state lost money that could be spent elsewhere, and to Gray that money could be best spent on adult education. R. J. Alderman of D. W. Alderman & Sons Company in Alcolu, South Carolina, wrote, "I am in favor of the adult school system ... but I am not in favor of compulsory education in any form. ... A compulsory system of education would start out harmless enough ... but it would ... be sure to develop into a semi-religious system of teaching with disastrous results."[92]

Inspired by the success of the adult schools, in 1921 Gray created the first of what became known as her trademark opportunity schools. "The flower of the adult work is the Opportunity School," she declared.[93] Her goal was for the students who attended the opportunity school to return after the summer program to their respective communities and "spread the gospel of health, citizenship, thrift and love for honest labor."[94] She also declared that "the three essentials to new advances in education are vision, faith, and friends," basics she relied upon to make her program a success.[95]

Gray modeled the opportunity school concept after Dutch folk schools and an adult program in Colorado she had studied while a student at Columbia University.[96] The opportunity school concept and the actual terminology originated with Emily Griffith, who opened a school in downtown Denver called the Denver Opportunity School in 1915 to provide educational opportunities for adult students. Gray's biographer and friend Mabel Montgomery suggested that she "borrowed the name from the Denver Opportunity School which was part of the Public School System." By World War I other southern states used the term *opportunity school* to describe adult schools, borrowing it, like Gray, from the Denver program.[97] Unlike the urban focus of the Denver school, Gray's opportunity schools reflected her training and interest in rural education and targeted rural rather than urban adults. Like the lay-by schools, they took place in July and August, when women and men could attend classes between the ebb of planting and harvesting on the farm. The school emphasized practical learning, an approach Gray believed was more effective than "poking book learning into folk."[98] The teachers, materials, and facilities employed each session were funded by a combination of charitable donations and state money. Students with sound body and mind and a desire to learn met the entrance requirements. "To make better citizens, to make better workers, to make better homemakers, to increase general information, and to effect improvement mentally, morally, and spiritually" were the express educational outcomes set forth by Gray.[99]

Gray's first opportunity school was held in Tamassee, South Carolina, at the school for neglected children owned by the Daughters of the American Revolution. As chairwoman of the board of Tamassee, Gray considered the facility ideal for her first summer program.[100] Seventeen women attended the first summer opportunity school, and they "accomplished so much during the short session that the feasibility of such a school was definitely established."[101] Gray chose the isolated location "so that in case the school failed, no one would be the wiser."[102] A student at the first camp recalled, "We had a real good time. We learned how to make handkerchiefs, we learned how to make pretty roses out of satin, how to set the table, table manners. And reading, writing and arithmetic."[103]

As residential boarding schools, the first two opportunity schools gave the chance to attend school to "girls over fourteen and women who in youth did not master the three R's but who now long for an opportunity."[104] The opportunity school was "more like a camp than a work site program," and it lasted a little more than a month. Gray claimed it was designed for "girls and women" with "the intense yearning in their hearts . . . to know how better to live so that they might come out of their corner of isolation and drudgery and become part of their community."[105] The curriculum included instruction in the three R's through practical application of tasks associated with daily living. This approach was successful the previous year at an Orangeburg mill school, where "a room full of women" learned how to read with recipes.[106] Each student brought their favorite recipe to class, where it was then read and prepared. Gray wrote, "I talked about foods, we prepared some, and I asked each person to tell something she wanted to know how to make. When a recipe was mentioned as 'lemon pie' I wrote this on the board and had it copied. Then I had each one to write the name of a dish she wanted so I could keep it and put her name on it. I had to write each name first."[107] This novel approach aimed to teach the students how to read with material that would train them not only to be able to read recipes but also to improve their skills as housekeepers, home economists, and citizens.

The cost of the first opportunity school was $100 for the salary of the teacher, Mamie McLees, who was the Spartanburg County supervising teacher.[108] An additional $24.95 was spent on groceries and $22 for the expenses of volunteers. The session started on August 2, and the school day started at six in the morning. The girls prepared their food, cleaned, participated in drills in the three R's, did arts and crafts, and "performed all work cheerfully even to the bringing of water from a distant spring."[109] The original cost was five dollars per student. When none could pay the fee, it was reduced to one dollar. Students had to bring commodities such as sugar, flour, or produce to make up for the reduction in fee.[110] One girl who had no money brought enough produce to make up for the lack of payment. After the event Gray followed up on three of the thirty-six pupils who attended the session. One went to work in a millinery shop, another continued in school, and a third attended the Lander opportunity school the following summer.[111] This first school established the pattern of payment that included bartering commodities to offset the cost of the program. Gray's friend and assistant Erin Kohn related that "one old lady paid her way with chickens."[112]

The following summer Gray held a second opportunity school at Lander College. Of the session she wrote, "The opening of the college for this purpose marks a new epoch in South Carolina's educational history, since it gives a chance for summer study and recreation of a high character to girls from a work-a-day world."[113] Her statement reflected her understanding of the lifestyle of laboring women and her desire to help them. Students ranged in age from fourteen to forty-one, and most of them had a third grade education. Board was $12.50 for the month, and the school day started at 7:30 A.M. Two of the pupils were from towns, nine from the country, and seventy-eight from the mill villages. Teachers were paid by the state and the cook and housekeeper by the County Board of Education. Many students received scholarships to attend given by local mill owners and women's groups. Gray claimed that there were more than fifteen thousand illiterate women in the state and that the Lander program "demonstrated the wonderful possibilities of such a school when backed by the sympathetic support of students and the public."[114] She also proclaimed that "since 1918, twenty-seven thousand adults have attended schools, twenty-seven thousand ignorant, prejudiced creatures have been transformed into enlightened, thinking men and women with ambitions aroused. . . . Every adult school is a factor in progress."[115]

To draw students to the opportunity school at Lander and raise public support, Gray announced the program in the *Southern Christian Advocate*, a popular regional magazine. She urged churches to support illiterate women who wanted to attend. "Believing that the Church should cooperate with the state . . . in the work of lifting the blot of illiteracy off our State . . . our Board of Education recommended the small sum of $300 be appropriated," declared Gray of the Methodist Episcopal Church, South's donation to the program. Tapping into the religious values of the public, she wrote that "the Master Himself declared that one of the outstanding credentials to His religion was the poor have the gospel preached upon them," thus linking her work to a spiritual mandate.[116] She argued that her work was a way to impart this spiritual imperative and thus deserved the religious community's financial support.

The opportunity school summer programs were funded by private and state funds. By 1930 the opportunity to attend these summer programs was provided in part by grants from the Rosenwald Fund, which donated $17,358 that year; local and county funds that totaled $23,074; and the Carnegie Corporation, which donated $5,000 in 1931. The American Legion was among the chief supporters and also supplied scholarship money for students to attend the summer programs.[117] But the real source of the moral and financial support came from "college authorities, church societies, patriotic organizations, civic clubs, textile officials, and public spirited citizens."[118] Between 1921 and 1946, Lander, Erskine, Anderson, and Clemson hosted the programs, and enrollment doubled each year, with schools for blacks beginning in the thirties at Seneca Junior College, Voorhees Technical School in Denmark, and later Benedict College in Columbia.[119] So successful were these summer schools that by 1929 enrollment averaged two hundred students per session, with Lander College the site of the women's program and Erskine College that of the male.[120]

The political value of literacy was established as a core theme in Gray's work during the 1920s, but she equally stressed the moral value of literacy as she marketed the adult education to the public. Gray claimed that "the constant yearning of the adult illiterates to read the Bible" was a primary cause for

Opportunity School students in Anderson, South Carolina, 1924.
Courtesy of Margaret Gray Choate.

the state to support adult education. In 1920 the South Carolina Federation of Women's Clubs considered the moral benefits of literacy so important that the organization donated five hundred dollars to publish a text called *The Bible Story Reader*. The book was written in part by Gray and used as a textbook in the adult schools.[121] In 1927 Gray wrote a text on civics education for adults in South Carolina that integrated Christianity as a core component of civic responsibility.[122]

Christianity was an important value to preserve in the context of the times, and state leaders in South Carolina had no problem advancing it as a core element of Americanization. They saw Sunday school to be as viable as a classroom in the propagation of state ideals. The binary to Christianity was atheism, the state religion in Communist Russia, and in South Carolina Christianity was an important foundation of the patriotism Gray initially built her campaign for adult literacy around. Often she reported to the General Assembly about the religious transformation of the adult students that accompanied learning to read to demonstrate the role it played in forging patriotism and citizenship.

Between 1919 and 1935, Gray revealed the moral awakening that came with literacy by sharing pupil success stories in her annual "Report on Adult Education" to the General Assembly. In one report she told a story about "a bright attractive girl who left school because sickness and misfortune" overtook her family. Gray claimed that the girl said, "I can't express what I have got out of this month. First, I learned table manners, something I wish every girl could learn. Next I learned to take care of my teeth and what to do to prevent T.B.... I know I have improved in many ways."[123] Although the girl made no mention of the three R's in her statement, she did convey knowledge of hygiene and etiquette that was gained at the adult school. Such elements in the curriculum reveal the progressive class values imparted in the literacy campaigns. Another student learned to read and "bought a large type Testament and Psalms and Hymn Book," and according to Gray, one family after a summer session in an adult school began to attend church on a regular basis.[124] In 1922 Gray included in her report a teacher's claim that "the majority" of her older students "joined the Sunday School and can read the Bible which is providing a source of joy to them."[125] Another teacher reported to Gray that the "laziest man in the community helped scrub house and asked for an individual drinking cup" after attending a night school.[126] Whether she used Christianity to appeal to the religious sentiments of politicians or to increase their fear that illiterates without an education were potential communists or atheists is unknown, but adult education leading to moral improvement was a persistent theme in her reports.

Gray's friend Kohn, in an article titled "South Carolina's Unique Adult Schools," included testimonials from students about the impact the opportunity school experience had upon their lives. One student wrote, "You know the first word I learned to read here was God, and now I see Him everywhere." Kohn claimed that "the burden of the song of all adult schools is better health habits and better citizenship." To bridge the gap between the spirit and the body, Kohn explained the significance of health education at the summer camps: "As a motivation ... there were tables for the too thin and tables for the over fat, lunches for the undernourished, and physical examination and exercise for all."[127]

In addition to the political and moral value of adult education Gray pitched to the public the economic value of literacy. Her appeals to the General Assembly for support took on an increasingly economic tone as the first decade of her work as supervisor of adult schools progressed. She chided the state for not enforcing a compulsory attendance law and struggled to get sufficient state funds to run the schools. Whenever the state cut the appropriation for adult schools, Gray noted in her reports the specific work that had to be halted or discontinued because of the lack of money. State appropriations for her adult school program were consistently inconsistent. In 1922 she wrote that "the reduction of the appropriation from $36,000 to $28,000 has greatly handicapped the work.... The pupils benefiting have never received from the State an education and this obligation has become an accrued debt. The expense per white pupil was $3.95, per negro pupil $1.52, a pittance in proportion to the value of better citizenship to the State."[128] Despite the 7 percent decrease in state illiteracy by 1929 and the increase in state appropriations from twenty-five thousand dollars in 1919 to sixty-five thousand in 1928, the funds could not keep up with the growth of the programs or the impending national economic crisis. State appropriations ebbed and flowed with the economic zeitgeist of each year. Although 142,000 students enrolled in the night schools between 1921 and 1931, in 1931 Gray wrote that "because of the decrease in appropriation, the withdrawal of the Rosenwald Foundation's offer, and county financial conditions, the number of schools decreased from 1,857 in 1930 to 360."[129] The next year she noted the continued struggle to grow her program without money. The reduced appropriation resulted in a decreased enrollment from 11,691 in 360 schools in 1931 to 8,999 for 307 schools in 1932, but the percentage of attendance increased in both black and white schools, a possible indication of the economic problems of the era.[130]

Gray persistently noted the waste of money in the public education system to illustrate that funds were available for adult education but that state money was spent inefficiently on public K-12 schools. In a pamphlet titled "Challenging Statistical Facts," Gray claimed the loss of public schools for nonattendance totaled $2,756,664 a year to the state. The cost per white student was $43.35 and per black $8.70, but the percent in daily attendance was a problem. She claimed that 126,521 young people aged fourteen to twenty-one were in school but 259,952 were out of school. She argued that money used wisely on adult education would benefit this age group instead of the state's spending money on the students who did not and could not attend regular school.[131] To Gray the existing system of funding was a complete waste of resources, but the lost revenue, if used to advance adult education, would produce results. By illustrating adult school enrollment numbers and perfect attendance statistics, she attempted to make politicians aware of their choice to waste money on day schools with poor attendance instead of investing in adult education. She wrote that if a child labor law and compulsory attendance law were passed in South Carolina, the state would be more productive. "In all candidness has child labor on the farms paid South Carolina? Iowa's put her children in school, her annual per capita income is $706; South Carolina kept her children out, her annual income is $437," wrote Gray.[132]

Gray believed that people in the state over fourteen years of age were illiterate not by choice but because of conditions that were out of their control. She listed poor schools, the lack of a compulsory education law, personal economic pressures that stemmed from necessity and greed, ignorance, and prejudice as constant culprits in the educational woes of the state.[133] She blamed the state in an acerbic indictment for its own stagnation. The ignorant masses were not interested in seeking wisdom and progress because the state kept them down.

"The uneducated mass cannot be interested in diversified farming rather than the one crop system, in home owning rather than renting, in home conveniences rather than automobiles, in securing financial independence rather than thriftless spending, in childhood investment rather than tobacco, in civic development rather than personal aggrandizement, in progressive statesmen rather than the noisy demagogue," she wrote.[134]

One way Gray marketed the economic value of literacy to mill owners and politicians was to offer proof that adult mill schools in the mill villages halted the exodus of skilled laborers from the state. "The value of this work cannot be overestimated. These teachers are reaching a group of people who have been neglected, and in their neglect, have been wandering from place to place in the blind hope that the next place will bring satisfaction," wrote Gray. She argued that adult education in the mill communities was an effective antidote to migration, and if administered to the community at large, adult education could prove to be a worthy investment for the executives: "In a number of instances the teachers have prevented families from moving by having the pupils work examples in school which proved that the moving was a losing game." She told a story of a husband who was unhappy with the mill and left his wife to find work elsewhere. His wife refused to go with him because she did not want to leave her school. Gray's happy ending to the story claimed "the husband went, only to return in a few days."[135] In a media broadside, Gray presented a disheveled man in a tattered coat and hat who stared at a sign that read, "Wanted: Educated Workers in SC."[136] The ad conveyed the message that an educated worker was stable and less likely to wander from place to place in search of work. Gray also attributed rural living conditions as a possible explanation for illiteracy and claimed that "dilapidated and impoverished conditions of the country people testify to lack of scientific methods of cultivation."[137] She argued that literacy attained through adult education taught the worker to increase their wages and stay put. This stability ultimately benefited his family, boss, and community. She also claimed that literate workers reciprocally assured the industrialist that their investment in the education of their workers returned in the form of a stable, skilled, more efficient labor force and, in turn, monetary profit. Gray marketed literacy as a win-win effort where every party that engaged in the work—student, activist, or donor—benefited.

Not every laboring and rural illiterate wanted to go to school. After a twelve-hour day in the mill and long hours on the farm, a classroom was the last place many wanted to rest after a hard day's work. These potential students had many excuses for not attending school. Student success stories were key marketing tools used by Gray to demonstrate to the public the transformative effect adult education had upon the illiterate, but her efforts to educate the disadvantaged often met resistance from the very group she aimed to help.

"Classification of pupils is nearly impossible," she wrote in 1921. "Everything will apparently be getting along right when the baby gets sick, company comes, the mill runs at night, a serial picture is shown, a patent medicine show giving away prizes, protracted meeting, etc. causes first one, then another pupil to be absent and so group work is practically made impossible."[138] Maggie Shirley, a teacher in Anderson County, shared with Gray excuses given by members in the community for not attending school. "About three or four days were spent going from house to house finding out who needed to attend school," she wrote. "Excuses of all kinds from bad eyes, indigestion and nervous troubles to protracted meeting, canning and lots of company had to be met and some plan by which to overcome had to be thought of."[139] When she pled for a mother to come to school with her two sons, the woman barred the door and with her hands on her hips said, "No, and I ain't a gwint a larn neither fur I'm too old."[140] Shirley also shared silly answers she received from adult students in class: "Sometimes a very funny answer was given to a question asked. One day we were having a lesson on the use of a silo and one pupil being asked what a silo is answered, 'That's a place where crazy people stay, ain't it?'"[141] Despite the implicit condescension, Gray shared the stories in her report to the General Assembly.

In addition to the resistance of students, Gray consistently received complaints from teachers about adult students. One teacher who taught in Berkeley County, an area plagued with the highest percentage of white and black illiteracy combined, complained about the character of her tenant worker students. Gray included her complaint in her annual report of 1928. The teacher wrote, "These people are ignorant and incapable and out of the abundance of their ignorance they are dissatisfied and restless. The end of the year finds them moving. There homes are mere hulls of houses in which they take little interest. . . . No conveniences or comforts are found, hardly the necessities. The word sanitary is not in their vocabulary and well balanced rations are generally impossible and not desired."[142]

Advocating for the education of black adults required a wholly economic strategy in the marketing Gray used to garner public support for adult educational programs designed to assist this group. To her black adult schools were essential for improving social and economic conditions in the state. To trap herself in a moral debate over whether blacks were inferior, worthy of state money, capable of learning, and so on was fruitless and counterintuitive to her goal of eradicating illiteracy from the state, so she argued the need for black adult education chiefly in economic terms. When marketing literacy as the only way to save the state from demagogues, communism, economic collapse, and self-sabotage, Gray placed black illiteracy at the top of the list of causes for the state's stagnation. By doing so she forced the public to recognize it as a crisis. In a 1925 report to the General Assembly, she declared: "Illiteracy in South Carolina is today chiefly a negro problem. . . . 51% of South Carolina's population is Negro of which 29% is illiterate—a much larger percent near illiterate. This means that practically one half of the population has low productive ability, thus a low purchasing capacity which in turn is reflected in all business. If the ability to read and write be economically valued at fifty cents per day, South Carolina loses annually because of illiteracy among negroes, $33,397,500."[143]

A decade later in 1935 Gray reissued the same proclamation in a letter to the *Charleston (S.C.) News and Courier* editor William Watts Ball. She wrote, "If illiteracy is to be eradicated, better educational opportunities must be given the Negroes. Is it fair to spend $42.25 a year on the white child and $8.70 on the Negro? Can such inequalities produce a descent [*sic*] standard of living under a democratic society?"[144]

Race was a topic that could render a law or an issue dead on arrival if presented to the public in a threatening way. In 1915 when a compulsory attendance law was set to be approved by the General Assembly, Gray and the teachers in the state teachers' association agreed that the word *negro* if included in their appeals would destroy their chances of success.[145] Although she advocated for black education, Gray did not protest separate but equal and instead set about her work within the framework of existing racial segregation in the state. To some degree she played into the prejudice of her region by refusing to engage in public protest against segregation. But equally she advanced opportunities afforded to black adults by working to provide facilities, teachers, and funds for black night schools. As a woman in a leadership position marginalized by virtue of her gender, Gray's approach was implicitly political.

Gray made the need to fund black adult night schools a key part of her literacy campaign. With approximately half of the state's population black, her appeal on behalf of a group systematically oppressed was a very progressive appeal and went against the grain of traditional social practice.[146] "The negroes have the sympathetic cooperation of their white friends supported by a fearless honesty on the part of their own race," she wrote. "It is a known fact that crime, disease, and economic poverty flourish among illiterate people and in our State this is true of the negro."[147] It was an economic plea with moral and political lining to inspire action on the part of the legislature and the public to assist black schools. "So long as one-half of our population is negro and so long as over one-half of the negroes are in the country and so long as one-half of this race has not really mastered the 3 R's, South Carolina will be looked upon as an ignorant State and incapable of great development," Gray wrote. "Therefore, in justice to both races the negro should be given a chance to acquire at least the rudiments of an education and thus become efficient, law abiding, understanding citizens."[148]

In 1919 the first night schools for black adult students opened in the majority of counties across the state. In the first four years of Gray's work as supervisor of adult schools, black night schools grew at a more rapid pace than white night schools.[149] With limited funds at her disposal, Gray asked teachers to provide their services as a sign of their belief in adult education. Initially the majority of black teachers who conducted these night programs volunteered their time. Her report of 1920 included charts with statistics on adult school development and enrollment. The chart showed 2,157 black men, 3,010 white men, 1,805 white women, and 1,366 black women enrolled in the schools. A total of 292 white teachers taught in 178 white schools, and 159 black teachers taught in 131 black schools. The salaries of the white teachers totaled $17,405, while the total salaries of the black teachers was $4,571, roughly four times less than that of the white teachers. The average expenditure for the state per black student was $1.29 and per white student $4.15.[150] For a one-hour session, white teachers were paid one dollar and black teachers fifty cents.[151]

Gray supervised black and white teachers in the state but did not directly deal with individual teachers. The county superintendents reported to her, and if they submitted a request for her assistance, she would travel to observe and train teachers as needed. "Where possible I have inquired into the fitness and quality of the work of the teachers," she wrote in her 1925 report. "Just recently three inquiries were written concerning negro teachers."[152] County supervisors often reported to Gray about black teachers under their supervision. In one case a supervisor declared that a black teacher in the district was one of the best in the county and doing excellent work; in another district a supervisor reported that the county trustees purposely refused to sign his report because of one black teacher who was no good; and in a third case, although the supervisor signed the application to receive money from the state for a black teacher, he claimed he knew nothing about the black teacher who worked in his district.[153]

This scenario is important because it demonstrates the complexity in terms of race and gender of Gray's leadership role as a state supervisor. She supervised many men who held county superintendent positions across the state, which in the scheme of gender expectations and relations in interwar South Carolina was uncommon. Further that the male superintendent in the third case regarding a black teacher signed the application for money without knowledge of the teacher demonstrates his distance from educational developments in the black community and in his district. Also it is unknown what assessment tool was used to evaluate the black teachers within county districts in the state. This is important when considering to what extent racism may have played a role in the second superintendent's claim that the black teacher was no good. Moreover the reports of these supervisors had an impact upon the lives of the black teachers. The first black teacher was paid; the second, "no good" teacher was not

Erskine Opportunity School, 1926. Courtesy of Margaret Gray Choate.

paid; and "in the third case payment was made for the application was properly signed by the superintendent and trustees" despite the fact the superintendent had no knowledge of the teacher for whom he signed a sheet for payment. Gray wrote, "If this work is to be effective, it must have the hearty cooperation of local white authorities."[154] It also required that they act in earnest. One female supervisor blamed a black teacher's delinquent report for her inability to get the work requested by Gray turned in on time. She wrote a lengthy excuse but provided the black teacher no opportunity to defend herself. These cases reflect the race relations of the era, and even if black schools developed, Gray relied upon local supervisors to ensure that money was effectively distributed and reports were truthful. As can be imagined, many local areas suffered as a consequence when Gray's efforts were not carried out effectively at the local level.[155]

By 1925 and with a state appropriation of $34,700, Gray reported the racial discrepancy in the use of funds for adult education and explained that "it is unfortunate that the increasing demand on the part of the whites forced a curtailment of the work among negroes, as seen by the growth of white enrollment and decrease in negroe enrollment. The supervisor appealed to the colored teachers for voluntary work and many responded."[156]

Model home built by Voorhees College students, 1936.
Courtesy of South Carolina Department of Archives and History,
Opportunity School Records, Columbia.

One of Gray's most potent appeals came in 1926: "So long as South Carolina has within her borders 38,000 whites and 181,000 negroes who cannot read and write ... the State cannot expect to develop as its native resources and climate would warrant."[157] She tied literacy to the economic development of the state and argued that "no one factor would be more instrumental in bringing about a New South Carolina than the elimination of illiteracy." When the state appropriations fell short of her needs, her reports often explained that demand for schools was greater than the ability to supply teachers and facilities. Black night schools were the first to be cut, and in 1926 Gray wrote that "no negro work was authorized" due to the lack of money.[158]

The rhetoric of opportunity inspired all people across the state to engage in the literacy campaign despite the reality that it was a separate and hardly equal opportunity. Gray must have followed this reasoning to ensure the lifespan of her adult education idea and to garner public support without stirring up protest or reaction from racist statesmen. Despite the limitations of what she did, her desire to improve the educational opportunities for black people was progressive in a state where lynching was still a practice, poverty a daily reality, and illiteracy a disease among many of its black citizens.[159]

CHAPTER 5

Democracy in
Black and White

————————

In 1974, when asked if she thought about race relations in South Carolina, Wil Lou Gray said, "I was like everyone else. I didn't."[1] Despite Gray's statement, apparently she did think about race relations in her home state, and often. In every report to the General Assembly between 1919 and 1935 as the supervisor of adult schools for the South Carolina Department of Education, Gray argued that the state could not prosper unless it gave equal attention and support to black adult education. Her reports forced the General Assembly to hear her pleas and brought racism and illiteracy center stage as impediments to state progress.

Gray's work to improve educational opportunities for black and white adults between 1919 and 1935 are commendable. Although she faced incredible obstacles in her effort to find money, support, qualified teachers, and pupils for her adult programs, she used her position in state government to make literacy a commodity needed by everyone, despite race, gender, or station in life.

Brought up in a white, upper-class household in South Carolina, Gray had been reared to accept the prevailing gender, class, and racial mores of her region. Yet by the 1930s she proffered a perspective on black life that defied the dominant regional narrative of black racial inferiority and used adult education as a portal to attack the racism that she believed stifled state progress. Regional progress in race relations depended upon whites envisioning black people as fully human with similar potential. Here projects conducted by Gray in the 1930s reveal she was instrumental in facilitating this process through her work. In 1931 she conducted an educational experiment (herein called the Seneca study), with the assistance of northern academics and a Carnegie Foundation grant, that proved there was little difference in the learning capacity of black and white adults when trained in favorable environments.[2] In 1935 she led four thousand black men and women on a one-day pilgrimage to the State House, and from 1934 to 1937, she held opportunity schools for black adults—four-week residential camps for adult illiterates—at Voorhees Technical College in Denmark, South Carolina. In addition to the three R's, the curriculum at these summer camps focused on African heritage and identity. In the context of De-pression-era South Carolina, where race violence, poverty, and illiteracy shaped the lives of many African Americans, her work marked a radical departure from the status quo. "Conflicts between the white and black groups is [sic] difficult to avoid because the races are so different in physical appearance, holdings, edu-cation, historical background and folkways. In many South Carolina commu-nities this inter-racial situation is the source of bitter discord and sometimes violence," explained Gray in a state pamphlet on statistics in South Carolina.[3]

Gray offered a unique portrayal of African Americans that had the potential to change white perceptions of race during an important transitional period in American history. Despite having come of age during the height of the Jim Crow era in the South, she produced three influential projects at a time when eugenics, scientific racism, segregation, and racial violence were widely accepted and when democratic institutions and values in the United States were sorely tested due to the global economic crisis. Totalitarian governments abroad pro-moted racial discrimination backed by the some of the same scientific theories that bolstered Jim Crow laws and involuntary sterilization at home, practices that reified the void between America's actions and democratic creed.[4] Against this backdrop Gray used tests and measurements, determination, and fearless-ness to promote democracy and social justice by casting aside stigmas assigned collectively to black people and revealing the individual black person's experi-ence and humanity.[5] Gray's friend Pulitzer Prize–winning author Julia Peterkin stated it clearly: "It is absurd to place all Negroes in one great social class, mark it 'colored' and make generalizations about its poverty, ignorance, immorality. . . . Negro individuals differ in character and mentality as widely as do people with lighter skin."[6] Gray agreed and proved this by using social science, ex-periential learning, and immersion camps to prove that shared the humanity of black and white people required that the state provide at least equality of opportunity in spite of the reality of social inequality.

Gray was part of an intellectual current in the South prefiguring the monu-mental policy changes of the 1950s that legally ended segregation. Historians have recently started to uncover significant civil rights activism in the decades before the 1950s, particularly among labor unions, the NAACP, and the Communist Party. Gray's work in the 1930s reveals the significant role that a handful of white women played in the decades leading up to the modern civil rights movements as they deviated from the racism that stifled the vast majority of white southerners.[7] Moreover the 1930s is an important period to analyze the system of segregation in the South because it was only one component of racial capitalism, what Jacqueline Dowd Hall argues advanced white privilege and the exploitation of blacks and poor whites in the region: "Black and white southerners engaged in constant and nuanced interactions. . . . The age of segregation might better be called the age of 'racial capitalism,' for segregation was but one instrument of white supremacy, and white supremacy entailed not only racial domination but economic practices. . . . Those practices involved low taxes, minimal investment in human capital, the exploitation of non-unionized, undereducated black and white labor, and the patriarchal control of families and local institutions."[8]

Aware of the systems of oppression that trapped her state from advancing, Gray through her work challenged the exploitation of blacks and poor whites by creating opportunities for these groups to attend school and learn to read and write, the starting point for social, economic, and personal improvement and enlightenment. Using social science as her weapon amid the despair and social crisis of the Depression years, in 1931 Gray conducted an experiment to test the ability of adult illiterates to learn to read and write at two coeducational summer camps, one for whites at Clemson College and the other for blacks at nearby Seneca Institute. Gray found little variance in the learning abilities of black and white adults and challenged the widespread idea of innate differences in the mental capacities of the two races.[9] By segregating the black and white student groups at different schools, excluding race from her vast list of research questions, and funding the experiment with money from the Carnegie Foundation, a source outside of the region, Gray worked around the limitations of regional race politics and achieved gains for black adult students.

By the early thirties, teaching universities across the nation produced scholarship related to adult education. In 1932 Columbia University, Vassar College, the University of Michigan, and Ohio State University received funds from the American Association of Adult Education to conduct research in adult education. Formed in 1926, the association served two purposes: to disseminate information on developments in the field through its publication, the *Journal of Adult Education,* and to fund research and scholarship. The association's main effort, however, was to "supply a medium of exchange for teachers and administrators actually in contact with adults," and by the early 1930s, it had direct contact with more than five hundred local, state, national, and international organizations.[10] Gray served as a member of the executive board of the association in 1931.[11]

Gray was well known across the nation for her work with adult learners and her signature opportunity schools. "She is one of the most outstanding women in the South. . . . Her contributions even to adult education is [sic] not only state wide but nationwide. Indeed, she has much to contribute even to China and India and every country of the world facing the dire dilemma of illiteracy," wrote Mabel Carney, a professor at Teachers College, Columbia University.[12] In 1921 Gray held the first opportunity school, for seventeen white women at Tamassee, South Carolina, and expanded the school in subsequent years to include men and black students. She used her position as state supervisor of adult education to bolster public and state tax support for her programs.[13] The South Carolina General Assembly was less inclined to supply money for her schools, and for the most part, funding for opportunity schools was a blend of state money and contributions from "college authorities, church societies, patriotic organizations, civic clubs, textile officials . . . public spirited citizens" and, in Gray's words, "faith."[14]

Between 1921 and 1946, numerous state colleges hosted opportunity schools, and enrollment doubled each year. Opportunity schools for black students took place in 1931 at the Seneca Institute in Seneca, South Carolina, and in 1934, 1935, 1936, and 1937 at Voorhees Technical School in Denmark, South Carolina.[15] In the summer of 1930, Gray submitted an application to the American Association of Adult Education for a subsidy of five thousand dollars to conduct an educational experiment at her summer opportunity school and received the money from the Carnegie Corporation. The purpose of the study was to discern the learning capacity of black and white adults with varied levels of education when taught in a "favorable" environment.[16] The study aimed to prove the effectiveness of adult elementary education on illiterate adults and provide a model for other states. William Gray of the University of Chicago (no relation to Gray) and J. Warren Tilton, a psychologist from Yale, directed the testing of the students and used materials designed by Edward L. Thorndike, a psychologist at Teachers College.[17] Gray used the study to promote her belief that the "lack of popular education is an expensive and increasing liability which can and which should be turned into rich assets."[18] She wanted all citizens of South Carolina, black and white, to receive tax-supported literacy education as needed, an unpopular and controversial idea at the time. Gray understood that the state government, already slow to support literacy education for white adults, was even more unwilling to support education for black adults, and hoped her study would justify and encourage such spending.

From July 23 to August 22, a combined summer school took place at Clemson College and the Seneca Institute. The five-thousand-dollar grant paid two

The Clemson Group, 1931. Courtesy of Margaret Gray Choate.

thousand dollars for the salaries of William Gray and Tilton (selected for the study by Thorndike) and two thousand dollars for scholarships, twenty dollars each for fifty black and fifty white participants. The remaining money paid for materials and testing supplies. Morse Cartwright of the American Association for Adult Education asked that the grant be made as an allocation against the Adult Education Experimental Fund (that contained sixteen thousand dollars of grant money from the Carnegie Corporation in 1930–31), because "South Carolina's program seems to be the outstanding state demonstration in the campaign against adult illiteracy."[19] Teachers were paid one hundred dollars, with board provided by the state.[20] To accommodate the racial demands of the region, the "colored Baptists" loaned the Seneca site to Gray for the black students' housing.[21]

Of the 288 pupils who attended, only the Carnegie-funded students were tested, and these students ranged in age from fourteen to seventy. The school day lasted from 7:30 A.M. to 11:00 P.M., with free time for exercise and chapel incorporated into the schedule. Gray noted that the first week was hard for many of the black students because they were older and struggled with eye-strain or poorly adjusted eyeglasses.[22] Out-of-class time was also different for

The Seneca Group, 1931. Courtesy of Wil Lou Gray Opportunity School,
West Columbia, South Carolina.

the black students. Because some of them worked as cooks, many participated
in cooking classes that focused on every aspect of the meal from cost analysis to
nutritional value. The black students also led their own vespers. Here they sang
spirituals "as only the colored race can," according to Gray, and recited from
newspapers and current events. Due to lack of equipment at the Seneca site,
moving pictures were absent in the curriculum provided the black students.
However a local theater manager invited them to attend on Saturdays, where
many students saw a "talkie" for the first time.[23] A local paper reported the
event and observed that "the Richardson theatre gave them a special show and
invited the entire school as their guests All accepted except some members of
the Holiness church, these thought this kind of entertainment a sin, so they
refused the invitation. It was an interesting study in psychology to hear the
reaction of those who had never seen, or heard, a play given on the screen."[24]

To determine the IQ of each student, verbal and nonverbal tests were
given during the month-long session to the Clemson and Seneca experimental
groups. Published after the experiment was completed, the Seneca study provided a comprehensive explanation of the rationale, objectives, findings, and
the decisive conclusions of the scholars involved in the project. The numerous research questions that guided the study were listed in the first chapter of

the report. These questions examined the impact of gender, age, income, previous schooling, and occupation on the intelligence and learning capacity of illiterate adults. Many of these factors later explained in part the differences between the black and white students' intelligence test scores. Although the study was clearly designed to determine whether or not race affected learning capacity, as written none of the research questions addressed race. The conspicuous absence of race in the research questions is important, because the two experimental groups of equal size were differentiated by race. Although age, gender, occupation, and education were assessed as key factors related to the differences in scores of the two groups, race, the most glaringly obvious difference and one fully loaded with cultural meaning, did not appear in any written question. It is likely that Gray purposely did not include a question about race in order to neutralize potential local controversy about the study, even though race was overtly a benchmark of the research. Only in the conclusion of the report did she mention race. Here she debunked the myth that learning capacity was innately tied to race and that racial difference was manifested in mental capacity by concluding that there was "little difference between the learning ability of whites and Negroes."[25]

The average age of the fifty-five students at Seneca was thirty-eight, and the group had an average of seven months of previous schooling. Since the grant paid for only fifty participants at Seneca, private donors paid the tuition for five additional students.[26] Collectively the black students were approximately thirteen years older than their white counterparts. Of the twenty-six black students reporting salaries, the average wage was a $1.50 per week for occupations that included farmer, cook, mechanic, laundress, and midwife. A local paper reported that "one man who is attending the school has 15 children but quit his job just to learn to read and write. Another earning $10.00 each week as a cook quit his job to learn to read and write."[27] None of the Seneca students worked in the mills, yet thirty of the students came from Oconee County, where the study took place, a cotton and textile center in the Upstate. In contrast two-thirds of the white students at Clemson worked in the textile industry and made an average salary of $9.04 per week.[28] Half of the Seneca participants were orphans, twenty-seven grew up in homes where there were ten to seventeen children, and the participants had an average of three children in their respective households. Despite significant socioeconomic differences from the Clemson group, the Seneca group read the same materials and took the same tests and measurements as their counterparts.[29]

In 1932 the *Peabody Journal of Education* reviewed the study as a "quantitative treatment of the results of short course schools for adults" and "a bit of definitive evidence in a field marked by many and diverse opinions."[30] Eight years later Gray summarized the 1931 summer experiment: "In 1931 ... the Carnegie

Corporation of New York City gave the school 5000k to finance an experiment to determine the learning ability of adult illiterates under favorable conditions. The findings of those four work-filled weeks were published in a book and sent all over this country and several foreign ones. We still have a feeling of pride when we see this book and remember the service we were able to render."[31] In 1931, when African Americans were still lynched in South Carolina and the global eugenics movement sprang from the premise that racial inferiority was physiological and scientifically verified, this was a bombshell of a study that found its primary reading audience outside of the state where the study took place. As a social scientist, Gray knew how to conduct a study, publish the findings, and use those findings as evidence to support her arguments and advance equality of educational opportunities for all the people of her state. And she used nationally recognized scholars as her research collaborators and used the most modern, cutting-edge academic testing measures as her tools, proof she was not willing to risk anyone attempting to undermine her findings by attacking her peers, methods, or tests and measurements. Clearly she knew what she was doing and did it with intent.

It is important to consider the curriculum used to educate the students at Seneca in relation to the findings of the experiment. All of the reading and writing material used at the Seneca site had both a racial and class bias, with everything from advertisements to etiquette lessons reflecting a white, upper-class lifestyle and environment. For example Seneca student Katy Smith, an African American women, wrote in her class scrapbook, "An attractive table makes the meal more appealing," above a picture of a table set for a wealthy, refined family. The caption beneath the picture read, "The dark beauty of Ebony and the clearness of Crystal are graciously combined in this setting for a formal luncheon. The Millefleur cutting on the square base tumbler is matched on the crystal service plate. The embroidered organdie cloth is Florentine."[32] It is unlikely that any of the students at either Seneca or Clemson could comprehend, much less find value in, this information beyond recognizing the picture of a table set with plates and utensils. How the black and white students understood, processed, and made sense of the teaching materials used by the instructors probably influenced the assessments of their progress administered during the term. The language and imagery used to teach core concepts—in an era before television, the Internet, and the advent of a primarily visual culture—likely appeared foreign to many of the students and in turn impacted their understanding of the concepts presented to them by the faculty.

Despite the biased curriculum used to instruct the students, the commencement exercises at Seneca were racially sensitive and reflected African American history and culture. At the final program, a group of students presented to the audience a booklet called "The Story of My Race" and sang what

Gray called a "farewell group of spirituals" at the conclusion of the program. "Every one," claimed Gray, "left the Seneca Institute with a feeling of satisfaction."[33] Although these closing ceremonies drew from black history, the question of who designed the program and chose the songs and specific black leaders to remember is significant since Gray was ultimately, in collaboration with the black teachers, responsible for designing and approving the program. With fellow educators such as Mary McLeod Bethune using similar approaches to the African American past in her work at Bethune-Cookman College, it is likely Gray was familiar with these ideas and incorporated them into the Seneca program. Bethune appealed to the white community on one front and the black community on the other. Whites honored her, says historian Elaine Smith, for her ability to get along with them and to "push them in the direction of the democratic ideal." She capitalized on her blackness, raising revenue for her school by "shamelessly exploiting the tourists at Daytona Beach" and marketing southern black culture for money. Too, as Smith suggests, "Bethune networked with influential whites to gain more opportunities." Her school in Daytona was an "interracial island in a sea of segregation" and promoted racial understanding and the gospel. The Sunday afternoon meetings drew tourists and locals, helped the local economy, and raised revenue for the school.[34]

Olema Wiggins, a student at Seneca, wrote to Gray after the summer program ended that "I have found no one so intensely interested in us as a race as you. All I can say will not express my gratitude to you for the interest you have in us."[35] Additionally the overall health of the Seneca students changed while in residence at the summer school. The local paper reported that "the pupils were given a medical examination at the beginning of school at which time each was weighed. On weighing the same pupils at the end of the month a gain of 11 pounds was noted."[36]

Gray's 1931 study put in scientific terms that race alone did not determine an adult illiterate's ability to learn. This result proved the power of democracy in education where equal opportunity meant equal potential for all people. With her scientific analysis as backing, Gray turned every argument against funding black education, and adult education, on its head and made the state's illiterate liabilities, both black and white, a point of national discussion. Numerous journals published her findings, dispensing this idea to a wide professional audience.[37] Through science Gray crafted a new conception of black potential.

Furthermore Gray's Seneca study offered audiences outside of the South virtual encounters with southern black culture. As a cultural text, the Seneca study conceptually linked a broad-based, literate audience to an image of black life that was positive and fostered a progressive view of South Carolina and its people.[38] Her work demonstrates that the printed word is more than just a reflection of what a culture believes or thinks it knows: it generates perceptions as well. Her 1931 experiment demonstrates how change came to the South piece-meal and from different sources, always in the shadow of tradition and often by indirect means.

The following year Gray attempted to secure funds for another study but was refused because "the activities of the [Carnegie] Corporation . . . had to be sharply curtailed."[39] For the next five years, she continued to seek support, urging the governor, private clubs, and local philanthropists to fund adult ed-ucation for both races, using her study to bolster her call for tax-supported op-portunity schools. In the wake of the success of the Seneca study, the economic crisis of the times took a toll on Gray's work, and she struggled to overcome depleted state appropriations for adult schools. But despite the lack of money, in 1935 enrollment in adult night schools totaled 18,746 students, 8,643 of which were black, more than double the 3,523 black pupils taught in 1919, the first year Gray started her work as the state supervisor.[40]

In the early months of 1935 Gray organized three massive field trips she deemed pilgrimages for adult students enrolled across the state. She wrote that "in order to foster State pride and to provide interesting drill, the spring work was centered on the study of South Carolina. As part of the project, pilgrimages to old cemeteries, to county seats and to cities were encouraged."[41] In March she led one thousand white students, teachers, and organizers to Charleston on a trip that cost three dollars per person for lodging, sightseeing, and en-trance into two gardens. A month later, on Sunday, April 7, she led six thousand white students representing every county in the state to the State House and the Township Auditorium. After the exercises of the day, vespers were held at four of the city's churches. "The pupils returned home with a new idea about State government as well as increased State pride and a store of happy memo-ries," Gray wrote.[42]

A week later, on April 14, Gray led approximately four thousand black stu-dents on the same tour of the State House given the preceding week to the white students. Although the black pilgrims visited the graves of Wade Hamp-ton and Ann Pamela Cunningham and viewed Confederate monuments on the State House grounds, at the end of the day they watched "a pageant titled *Van-guards of Our Race*" at the Township Auditorium. "This told the story of the Ne-gro's contributions to poetry, science, literature, music, and inventions," Gray reported. "Dr. Channing Tobias, Negro leader, made a stirring address."[43] At the pageant the crowd sang "Lift Every Voice and Sing" and the spirituals "Steal Away to Jesus" and "We Are Climbing Jacob's Ladder." The program included a presentation on historic black leaders Crispus Attucks, Booker T. Washington, Mary McLeod Bethune, Benjamin Banneker, Washington Carver, Ernest Just, Phillis Wheatley, Countee Cullen, Langston Hughes, Paul Dunbar, Kelly Miller, and W. E. B. Du Bois.[44] A Georgia native, theologian, and nationally recognized

Black pilgrimage to the state Capital, 1935. Courtesy of
South Carolina Department of Archives and History,
Opportunity School Records, Columbia.

———————

leader, Channing Tobias served as the senior secretary of the YMCA's Colored
Work Department from 1923 to 1946, as associate director of the Commission
on Interracial Cooperation, and on the YMCA's executive committee of the National Interracial Conference.[45] His participation in the event reveals Gray's
knowledge of and connection to professional African Americans involved in
reform and uplift campaigns across the nation.[46] Equally it illustrates Tobias's
interest in the pilgrims' progress and his support of Gray's efforts. He wrote to
Gray, "Your office is to be congratulated upon making this opportunity possible for the Negro students of the Adult Schools in your state. It should go
a long way toward building up, on the part of these students and those with
whom they are related, a larger interest in their state and a greater concern for
its welfare and progress."[47] The YMCA no doubt was a critical link between
Tobias and Gray. At the end of the pilgrimages, both black and white students
brought a penny to Columbia as an expression of their appreciation. "The contribution will be invested in a tree planted in the Capitol Square under which
a seat will be placed," wrote Gray.[48] Of the event a black teacher wrote, "My
pupils are glad to visit the capital city as a place of joy instead of a place of im-
prisonment, to be carried to the penitentiary by some officer."[49]

A pilgrimage is a journey to a sacred place or shrine that has moral significance. Although segregated, the pilgrimages of 1935 were Gray's effort to democratize public space by claiming state monuments and sites for all the citizens of the state, black and white, poor, dispossessed, and illiterate, at a time when most South Carolinians struggled to put food on the table. In these mass public spectacles, thousands of pilgrims paid homage to the state under the guidance of Gray. They asserted their claim to state sites and history by physically engaging in public spaces filled with important state relics, although the monuments excluded reference to the history of the black students.[50]

In preparation for the pilgrimages, Gray sent a checklist to teachers expected to attend with their students. It provided the location of bus pickups and public bathrooms and provided directions to meeting points. Students were reminded to bring a penny to help beautify the Capital Square and to leave the city clean "with no evidences of lunches" at the end of the event. One important prepilgrimage directive was the location where pilgrims and their teachers were to assemble at the start of the event. The white students and teachers were to meet at the piazza of the State Teachers Association building on Senate Street. The black students and teachers were to meet at the "Side Road Entrance, State Office Building, Corner Senate and Sumter." Despite the different rallying points based on race, all students were asked to learn the song "Carolina" and "The Star-Spangled Banner" to perform at a pageant at the end of the day.[51]

Gray's checklist symbolizes the contradictions that defined her life and work. On one hand she followed the rules. The spatial segregation of her black and white pilgrims showed she did not violate Jim Crow. By singing the state and national anthems, her students exhibited patriotism and civic commitment, important components of her citizenship education curriculum. Despite endemic racism, segregation, poorly funded schools, and political lethargy, Gray's pilgrims descended upon the capital, with penny in hand, to show pride and respect for a state that had dealt them a hard hand.

On the other hand, she broke all the rules. Hers was a pilgrimage to pay homage to the state, but it was equally a protest against the state's apathy about the polity's real needs, especially the needs of illiterate black adults. The pilgrimage was an organized spectacle intended to force the state to see the pilgrims, black and white, as devoted citizens hungry for opportunity. The event was a radical act carried out by Gray, teachers, and adult students, black and white, from across South Carolina. Gray put thousands of faces on illiteracy and forced the state to notice. Her message was that the pilgrims desired civic participation, loved the state, and demonstrated citizenship training in action, training that came by way of adult education, a defined field the state needed to fund. The pilgrimage was a wakeup call for the state disguised as a tribute delivered by Gray in the form of thousands of pilgrims to the State House door. The event captures the complexity of her actions and their hidden meanings.

Black adult education was not a priority for politicians and white citizens, and Gray struggled to raise funds and provide opportunities for black students during her tenure as the supervisor of adult schools. Black schools were notoriously underfunded and poorly equipped. After holding summer opportunity schools at Voorhees Technical College, for black students between 1934 and 1936, Gray obtained federal money in 1937 to supplement the costs of the program.[52]

In 1936 Gov. Olin Johnston wrote to Gray, "Now is the logical time to begin our renewed efforts for the eradication of this menace to our State's welfare. Looked at from every angle, illiteracy is expensive.... We still have 36,000 white and 156,000 colored illiterates who, themselves, in 1930 admitted they could not write their names."[53] Gray wrote to the *Charleston (S.C.) News and Courier* editor William Watts Ball that "if illiteracy is to be eradicated, better educational opportunities must be given the Negroes. Is it fair to spend $42.25 a year on the white child and $8.70 on the Negro? Can such inequalities produce a descent [sic] standard of living under a democratic society?"[54] In 1936 the NAACP made a documentary to convey to a national audience what "separate but equal" looked like in South Carolina. The film canvassed school facilities, public school transportation, and statistics on the disparity in funding between black and white schools. Grim shots of pitiful places brought to the big screen and to a national audience the deplorable state of black education in the South Carolina.[55]

That same year a fourth opportunity school for black adults was held in July. Fifty-three students enrolled in the program at Voorhees and represented many of the counties in the state. Thirty-nine of the students were women. "If you want to be somebody and try to be somebody, I am sure others will help you" was the motto of the program.[56] This reflected the core theme of the statewide literacy campaign that had been conducted in the media for more than a decade. For example the Barnwell paper urged its citizens to "teach ... your cook, your washerwoman, your hired man anyone who can't write. Remember, Negroes are citizens of our state and our rating in illiteracy is judged by total, not by white illiteracy," conveying in its call to arms its assumptions about black occupations.[57] Likewise a white Barnwell county illiteracy campaign organizer revealed the implicit condescension in illiteracy work when she proclaimed that "every thinking person knows something of the problems which the Negro confronts in trying to adjust himself to the exigencies of life in a white civilization of America, and of the handicaps growing out of his position here.... I do believe that because of this effort put forth on his behalf you will find him a better citizen as well as laborer."[58]

Like the 1935 summer school, a central theme of the 1936 opportunity school at Voorhees was the home and how to maintain it. A model home was built to teach the black students what a "good" home looked like and the items it housed—books, music, health habits, and morality.[59] A teacher at the session described this work:

> Economy and thrift have been taught through the use of such things as shucks, burlap bags, meal sacks, mayonnaise jars, discarded tin cans, and orange crates. The lesson has been driven home that any rural home can be made attractive, comfortable, and happy with little expense.... The young men repaired, whitewashed, and screened the entire house, built a kitchen cupboard, three pair of steps, and laid new floor boards for the porch.... The young women transformed the interior of the home by doing much of the actual cleaning, varnishing the picture frames, painting several pieces of furniture and made flower cans. They dyed and made burlap draperies and rugs. Two chairs received shuck bottoms and a washstand was made of an orange crate.[60]

The curriculum focused on African heritage, health education, home repair, and domestic training. Students at Voorhees responded positively to the program. John Groves wrote, "We have made fans about the colored people we have talked about."[61] Another student, Frankie Walker of York, wrote that she loved the dress she made at the school and declared that "I am going to do all I can to teach someone else the things that I have learned." As a sign of support, Modjeska Simkins visited the site.[62]

An important development at the 1936 opportunity school, as opposed to the first black opportunity school held at Seneca five years earlier, was Gray's use of curriculum that highlighted the African American experience. Although African heritage was a component of the closing program at Seneca, the core curriculum reflected white, upper-class values. At Voorhees in 1936, the curriculum addressed practical needs of students that related to home economics and health. Closing ceremonies highlighted the traditions and heritage of the African American past in the South. The students performed a pageant that depicted the trials, advancements, and contributions of African Americans. Episode 1 was titled "African Background" and Episode 2, "Slavery." In this scene students sang "Steal Away to Jesus," "Nobody Knows the Trouble I've Seen," "Old Black Joe," and "Freedom." Episode 3 was titled "Freedom," and the music included "America the Beautiful," "We Are Climbing Jacob's Ladder," "Give Me That Old Time Religion," and the "Negro National Anthem," "Lift Every Voice and Sing."[63] Five months later Gray received a Christmas letter from an "old Negro woman," sixty-eight-year-old Emma Gilliard of Hartsville, South Carolina. In a display of the skills she had learned, she wrote, "I like my school fine."[64]

In preparation for the event, Gray asked the staff of the college to anticipate eighty to one hundred students, more than double the forty-four that actually boarded. At the end of the session, the president of the college, J. E. Blanton, wrote to Gray and requested that the state reimburse his school seventy-five dollars for the loss it took as a consequence of her inadequate estimations.[65] A week later he wrote that "it will give us a great deal of pleasure to cooperate in the future" and informed her that the financial problem had been resolved.[66] But the financial issues at this camp did not end with Blanton. A black teacher returned a check to Gray's office and explained that it bounced when she attempted to cash it. It is unclear whether Gray paid the teacher, but it is clear that black teachers, institutions, and students endured a great struggle to get money and support from the state for their efforts to advance black literacy. "Much of South Carolina's illiteracy is accounted for by the high percentage of Negro population," claimed Gray, who turned to philanthropist Bernard Baruch, owner of Hobcaw Barony in Georgetown, for support when the state cut appropriations for adult education in 1939. She explained to him that the lack of money for adult education was the reason South Carolina remained the most illiterate state in the Union in 1930 and lamented that the state planned to appropriate a mere fifteen thousand dollars in 1940.[67] Gray appealed to Baruch to fund a study specifically aimed to help blacks, 26.9 percent of the illiterate population (156,065). "Because Negro illiteracy is the major problem, we will concentrate on that group," she wrote and asked for ten thousand dollars.[68]

With the emergence of New Deal divisions such as the National Youth Administration, Gray's work to promote black education gained momentum. In 1938 she invited fellow South Carolinian Mary McLeod Bethune to speak at the Washington Street United Methodist Church. Bethune was the director of Negro affairs in the National Youth Administration from 1936 and 1944 and chair of an unofficial black cabinet that met with President Franklin D. Roosevelt to direct policy for social change. The congregation, particularly the women of the church, endorsed Gray's request for Bethune to speak at a Sunday evening service, and Gray received the blessing of pastor J. W. Shackford. But many church members, specifically the race-baiting demagogue Coleman Blease, adamantly opposed the invitation. Despite their protest the meeting occurred as planned, and Gray asked the ushers to treat kindly the black visitors in the congregation. At the end of her speech, Bethune said that "she could only feel in her heart what Queen Esther had experienced when the king granted her request to honor her people, gratitude to God."[69]

Although Gray claimed to not think about race, her actions reveal that she did. That she did anything to advance educational opportunities for African Americans in the South Carolina is commendable. By adhering to separate but equal, her efforts did not directly agitate against regional race practice, but she did make her state recognize that black education was critical to the advancement of the state through the Seneca study, pilgrimages, and opportunity schools.[70] Equality of opportunity was the first step toward a more democratic state, a goal Gray worked toward during the 1930s.

It is easy to view Gray through a modern lens and argue that she did not do enough to undermine the structural and social inequalities black South Carolinians struggled against in their daily lives. Civil rights activist and fellow South Carolinian Modjeska Simkins claimed she never forgave Gray for calling her school the Opportunity School and opening it to whites only.[71] She recalled a meeting where "Miss Wil Lou was doing a whole lot of talking and heaping accolades upon herself and what she had done." She leaned over to a friend and said, "I think we ought to get this old sister right now, because she doesn't need all that praise, because she couldn't see that opportunity was needed by all youth in South Carolina." The friend was Alice Spearman Wright.[72] Wright asked Simkins to not bother Gray, who she argued had done the best she could with the vision she had. Simkins recalled: "She knew I'd run roughshod, you know.... I think she has done a good work as she saw it.... A person can be the product of his time and his environment, you know.... It seemed to me that she should have felt that black youth needed opportunity as well as white youth. And I've never forgiven her for not being able to see that."[73]

Race ideology complicated Gray's efforts to eradicate illiteracy in South Carolina and required ingenuity in the way she advanced educational opportunities for black adults in a passive, racist state. Countless black teachers and professionals supported Gray's work, and their help made her vision possible. "Among my choicest memories of cooperation is that of my Negro co-workers. . . . Without such assistance, I could have done nothing," wrote Gray.[74] In recognition of her service to the black race, South Carolina State College in Orangeburg awarded Gray a certificate of merit, a loving cup, and flowers at the Seventh Annual Conference on Adult Education and the Negro on April 6, 1949.[75]

Gray's efforts in the 1930s to advance black literacy reveal the mechanics of progress in a region limited by tradition and defined by social inertia. Gray, through the Seneca study, the pilgrimage of 1935, and opportunity schools for African American men and women in the 1930s, initiated a shift in perception about black potential that must be considered a stepping-stone in the path of regional progress. These projects demonstrate how Gray, when viewed collectively with other southern writers, activists, and educators, made small ripples, albeit intellectually, that led to the sweeping social changes implemented through policy in the 1950s. Reflecting on black educational progress, Gray wrote Dr. William Cooper of the Hampton Institute that "we should not attempt to measure progress by days and months, but rather by years and decades."[76] Gray devoted her career to the advancement of literacy for all people, despite race or caste, and used her work to forge a new direction in the mindset of her region.

Conclusion

Wil Lou Gray emerged an unlikely leader in South Carolina during a period of great change. She was a waged, female state worker who used her position as a supervisor to challenge regional inequality and education as the vehicle to conduct the attack. She was an anomaly in everything she represented in a region rigidly defined by traditional ideas about race, gender, and power, but despite this she carved out a unique place for herself by working on behalf of the state to empower marginalized groups. Although she reinforced inequality by working within existing social customs to advance her career, her work in the first decades of the twentieth century projected a belief in human potential and a shared humanity affirmed by social science and experimentation.[1] Through her own educational experiments and by putting the outcomes in print, she made her work accessible to audiences within and beyond her region and drew national attention to the problems in her state and the innovative solutions she designed to address them. Professionalization of her research was key to establishing the precedents she used to argue for change in funding and policy related to adult education.

The economic crisis that defined the 1930s took a toll on Gray's work to eradicate illiteracy in South Carolina. She struggled to overcome depleted state appropriations for adult schools, and in 1933 she went to Washington, D.C., to confer with the secretary of the interior and the Bureau of Education about the implementation of emergency relief education.[2] By 1935 teachers in adult schools were paid with federal funds, and federal regulation required that Gray hire only teachers on government relief. Concerned by the impact of these changes on her work, Gray reported to the General Assembly that "the work has been greatly handicapped because only teachers on relief could be employed and because the term could not be continuous. Naturally teachers and pupils found it difficult to work intelligently when constantly ordered to stop and start."[3] Federal relief abruptly undid many of the credentialing standards Gray developed in the first decade of her work as supervisor of adult schools, and she explained the predicament to the General Assembly: "Since only persons on relief could be employed the problem which confronted the counties…was to secure more capable teachers who could qualify under relief requirements. This was impossible under existing certification standards, therefore, temporary certificates marked 'Emergency WPA' were issued to those best qualified to teach."[4]

Gray complained that "the prospective teaching force had little or no conception of the aims and philosophy of adult education," which was an essential element of the credentialing standards she had developed in the previous decade. The problem led her to establish "training schools of one week" for the "emergency WPA" teachers.[5] The University of South Carolina hosted the white teachers, and Benedict College and Allen University the black teachers. These training sessions focused on goals teachers were to accomplish in the classroom. Topics included enrolling illiterates and semiliterates in adult classes; instilling a love of reading in the students; developing individual responsibility toward home, county, state, and nation; appreciating beauty in life and improving manners; and inculcating good health habits. The reading material at these sessions and later used in adult classrooms included two texts written by Gray and her friend Mabel Montgomery, *Worthwhile South Carolinians* and *The Adult School Messenger*. School newsletters, picture sheets about history and industry in South Carolina, and plays about health, taxes, thrift, Christmas, and state pride written by Gray's friend Erin Kohn supplemented these. A total of 18,746 students enrolled in night schools in 1935.[6]

In the same report to the General Assembly, Gray noted the ingenuity of adult students who suffered in the harsh economic conditions. She shared a story passed on by a teacher she had employed to teach forty-five women workers on relief how to write their names. Since 1923 a chief component of Gray's adult educational philosophy had been the necessity that the student learn to write their name. She believed the representation in print was useful and urged her students to write their names in the guest registers when they traveled on pilgrimages to state sites and when they cast a vote.[7] Gray believed this was an important process that made the student acutely aware of their identity as a participant and citizen of the state. The teacher claimed that after four weeks of instruction, the director of women's work refused to give paychecks to any of the workers who could not write their name. Gray conveyed the trauma one student experienced: "One woman failed ... her sobbing was heard by the group.... A second woman who could not sign her name went to the first and said, 'What's the use to cry. Come on and lets get a copy and practice quick.' ... When all had signed ... they too, were ready to write something which was accepted, provided they would do better by next pay day."[8]

Instead of condemning the harsh method employed by the director of women's work who withheld the pay of the illiterate women, Gray celebrated the ability of the workers to help each other figure out how to write their names under pressure. The story gives insight into her belief that writing a name was a victory despite the context in which it was won. Writing one's name did not make a person literate, but it did provide a person representation in print that was far more personal and meaningful than a mark. The draconian and possibly illegal method the director used in an era of economic and social chaos and the blind eye Gray turned to such behavior is evidence that she focused on outcomes not context.

Gray looked to both the government and the private sector to aid her efforts. Between 1919 and 1935, with the support of countless teachers, public-spirited citizens, and private organizations, she worked tirelessly to improve the literacy rates in South Carolina. She believed that it was the state's responsibility to supply all of its citizens with the rudiments of an elementary education, and when New Deal programs such as the Civilian Conservation Corps and the National Youth Administration formed, she praised these agencies as progressive. By 1936 the National Youth Administration's Rural Life Improvement Project provided the means for one hundred youth from relief families to earn $15.00 while attending the Clemson Opportunity School. The expense of the camp was $18.50, and two youth from each county were chosen to attend. Gray offset the cost with scholarships provided by private groups such as the American Legion.[9] Only students between the ages of sixteen and twenty-five who had no schooling beyond the seventh grade could attend.[10] The government-sanctioned financial incentive coupled with Gray's ability to garner scholarships to cover differential expenses undoubtedly drew attendees to the program. Despite these alluring perks, Gray's assistant claimed people enrolled in the program for "social improvement, to get ahead, some because friends ... and some for a vacation that they profit from in terms of recreation and learning."[11]

Federal relief money dictated the terms of how Gray conducted her work after 1935 and, in many ways, undid the credentialing standards she had established in the previous decade. Her faith in the role of government was challenged, because work relief programs created new challenges to her effort to eradicate adult illiteracy. In 1936 she appealed directly to Eleanor and Franklin Roosevelt for help. "I have struggled for twenty three years for illiteracy—not simply to teach the basic tools of learning but rather how to use these tools as a medium for personal growth and a better understanding of citizenship and all its implications. We have struggled without money, holding on each year hoping that either the state or the national government would recognize the education of the masses as a functional need, and one which should be met along with vocational education."[12]

She complained that the Civilian Conservation Corps and the National Youth Administration, programs she readily supported at the start of the relief work, impeded her capacity to eradicate illiteracy because the nation's call for skilled workers interfered with her efforts to educate adults. She argued that general education was essential to the skilled worker's success and told the Roosevelts that "we covet your active support in securing Federal aid for a program of adult education." In a pencil edit at the base of the draft copy, Gray in an afterthought added, "to sacrifice the cream of our manhood to war while we stand idly by and leave this group fertile soil for the demagogues," a dated message she often used in her early literacy media slogans that carried immense historic meaning to many familiar with the power of demagogues in the area. Her intent was to add it to the final draft to strengthen her appeal.[13]

Gray was cautious in her early work as the supervisor of adult schools to keep public opinion and support on her side. By serving in the 1920s and '30s on the national boards of the General Federation of Women's Clubs, the National Education Association, and the American Association of Adult Education, Gray connected her work to the national landscape of social reform. She also formed the Southeastern Conference on Adult Education, an organization that held annual meetings in the interwar years and pursued graduate study at Teachers College, Columbia University, writing a book on citizenship during a tenure at the school in 1926. Through these associations she met influential leaders in her field and shared her work in South Carolina, causing it to emerge as a model for rural adult education across the country and abroad.[14] This cast a spotlight on South Carolina and drew national attention to her work and the state's internal problems which in turn put pressure on state leadership to act. By the 1930s Gray, who was fifty years old in 1933, took more aggressive steps to force South Carolina to address the needs of its illiterate adults. Her work to advance educational opportunities for black adult students in this decade directly challenged ideas about race, intelligence, and human potential. Even though Gray was dogmatic in her efforts to eradicate illiteracy, illiteracy was persistent in South Carolina and costly. When black illiteracy constituted 26.9 percent and white illiteracy 14.9 percent of the state population on the eve of World War II, Gray reverted as she had done two decades earlier to patriotism as a rallying cry to the public.[15] Gray relayed a story shared by a male teacher about his students enrolled as workers in the Civilian Conservation Corps. "In a class of 28 boys I was teaching, less than 10% knew the meaning of Thanks-giving, only 12% knew who Hitler was, and 5% knew the meaning of Armistice Day," he wrote.[16]

Her connection to national organizations gave her a platform to discuss her work with experts and thrust her into the inner circle of leading educa-tors of the day. Surely this contributed to the recognition and support her work received in and outside of the South. Lillian Smith, Julia Peterkin, Channing Tobias, E. L. Thorndike, Ida Tarbell, L. R. Alderman of the United States Bu-reau of Education, Calvin Coolidge, Eleanor and Franklin Roosevelt, Bernard Baruch, and the Carnegie Foundation all knew about Wil Lou Gray. This dem-onstrates her politics. When her state failed to meet the needs of her students, she linked her work to a national arena of renowned intellectuals, financiers, philanthropists, and reformers to challenge the state's apathy toward her cause and to draw attention to her innovative work. Equally her connection to Thorn-dike, Albert Shields, and Mabel Carney, all professors at Teachers College, and southern educational leaders such as William Knox Tate took her ideas to an audience of scholars in classrooms in New York and in Nashville.[17]

Before World War I and in the subsequent decade, Gray forged the state-managed infrastructure upon which federal relief efforts by the mid-1930s dis-pensed money into the state and organized agencies to aid the needy. Before the New Deal brought federal relief to the state, Gray's work was distinct, vis-ible, and funded for the most part by state allotments. Published each year in the General Assembly reports was the state appropriation allotted for her work. Equally visible was the support she received from a mélange of volunteers, civic groups, and private individuals who helped raise money, craft reading materi-als, and campaign on her behalf. After the sweeping changes brought into the region with the relief agencies of the New Deal and later the draft and World War II, the visibility of Gray's efforts diminished. The flood of federal money, relief work, and federal programs reshaped the environment of her work as edu-cation and literacy found new meaning on the eve of war. She was forced to reconcile the progress she had made in adult education with the new landscape of the times.

In 1946 the state awarded Gray the land and physical plants of the for-mer World War II Columbia air base for the development of a permanent, year-round adult opportunity school. The following year 275 students attended what became known as the South Carolina Opportunity School.[18] Endowments were essential to the growth and longevity of the fledgling institution. Gray was sixty-five years old when she obtained the property in 1947 and returned all of the salary she received from "that time forward" to the school in the form of a scholarship.[19] Gray described the scholarship as a thank you "to the South Carolina legislature, churches, civic and fraternal organizations, businesses and industry, and many individuals too numerous to mention who have made it possible for the school to be giving such wonderful service to the people of the state."[20] She worked to develop the trust into a $1.5 million fund designed "to enable all the young and older persons who have been deprived of an education to have at least a high school education."[21]

Between 1921 and 1956, South Carolina spent $1,087,838 in appropriations for Gray's adult education program. The decline in illiteracy justified the expenditure, and Gray argued that adult education produced better-informed and contributing citizens familiar with ideas about taxes, education, budgeting, "loss of time from preventable illness," and the detriments of moving from place to place, issues "canvassed in the classroom and debated in the evening get-togethers." In 1951 the *Carolina Pioneer*, the newspaper of the South Carolina Opportunity School, asked "Does Education Pay?" The paper claimed adult education led to "increased lifetime earnings of a small group of graduated students." Gray estimated that this group would gain $24,713,000 over the course of a lifetime, ample economic proof that literacy paid.[22]

"In the history of the world there have been people who have become famous painters, famous scientists, famous writers, famous military leaders. Dr. Wil Lou Gray is the only person I know who has become famous in the field of adult education," wrote Opportunity School graduate James F. Miles. "Although she has worked in a small area . . . her fame has become national and even international."[23] "The personal is political": a central tenet of the second-wave feminist movement, this phrase represents the belief that personal choices have political implications.[24] Gray's personal politics shaped everything she did in both her public and private lives, and by personalizing her political action, she never failed to rally a force behind a cause she found worthy. A friend claimed that "perhaps her greatest asset is that charm and enthusiasm that have tempted all kinds of people to drop what they were doing and help with her work."[25] Equally Gray neutralized her politics when her personal life demanded and thus easily engaged with people of diverse political, economic, and racial backgrounds while remaining in every way a genteel southern lady in the good graces of the public and her personal circle of family and friends.

Although she did not define herself as a feminist, Gray represented the new woman of the era: professional, single, economically self-sufficient, and well educated. It is interesting that she rarely articulated a feminist viewpoint, but she was clearly aware of her role as a female leader in a time of change. In a letter to her family written two years after her retirement in 1960, she wrote, "Certainly at some stage in my life I might have felt that the woman who did not work for a check had little to do."[26] It is possible that in retirement Gray sought to justify her newly acquired status in light of what she believed—that unpaid domestic responsibilities, although time-consuming, were devalued in a society where the wage delimited the value of women's work.[27] Scholar Harvey Neufeldt suggests that her work was implicitly feminist: "Adult education did not carry professional prestige—it enabled women like Wil Lou Gray to rise to the top since males would be found in the more professionally prestigious areas.... Adult education, like social work and ... school librarian positions were at first open to women because these fields lacked a clear professional status."[28]

Gray found a niche in adult education, a field unregulated and open to experimentation. At a time when few women worked as state-level supervisors, especially in the southern region, her job as supervisor of adult schools was the key to her success and public legacy. She was conscious of the politics tied to her position, and to keep her job was as important as implementing her social vision. How she did both without losing favor with the public speaks to her personal politics.

Equal opportunity for women was a major theme within the broader social liberal discourse about equal rights of citizens in the period before World War I. During this time government "was not just a contractually engaged enforcer of contracts but had a moral or ethical nature of the kind previously associated with the private sphere," states political scientist Marian Sawer. "Not only did the social liberals believe that the state should take on roles previously identified with women, they also believed that the state had a duty to ensure that women received equal developmental opportunities."[29] In South Carolina Gray carried out the role of public caregiver for the state as a paid state worker from 1919 to 1947, a definitive example of a developmental opportunity given to a woman with its gendered responsibility to extend moral and ethical care to fellow citizens. Her surrogate family included the state and the illiterate masses. She nurtured this virtual home ultimately to bolster the state's image within the nation and to fulfill, by proxy, the role of mother to the disadvantaged. Her gendered reconstruction of the public sphere was bolstered from above and from below. From above hers was a public domesticity where her duties centered on social uplift, but uplift for which she was paid in real terms. She engaged in a lifelong, committed partnership with the state.

Likewise from below those she aimed to help reinforced her public motherhood. She called her students "children," and on Mother's Day one student wrote to Gray, "For while my mother gave birth to me physically, you are responsible for the birth of my mental development."[30] The values she imparted to the illiterate through her educational programs benefited the health of the state. "A state grows in power as its citizens become enlightened," wrote Gray, who defined what that enlightenment looked like.[31] Good manners, thrift, health, budgeting, life and death insurance, and the machinations of local, state, and federal governments constituted the table of contents of a civics text she wrote for adult pupils in 1921. "Good manners are not learned. . . . They come from within. . . . A person who won't learn, who giggles at church, who wears too loud clothes, who talks too loud on the street is just common," wrote Gray. Two etiquette rules presented in the text: "Toothpicks should only be used in private," and "Do not spit on the floor. Spitting is filthy."[32] Gray described the goals of adult education: "to make better citizens, to make better workers, to make better homemakers, to increase general information, and to effect improvement mentally, morally, and spiritually."[33]

The intended recipients of her message were not passive in the encounter but active in this exchange as eager consumers ready to emerge from the darkness of illiteracy as viable commodities to industry and local politicians. Like a mother she guided their way by imparting values tied to her class and heritage. She wrote of these students, "On each face there was a look that seemed to say: Thank God for the leader who believes in me; thinks I am worthy of a second chance. May I do nothing to reflect dishonor on her and her colleagues."[34] She was there to help them advance "in wisdom, in stature, and in favor with God and man."[35] In her public home, she found purpose, and the many individuals and facilities that currently bear her name testify to the enduring legacy and impact of her work.

Adults who attended adult schools improved their hourly wage and their moral vision. A black teacher in Cherokee County claimed that "men who have been gamblers in attendance publicly declared they mean to lead different lives."[36] The result of this instruction was evidenced by one pupil's intent after a summer program not to climb higher in the mill but to plant trees so that "someone else can enjoy the shade."[37] Others responded with vows "to be nicer to everyone at home, especially my husband," and "to do better on my job, save more money, and put more time on studying."[38] Despite her efforts some pessimists expressed the unlikelihood of a permanent transformation of the underclass Gray aimed to elevate. "I think a Birth Control Act or Sterilization Law as well as Compulsory School Act law for this class would not be too much. . . . They know nothing to do and have nothing to think of except to breed like rabbits. . . . They are only liabilities rather than assets," wrote a graduate school classmate of Gray.[39]

Did Gray make a difference? Illiteracy declined in South Carolina, and adult education emerged as a legitimate field as a consequence of her work. In the decade after World War II, adult education was transformed in South Carolina due in part to the impact of compulsory school attendance, child labor, and public-welfare laws and in the use of the GED by 1942 as a credentialing tool.[40] Historian Norfleet Hardy suggests that "by the early forties . . . the Opportunity Schools had become an integral and complementary part of the

State's over-all program of public education. At the same time . . . these schools were changing from residential adult education to adult education in residence, with short-term residential institutes as a secondary function."[41] In 1942, the first year the GED was used nationwide, 2 Opportunity School students received a GED. More than a decade later, in 1956, 280 Opportunity School students received the certificate.[42]

Despite advances South Carolina repealed its compulsory attendance law, originally passed in 1937, in 1955 in reaction to the *Brown v. Board of Education* ruling. "The seeming general lack of concern in the State over the repeal . . . reflected what some social historians say is the widespread lack of belief in South Carolina in the value of education for everyone," wrote Hardy.[43] By the 1960s adult education moved from a separately funded entity into a function of secondary education, agricultural extension programs, vocational education, and community college technical training centers.[44] Other areas of education absorbed the field, and the function of the South Carolina Opportunity School transformed to accommodate at-risk secondary students.

This story of Wil Lou Gray does not offer an explanation of the complex relationship of power, race, and gender in the New South, but it does illustrate how Gray reconciled her status as both a southern woman and a public figure in relation to these issues as they intersected in her public work and private life. Gray was a political agent paid by the state, and despite living as the exception rather than the rule, she rose to the top of her profession, financially supported herself and members of her family, surrounded herself with like-minded people in philanthropic and academic circles, and challenged racism and sexism in subtle but meaningful ways. By not making her status or her views radical issues, she made an impact on South Carolina without directly agitating against tradition.

During her career Gray stood at the forefront of the opposition to the status quo that fueled progressive changes in South Carolina and the southern region. Her opposition was not aggressive or overtly radical as displayed in the 1960s but rather manifested in a skilled, political assault orchestrated from inside state government that opened the way for subsequent achievements in education for all people in her region. By challenging the status quo, she confronted the essence of who she was in terms of heritage, class, and race. These values, traditions, and social inequalities defined her place in the social fabric of her region and also endowed her with connections and status that made her capable of achieving what she did. The very systems that empowered her and her class to direct the economic, social, and political progress of the state were the exact ones she opposed. She did not dismantle the structural inequalities that defined the social system that made her who she was, but she was aware of how this stagnated state progress. By virtue of who she was as an elite South

Carolinian, she used her access to power to create opportunities that otherwise would not have been afforded to the disadvantaged poor of her state and, in so doing, created a special space for herself in the social fabric of a hyper-gendered region and crafted the new field of adult education. She was part of a disparate group of southern educators, intellectuals, writers, and artists who challenged the grim social realities of illiteracy, poverty, and racism by advocating for regional progress. Her pioneering work in adult education intersected with major revolutions in transportation, consumerism, communication, urbanization, and public education that came to the South by World War II, and she used these developments to market her social vision to the public.

It is useful to think of her as moving from a position of reform, particularly in the early decades of her work, when she led the efforts to consolidate and organize rural schools under state auspices, to one of protest by the 1930s, when she used social science, outside funding, and burgeoning academic fields such as adult education to challenge regional inequality. Her use of print capital to expand the scope of exposure to her work was a powerful weapon that drew national and international attention and interest to her ideas and methods. By publishing studies about the outcomes of her work with adult learners, she gained national recognition as a scholar and emerged as a key innovator in the adult education movement.

Despite an incredible work ethic, Wil Lou Gray was human. She was known to be forgetful, leaving her mother's pearls on a train when she was in college and often losing her keys. She was known to do crazy things, for example catching a ride in the middle of the night from a group of strange men when her car broke down on a rural road. She was trusting, hopeful, and even daring, taking steps to force new ways of thinking about people and their abilities on everyone she encountered. She kept this up well into her retirement. She hosted the first interracial luncheon in Columbia in the early 1950s and often took her maid, Evelyn, who worked for Gray from 1958 to 1984, to meetings and luncheons designated for whites only.[45] She believed advancing South Carolina was worth her effort, even if it put her in harm's way or caused some to raise their eyebrows in dismay. Whatever impediments she faced, she worked through them. Gray candidly revealed that when things got tough, she'd cry a spell but get back up and keep on going.

She was unique because of her leadership position as a woman and her progressive vision of government welfare. She was the harbinger of progress in a stagnant state. She was educated in the Progressive Era, influenced by progressive ideology, and used education—the one field government regulated to a greater degree than others by World War I—as a laboratory for her ideas. She understood what had to be done and did it in spite of immense financial and political obstacles. The material testament to the adoption of her vision by state leaders was the gift of the airbase given to her by the state to develop the South Carolina Opportunity School in 1947. Although it was segregated, I deeply believe she would have chosen otherwise had the times been different. 1947 was a difficult year in South Carolina. Strom Thurmond was governor, and the postwar tensions, especially pertaining to integration, led South Carolina briefly to secede from the Democratic Party to embrace the Dixiecrats. In this chaotic moment, she remained among a small minority that supported integration surrounded by a majority who feared it and adhered to the racial values deeply rooted in regional culture. Unwilling or unable to fight—she was sixty-three years old and about to retire from a position she had held since 1918—she compromised by accepting the airbase and developing her school for whites only. To sacrifice that gain for the sake of a race battle she could not win alone in 1947 was not worth the cost of losing a school that would benefit thousands of adults in the state.

It is interesting to think about the small select group of people who thought as she did. She did not surround herself with opposition. She was known to cut off those who were not of a common mindset. She was a lifelong Democrat. Until her death she supported teacher unions, feminist issues such as reproductive rights and equal rights, minority candidates—she gave James Clyburn two hundred dollars for his 1972 campaign—Medicare, and government programs to aid the needy. It is safe to say she was a southern liberal with a tremendous dose of refinement.

She was not alone and shared common principles with other enlightened South Carolinians of the times. Early in her career, she advocated well-funded public education, compulsory education, economic progress, the silencing of demagogues, social justice, equality for women, woman suffrage, and equal opportunity given to all disadvantaged groups whether they be African Americans, poor millworkers, or disfranchised women. But her principles were prioritized, and first on the list was eradicating illiteracy. To her the advancement of South Carolina hinged on a literate population. All other social issues ran secondary to the primacy of wiping out illiteracy. Gray believed illiteracy to be the wellspring of racism, poverty, ignorance, and localism. Fifty percent of the state could not read or write when she started her work. Literacy was the backbone of Americanization, citizenship education, economic progress, and political justice. Gray earned a state leadership position, carved out a national identity as a pioneer in adult education, and led the way to the creation of adult and vocational education as a part of the public school system. Did her work make a dent in illiteracy? When she started her work in 1918, the bulk of illiterates were older people reared in the era when the Civil War and Reconstruction had excluded most from attending the barely extant public school system. She initially focused on this group, but as many of them died off, illiteracy percentages dropped. Once the oldest generation of illiterates died off and the state passed a compulsory school attendance law in 1937, illiteracy began a gradual decline egged on by the adoption of the GED and vocational education in the 1940s as components of the state educational system.

In a modern world where a forty-hour workweek is standard, it is hard to imagine that almost one hundred years ago Gray worked eighty to one hundred hours a week as a field secretary for the Illiteracy Commission. In 1918 she was a thirty-five-year-old, unmarried woman riding on trains as transportation to various counties across the state to do her work, without a car, dependent on charitable friends and peers to house her as she traveled and a meager state wage as the economic backbone of her atypical household. It is amazing that she did it, because she did not have to. It was not as if she was foreigner in some strange community doing mission work. She was at home in South Carolina in a place where she had an identity and a history generations deep. Friends, family, and class connections aided her efforts to implement reform. She understood the system of rural schools, having served as a rural school supervisor before World War I. She understood rural people, localism, and the psychology of the communities she aimed to help as a product of a rural upbringing. She understood the vicissitudes of state politics, with a family of Bourbon Democrats, a state senator as an uncle, and a father who served as member of the General Assembly in the 1920s. She recognized the shift in the nature of the workforce from volunteers to professionals under way in the interwar period and led the transformation as a leader in the state educational system. She understood the nuanced sources of funding for black and white education and found ways to advance opportunities to poor adults. She believed in progressive government and worked during her lifetime to advance state control of education and state intervention in social welfare. Gray should not be remembered as an educator but as an innovator who used education, one of the only fields open to women of her education and training when she began her career, as a vehicle to challenge the social and structural inequalities that disempowered many people in her state. Moreover she did it as a leader in state government when women barely had the vote and found a place in a rigidly defined social system that gave her viability in a region where she was outside the normative role of a southern woman. She was a powerful and ambitious, skilled politician and understood that progress required determination and commitment, two skills she exhibited over the course of her career.

Why and how she went about embracing disadvantaged people and inspiring them to learn is important to analyze. How did she get them to come to the table? How did she get local teachers and local school boards to support her work? How did she get politicians to support her, especially when her work by the 1930s overtly advanced the idea that African Americans were human beings capable of anything if given an equal opportunity, radically challenging presumed ideas about intelligence and race? How did she craft a public image resistant to public criticism? Why did adult students attend school? Did they come for a paid vacation at a moment when the workday was long, hard, low-paying, and tedious? Or did they come to elevate their station in life? Did black teachers take offense at their wages (fifty cents versus one dollar per hour) to teach adult students? And who were the black teachers who helped her and did not get paid? Why did Gray advocate for black educational progress but stop short of calling for integration and civic equality? Why did she develop the opportunity school when there were other options in place to educate adults, and how did she eventually get the state to support the creation of a year-round school in 1947? How did this impact her work with black people? By not integrating the school, did she sacrifice them on the altar of her acquisition? The records reveal little about her relationship with black teachers, her role in challenging segregation, and her personal views on the topic other than how it related to illiteracy.[46] These are critical questions that will inspire future scholarship on this amazing American woman and notable South Carolinian. In 1963 Gray wrote, "Children can still be deeded in S.C. so I try to keep my faith up for I believe the things I yearn for will eventually come."[47] She lived long enough to see her state progress out of its troubled past and be an instrument of the process.

Notes

Introduction

1. Tom Baldwin, "Schools Are Still Crumbling in 'Corridor of Shame' Haunted by the Old South," *The Times* (London), January 25, 2008, http://www.timesonline.co .uk/tol/news/world/us__and__americas/us__elections/article3248449.ece; Stephanie McCrummen and Elahie Izadi, "Confederate Flag Comes Down," *Washington Post*, July 10, 2015, http://www.washingtonpost.com/news/post-nation/wp/2015/07/10/watch-live-as-the-confederate-flag-comes-down-in-south-carolina.

2. Shankman, "Jury of Her Peers"; Wil Lou Gray to Harriet Blackwell, June 3, 1963, letter held by author.

3. Statement of Gov. Ernest Hollings, read at testimonial dinner honoring Dr. Wil Lou Gray, May 15, 1961, transcript held by author.

4. For a history of the adult education movement in the United States, see Knowles, *Adult Education Movement;* Stubblefield, *History of Adult Education;* Stubblefield and Keane, *Adult Education in the American Experience.* See box 24, Wil Lou Gray Papers, and Bernard, "Culture and Environment II," 48. For a history of tax-supported adult education in South Carolina, see Hardy, *Farm, Mill, and Classroom.*

5. "She Always Had a Project," *Columbia (S.C.) State,* March 11, 1984; "Dr. Wil Lou," *Columbia (S.C.) Record,* March 13, 1984.

6. Gov. Richard Riley at the unveiling of Wil Lou Gray's portrait at the State House, 1985, http://www.scstatehouse.net/sess106__1985-1986/hj86/19860514.htm, accessed January 20, 2006.

7. DaMaris Ayres, "Crusader: Wil Lou Gray Has Fought to Wipe Out Illiteracy in South Carolina," *Columbia (S.C.) State Magazine,* October 7, 1979, 9. Gray is recognized as a pioneer in the field of adult education. See Strom Thurmond, "Tribute to Wil Lou Gray," *Congressional Record,* vol. 130, no. 37, March 27, 1984, S3179–S3181. Spears labeled Gray a modern Wilberforce in *One in the Spirit,* 109.

8. *Congressional Record,* vol. 130, no. 37, March 27, 1984, S3178.

9. This is one of the best-known descriptions of Gray and is commonly cited in material about her. See Mabel Montgomery, *South Carolina's Wil Lou Gray*, 39. Montgomery asserts that Hammond said the state appropriations for Gray's work were given "mostly to get rid of her." James Henry Hammond (1885–1970) was the namesake of the famous governor, senator, and congressman from South Carolina who led the state in the antebellum period. For a history of the grandson and the establishment of Forest Acres, see Warner M. Montgomery, *Forest Acres*, chap. 4 ("Cooper and Hammond Bring New Direction").

10. Quote by Mabel Montgomery in Laverne Prosser, "Wil Lou Gray's Story 'Important,'" *Florence (S.C.) News and Courier*, April 5, 1964, Harriet Gray Blackwell Papers, records held by author.

11. George Smith, *Opportunity Schools*, 8.

12. Many of these awards are located at the Wil Lou Gray Opportunity School in West Columbia and are on display in the banquet room at the facility; File of Certificates, box 32, Wil Lou Gray Papers.

13. Program, Seventh Annual Conference, Adult Education and the Negro, South Carolina State College, Orangeburg, April 6–9, 1949, Miller F. Whittaker Library, Archives and History Center.

14. "Biographical Data, Wil Lou Gray, Teacher and Educator," in George Smith, *Documents of the Early Beginnings*, 2; "Services Held for Educator," *Columbia (S.C.) Record*, March 12, 1984.

15. Folder, "Biographies," Wil Lou Gray Opportunity School Archive.

16. Gray died March 10, 1984. For information on these awards, see Wallace, *History of Wofford College*, 267; Wil Lou Gray, Series 38, Clemson University Biography Files, Special Collections, Clemson University Libraries, Clemson, South Carolina; "List of Honorary Degrees Given 1966–1986," Commencement Records, W417 box 1, folder 3, Winthrop University Archives and Special Collections, Dacus Library, Winthrop University, Rock Hill, South Carolina; Columbia College Alumni Office, telephone interview, November 12, 2007; *Congressional Record*, vol. 130, no. 37, March 27, 1984, S3178. For information on the establishment of the Wil Lou Gray Opportunity School, see George Smith, *Documents of the Early Beginnings*. The portrait of Wil Lou Gray hangs in the stairwell in the South Carolina State House.

17. Remarks by Gov. Richard Riley in eulogy for Wil Lou Gray at the Washington Street United Methodist Church, Columbia, March 12, 1984, transcript held by author.

18. *Congressional Record*, vol. 130, no. 37, March 27, 1984, S3178. The South Carolina Opportunity School was renamed the Wil Lou Gray Opportunity School in 1976. On May 14, 1986, during the administration of Governor Riley, Gray's portrait was placed in the South Carolina State House. She is the third woman in the history of South Carolina to receive the honor.

19. "State Must Not Forget Wil Lou Gray," *Columbia (S.C.) State*, October 19, 1988.

20. George Smith, *Documents on the Early Beginnings*.

21. George Smith, *Documents on the Early Beginnings*.

22. Night schools existed in the mills but not in rural communities. Gray credited Cora Wilson Stewart's moonlight schools as her inspiration; interview, Wil Lou Gray, February 11, 1975, Museum of Education, South Carolina Educational Television. For information on the first rural night school experiment, see Gray, *Night School Experiment*, South Carolina Department of Archives and History, Columbia (hereafter

SCDAH); Mary E. Anderson, Executive Secretary, Alumnae Association of Converse College, "Late Miss Julia Selden Pioneer in Work for Adult Illiterates," box 24, Wil Lou Gray Papers; Hardy, *Farm, Mill, and Classroom,* 101–44.

23. In 1918 New York and South Carolina were the only two states to employ full-time supervisors of adult schools. See Knowles, *Adult Education Movement;* Hardy, *Farm, Mill, and Classroom,* 44. Gray was actually appointed in 1918 but assumed her position in January 1919. Her official title at the time was state supervisor of night schools and later adult education supervisor. See George Smith, *Documents on the Early Beginnings.*

24. "Wil Lou Gray to Be Honored at Ceremony," *Laurens County (S.C.) Advocate,* October 19, 1990.

25. To avoid confusion with the year-round school that opened in 1947, I do not capitalize the term *opportunity school.* By World War I other southern states used the term to describe adult schools. See Mabel Montgomery, *South Carolina's Wil Lou Gray,* 42, and Akerson and Neufeldt, "Alabama's Illiteracy Campaign."

26. Blackwell, "Wil Lou Gray, Educator," 12.

27. See Hardy, *Farm, Mill, and Classroom,* 36n6, 40n23.

28. Wil Lou Gray, "History of the Opportunity School," uncatalogued papers, Wil Lou Gray Opportunity School Archives, copy held by author.

29. See Hardy, *Farm, Mill and Classroom,* 96–97; Ayres, *Let My People Learn,* 160–61. See also the State Superintendent of Education annual reports for 1934 to 1939, SCDAH.

30. "Wil Lou Gray, South Carolinian Extraordinary," *State Service Magazine,* December 1957, 19; James F. Miles, "Wil Lou Gray—Noblesse Oblige," Opportunity School Founder's Day Address, November 26, 1963, transcript held by author. Miles was the first South Carolina Opportunity School graduate to earn a Ph.D. Mabel Montgomery, *South Carolina's Wil Lou Gray,* 98. See George Smith, *Documents of the Early Beginnings.* As part of the state system, the school followed the separate but equal practice codified by *Plessy v. Ferguson* in 1896. Gray received criticism from black leaders such as Modjeska Simkins for her willingness to allow only whites to attend the school. See Jacquelyn Dowd Hall, interview with Modjeska Simkins, transcript located at http://docsouth.unc.edu/sohp/G-0056-2/G-0056-2.xml, accessed January 5, 2008.

31. Qtd. in Mabel Montgomery, *South Carolina's Wil Lou Gray,* xi.

32. See "Miss Wil Lou's School," *Columbia (S.C.) State,* July 7, 1976, newspaper clipping held by author. For an explanation of the motto, see David Abeel, "The Thousand Opportunities," *South Carolina Schools,* May 1957, 10. It is interesting that the Denver Opportunity School's motto was "You Can Do It." See Akerson and Neufeldt, "Alabama's Illiteracy Campaign," 174.

33. Ulrich, *Well Behaved Women,* xxxiii; Geertz, "Thick Description," 9.

34. Kett, "Women and the Progressive Impulse," 175–76.

35. See Link, "Privies, Progressivism, and Public Schools."

36. Anne Firor Scott, "After Suffrage."

37. Cooper and Terrill, *American South,* chaps. 22–23; Anne Firor Scott, "Progressive Wind"; Grantham, *Southern Progressivism.*

38. For an interesting interpretation that addresses these three types of schools, see Whisnant, *All That Is Native and Fine.* Whisnant examines the Hindman Settlement

School in Kentucky, the Campbell Folk School in North Carolina, and the White Top Folk Festival in Virginia in the first three decades of the twentieth century.

39. Stewart's "moonlight" schools were held in the evening so adults could attend school. See Stewart, *Moonlight Schools*. For a more recent interpretation of Stewart, see Baldwin, *Cora Wilson Stewart*.

40. Wilson Gee, "From South Carolina," *New York Times*, February 29, 1920. See "Report on Adult Education" (1922).

41. The term *New South* first appeared on March 14, 1874, when Henry Grady published an editorial in the *Atlanta Daily Herald* titled "The New South," in which he argued that industrial development could help solve the postwar South's economic and social troubles. "Henry W. Grady (1850–1889)," *New Georgia Encyclopedia*, http://www .georgiaencyclopedia.org/nge/Article.jsp?id=h-2451, accessed October 4, 2009. See Nixon, *Henry W. Grady*.

42. For a discussion of the economic centrality of textiles to the state in the first three decades of the twentieth century and the industry's impact on the development of state political culture, see Simon, *Fabric of Defeat;* Hayes, *South Carolina and the New Deal;* Hardy, *Farm, Mill, and Classroom;* Wallace, *South Carolina;* and Edgar, *South Carolina.*

43. See Cohen, *Making a New Deal*, for a description of this transformation.

44. For South Carolina during the 1930s, see Hayes, *South Carolina and the New Deal.*

45. See Lois M. Quinn, "An Institutional History of the GED," http://www4.uwm .edu/eti/reprints/GEDHistory.pdf, accessed February 20, 2010; Knight, *Public Education in the South*, 446; Hardy, *Farm, Mill, and Classroom*, 99.

46. See interview, Wil Lou Gray by Constance Ashton Myers, June 14, 1974, Columbia, Constance Ashton Myers Collection, South Caroliniana Library.

47. By the 1930s the federal government began efforts to aid the nation through the New Deal, and numerous new state divisions assisted Gray in her work to advance adult literacy. The National Youth Administration and the Civilian Conservation Corps were two she worked with.

48. Historian Anne Firor Scott has discussed this image issue in many of her works. Her seminal work, *The Southern Lady: From Pedestal to Politics 1830–1930* (1970), and her collection of essays *Making the Invisible Woman Visible* (1984) provide the analytical starting point for my interpretation of Gray.

49. South Carolina ratified the amendment on July 1, 1969 and certified it on August 22, 1973. Information located at http://www.usconstitution.net/constamrat.html, accessed May 1, 2010.

50. "South Carolina's political gender gap is not just a gap … it's a Grand Canyon!" Southeastern Institute for Women in Politics, http://www.scelectswomen.com/about/, accessed February 10, 2011.

51. Kessler-Harris, *In Pursuit of Equity*, 4.

52. Glazer and Slater, *Unequal Colleagues*, 210.

53. Dr. Nicholas Mitchell, dean of the College of General Studies at the University of South Carolina, qtd. in Hardy, *Farm, Mill, and Classroom*, x.

54. Gilmore, "Gender and the Origins of the New South."

55. Anne Firor Scott, "After Suffrage," 300. For a detailed history of the origins of the cultural image of the southern lady, see Scott's *Southern Lady*. Scott is the primary

authority on the topic of the emergence of the new woman in the New South era. Scott's work on clubwomen, women's associations, black women's activism, and the invisibility of women in the master narrative has shaped the field of women's history. See also her other works *Natural Allies, Making the Invisible Woman Visible,* and *One Half the People.* For black women see Scott's "Most Invisible of All."

56. Blackwell, "Wil Lou Gray, Educator," 12.

57. Collins, *Fighting Words,* 5.

58. Untitled review of Collins's *Fighting Words,* Stumptious.com, http://www.stumptuous.com/comps/collins.html, accessed April 5, 2010.

59. Diana Philips, "Feminist Pedagogy: Issues Challenging Today's Instructors," graduate paper, Department of Women's Studies, Towson University, September 11, 2009, http://wwwnew.towson.edu/itrow/documents/Feminist_Pedagogy_Project091109.pdf, accessed November 5, 2009; Tétreault and Teske, *Partial Truths and the Politics of Community.*

60. Butler, "Gender and Performance," 42; Butler, *Gender Trouble.* I am also fascinated by the impact of psychoanalytical theory on gender identity. Although dated, see Joan Riviere, "Womanliness as a Masquerade," and Hughes, *Inner World and Joan Riviere.*

61. See Sullivan, *Days of Hope;* Hall, "Long Civil Rights Movement"; Gilmore, *Defying Dixie.* The debate around this topic is whether the small number of white women who helped advance opportunities for African Americans in the decades before *Brown v. Board of Education* actually reinforced rather than broke down racial inequality.

CHAPTER 1: ANCESTRY AND HERITAGE

1. Eudora Welty and James McBride Dabbs are just two of the many southern writers who wrote about the "sense of place" that belied the southern character. To southerners their place—community, family, and class—underscored every breath of life. Place was a reaffirmation of self. It defined who and what a person was within the mainstream world. Margaret Wolfe in *Daughters of Canaan* states that her grandmother "was rooted in tradition, sustained by her abiding sense of family, and deep religious faith," qualities she shared with other southern women of her time. See Wolfe, *Daughters of Canaan,* 6.

2. Wil Lou Gray to members of the Gray and Dial families, photocopied handwritten note, August 6, 1975, letter held by author.

3. I mean the women in her direct maternal and paternal lines. None had a public career, although her mother had a college degree.

4. See *Federal Census of the United States, Slave Schedule,* 1810, roll 865. See also Wil Lou Gray Ogden, "The Gray Family History," 105–16, booklet held by author.

5. South Carolina Pre-Revolutionary War Plates, vol. 16, 198; Grants, vol. 25, 474; Memorials, vol. 11, 284, SCDAH; records also available online at http://www.archivesindex.sc.gov/onlinearchives, series S213190, v0008, 397; v0017, 18. Family history pamphlet on Gray genealogy held by author.

6. Ogden, "Gray Family History," 107. His service is recorded on a receipt he signed for "60 wate of pork for Colonel Casey's milisha." See South Carolina Revolutionary War Folder AA3049, also shown in SE S-502. SCDAH.

7. W. Roy Smith, *South Carolina as a Royal Province*, 182; Ward, "Dial Family of Laurens County," 162. Issued in 1767, the grant deeds land in Craven County to Hasting Doyle. Henry Arthur Dial was the grandson of James D'Oyley, the grandson of Lady Lindsley. This may explain why the grant was issued in the name Doyle rather than Dial. The history of the county claims that "from 1682 to 1768, four South Carolina counties—Craven, Berkeley, Colleton, and Carteret/Granville—were never surveyed or properly laid out; all were fairly ambiguous geographical areas with no real governmental seat or political connotations to their existence. . . . In 1768, South Carolina eliminated all counties, including Craven County and established seven new 'Districts,' with governmental seats in each district. From 1768 to 1785, these districts remained intact, however, the district seats did change some during that time-frame." The Ninety-Sixth District grew from this reorganization. "A History of Craven County—One of the Three Original Counties of Carolina," http://www.carolana.com/Carolina/Settlement/craven__county__original.html, accessed May 12, 2010.

8. W. Roy Smith, *South Carolina as a Royal Province*, 160.

9. Ibid., 193–94, 412. Gray family members who have joined the St. Andrews Society and the Colonial Dames have used this genealogy.

10. Ward, "Dial Family of Laurens County," 162. Excerpts from books that refer to the Cane Brake battle are located at John A. Robinson, "Great Cane Break," *Global Gazetteer of the American Revolution*, http://gaz.jrshelby.com/greatcanebrake.htm, accessed January 10, 2011. During the Revolution Martin served eight months under Captain Ridgeway and Colonels Hayes and Kilgore. It was stated that Martin claimed his brothers were Tories. He was one of the few survivors of the Cane Brake Massacre. Facing execution by the British, his life was spared by his brother Col. Hastings Dial, an officer in the British Army.

11. Ward, "Dial Family of Laurens County," 162; Libby Rhodes, "Historical Marker Unveiled at Dial's Methodist Church in Gray Court," July 26, 2010, http://www.go laurens.com/index.php?option=com__content&view=article&id=4377:historical -marker-unveiled-at-dials-united-methodist-church&catid=25:news, accessed October 10, 2010.

12. Wil Lou Gray, manuscript application to the Daughters of the American Revolution, transcript held by author.

13. *Federal Census of the United States, Slave Schedule*, 1820, roll 865; see also Ward, "Dial Family of Laurens County," 160. The descendants of Hastings Dial were Baptist.

14. *Federal Census of the United States, Slave Schedule*, 1810, roll 865. See also Ogden, "Gray Family History," 105–16.

15. Dial, *True to His Colors*.

16. *Federal Census of the United States, Slave Schedule*, 1850, roll 865.

17. Blackwell, *Candle for All Time*, 84.

18. "The 1970 Gray Reunion," 3; booklet held by author.

19. Wallace, *History of South Carolina—Biographical*, 4:888.

20. Snowden, *History of South Carolina*, 8.

21. Ward, "Dial Family of Laurens County," 160. He is listed as a private, not a captain, in the Ninth South Carolina Regiment reserves along with Robert Lee Gray. "Soldiers and Sailors Database," National Park Service, http://www.itd.nps.gov/cwss/soldiers.cfm, accessed February 12, 2009. For a recent interpretation of the origins of

the terms *carpetbagger* and *scalawag*, see Tunnell, "Creating 'the Propaganda of History.'"

22. Slaunwhite, "Public Career of Nathaniel Barksdale Dial," 7.

23. Ibid., 1; Snowden, *History of South Carolina*, 8.

24. Snowden, *History of South Carolina*, 8.

25. Woodward, "In Search of the Southern Identity," 5; Wolfe, *Daughters of Canaan*, 8. Woodward's scholarship is the starting point for any work that discusses the transitional period in the South between 1877 and 1913. His book *The Origins of the New South* spawned the field of scholarship on southern history that addresses this period.

26. Dean flower, "Eudora Welty and Racism," *The Hudson Review*, vol. 60 no. 2 (Summer 2007), quote from Welty's 1956 essay "Place in Fiction" located at http://www.hudsonreview.com/flowerSU07.pdf, accessed 12 February 2009.

27. Blackwell, *Candle for All Time*, 6.

28. For a discussion of southern politics in the early twentieth century, see Key, *Southern Politics;* Lander, *History of South Carolina;* Wallace, *Short History;* Cash, *Mind of the South;* and Woodward, *Origins of the New South.* For a discussion of how some southerners felt about the effects of the "New South," see Simpson, *I'll Take My Stand;* Edgar, *South Carolina;* Simon, *Fabric of Defeat.*

29. See Hayes, *South Carolina and the New Deal;* Edgar, *South Carolina.*

30. Valerie Cook, librarian, interview by author, Clinton, S.C., April 1, 1996.

31. Ayres, *Let My People Learn*, 2; Blackwell, *Candle for All Time*, 25.

32. Ayres, *Let My People Learn*, 7.

33. For a discussion of this situation, see chapter 1 in Mabel Montgomery, *South Carolina's Wil Lou Gray*, 1–10. See also Hardy, *Farm, Mill and Classroom.*

34. Bolick, *Laurens County Sketchbook*, 66.

35. South Carolina first enacted a compulsory attendance law in 1915 but did not formally support it until 1937. It eliminated the law in 1955 in response to *Brown v. Board of Education* and reinstated it in 1967. See Hardy, *Farm, Mill, and Classroom*, 47, 69, 189.

36. Bollet, "Politics and Pellagra"; see also Etheridge, *Butterfly Caste.* As Bollet writes, records for 1907–11 for eight southern states reveal that there were 15,870 cases, with a fatality rate of 39.1 percent. See also the brief summary of the disorder in the *New World Encyclopedia*, http://www.newworldencyclopedia.org/entry/Pellagra, accessed January 10, 2011.

37. The "Negro Question" regarded whether or not to allow blacks civil liberties and, if so, to what extent. The question plagued every southern state after the Civil War, but between 1877 and the turn of the century, the question was answered by the implementation of Jim Crow laws designed to limit the freedom of black people. By the end of the nineteenth century, Jim Crow was well established across the South. See Cabell, *Negro Question;* Bryce, "Thoughts on the Negro Problem"; Weaver, "Failure of Civil Rights"; Simkins, "Race Legislation in South Carolina"; Woodward, *Strange Career of Jim Crow;* Wiener, "Planter Persistence and Social Change"; Mandle, "Re-Establishment of the Plantation Economy"; Nieman, *From Slavery to Sharecropping.* For recent scholarship on the black response to this era, see Hahn, *Nation under Our Feet;* Blight, *Race and Reunion;* Gilmore, *Gender and Jim Crow;* Harlan, *Booker T. Washington.*

38. The black population made up 60 percent of the population of Laurens County

in 1880 and 51 percent by 1920. It was among the most racially violent counties in the state. See Moore, *Carnival of Blood*, 129, 217 (statistics for Laurens County).

39. The Federal Census of 1880 indicated that only about 20 percent of all black children attended school and that the literacy level of the group at large was less than 10 percent.

40. See Moore, *Carnival of Blood;* Wood, *Lynching and Spectacle;* Brundage, *Under Sentence of Death;* Hale, *Making Whiteness;* Ayers, *Vengeance and Justice;* Finnegan, "At the Hands of Parties Unknown"; Feimster, "'Ladies and Lynching.'"

41. Leland, *Voice from South Carolina*, 55–60, located at http://oocities.org/gene brooks/laurens1.html. See also Baker, "Under the Rope." For a brief description of the 1870 riot, see "Laurens, South Carolina during Reconstruction," accessed October 20, 2010.

42. Trelease, *White Terror*, xiv, 351, 403–4, 406. Trelease explains the origins of terrorist activity in South Carolina in his look at the Klan's development in the South. See also John David Smith, *Disfranchisement Proposals*.

43. Ball, *Boy's Recollection*. See also Poole, *Never Surrender*, 122.

44. Poole, "Religion, Gender, and the Lost Cause"; Zuczek, "Last Campaign of the Civil War"; Rable, *But There Was No Peace;* Ball, *State That Forgot;* Foner, *Reconstruction;* Drago, *Hurrah for Hampton!;* Edgar, *South Carolina;* Beeby, "Red Shirt Violence."

45. Blackwell, *Candle for All Time*, 15.

46. "Chester County," http://memory.loc.gov/cgi-bin/query/D?wpa:18:./temp/~am mem__MU5Z:, accessed July 30, 2006.

47. Bailey, *Liberalism in the New South*, 18. See also Kantrowitz, "Ben Tillman and Hendrix McLane," 523; Bartley, "In Search of the New South," 153; Burnside, "Governorship of Coleman Livingston Blease"; Selden Kennedy Smith, "Ellison DuRant Smith"; Mixon, "Senatorial Career of Coleman Livingston Blease"; Gilbert, "Dictators and Demagogues"; and Dorgan et al., *Oratory of Southern Demagogues*.

48. Sosna, *In Search of the Silent South*, 11; see also Simon, *Fabric of Defeat*, for the role that these politicians played in the politics of mill workers in the state.

49. Carter, *Politics of Rage*, 69; qtd. in Simon, *Fabric of Defeat*, 248n14.

50. Dial, *True to His Colors*, 102.

51. Holt, *Black over White*, 183–84, 202–3, citation located in a summary of the Riot of 1870 in Laurens in "Laurens County, South Carolina during the Reconstruction Era," http://www.oocities.org/genebrooks/laurens1.html, accessed September 9, 2010.

52. This spectacle assured Hampton's victory, although Chamberlain protested the vote and took the oath of office. When the contested presidential election between Rutherford B. Hayes and Samuel Tilden ended Reconstruction and federal occupation of the South, Hampton officially became governor in April 1877. For a summation of Hampton's governorship, see Edgar, *South Carolina*, 408–29.

53. Poole, *Never Surrender*, 128. Poole builds his argument from Stephanie McCurry's work on the household as a central rallying point for secessionists during the Nullification Crisis of the 1830s. See McCurry, *Masters of Small Worlds: Yeoman Households and the Political Culture of the Antebellum South Carolina Low Country* (Oxford University Press, 1995).

54. Blackwell, *Candle for All Time*, 24. According to Huff, *Tried by Fire*, the "Lost Cause" was a common topic preached from the pulpits of Southern Methodist churches,

although the subject violated the Methodist tenet of the Social Gospel. See Cox, *Dixie's Daughters*, and Foster, *Ghosts of the Confederacy*.

55. Elliott, Gray, and Tolbert, *Distinguished Women of Laurens County*, 105. History of the Kappa Alpha Order, http://www.kappaalphaorder.org/ka/history, accessed March 10, 2006.

56. J. C. Garlington, "Men of the Time: South Carolina," biographical clipping located in private papers of Harriet Blackwell Gray, collection held by author. See Blackwell, *Candle for All Time*.

57. Sarah Dial's college major is unknown.

58. Blackwell, *Candle for All Time*, 88.

59. See Poole, "Religion, Gender, and the Lost Cause," for a good history of the events of that election cycle. See also Edgar, *South Carolina*, chap. 18.

60. For Gray's later career achievements, see Snowden, *History of South Carolina*, 194. There are letters between Wil Lou Gray and her father and material about him in the Wil Lou Gray Papers, box 32.

61. *Scrapbook*, 202.

62. Snowden, *History of South Carolina*, 194.

63. Dial, *True to His Colors*, 94.

64. Moore, "Redeemers Reconsidered"; Moore, "Historical Context."

65. For a narrative about this transitional period, see Lumpkin, *Making of a Southerner*. For more information about the life of Lumpkin, see Hall, "Open Secrets."

66. Ford, "Rednecks and Merchants."

67. See Blackwell, *Candle for All Time*; Mabel Montgomery, *South Carolina's Wil Lou Gray*; Dial, *True to His Colors*; Elliott, Gray, and Tolbert, *Distinguished Women of Laurens County*.

68. Ford, "Rednecks and Merchants," 317.

69. Nicholls, *Southern Tradition*, 7; see also Grantham, *Southern Progressivism*, and Kousser, *Shaping of Southern Politics*.

70. Nathaniel Dial was a lawyer, mayor of Laurens, and a United States senator from 1919 to 1925. His father, Capt. Albert Dial, suffered financial losses during the Civil War but later served as president of a bank. Wallace, *History of South Carolina—Biography*, 4:888.

71. Slaunwhite, "Public Career of Nathaniel Barksdale Dial," ix.

72. See Cal M. Logue and Howard Dorgan, "The Demagogue," in Dorgan et al., *Oratory of Southern Demagogues*, 2.

73. Slaunwhite, "Public Career of Nathaniel Barksdale Dial," 128; Kantrowitz, "Ben Tillman and Hendrix McLane," 523.

74. Snowden, *History of South Carolina*, 8.

75. Slaunwhite, "Public Career of Nathaniel Barksdale Dial," 191–97.

76. Shankman, "Jury of Her Peers," 121.

77. *Scrapbook*, 33.

78. Gray to extended family, April 13, 1965, n.p., mimeographed letter with a handwritten message to Wil Lou Gray Ogden held by author.

79. Blackwell, *Candle for All Time*, 121.

80. Ayres, *Let My People Learn*, 9.

81. "In Recognition of Outstanding Public Service The Anderson Daily Mail

herewith inscribes this Scroll of Honor to this Distinguished Citizen, Miss Wil Lou Gray," newspaper clipping, *Anderson Daily Mail*, n.d. [1942?], clipping held by author.

82. Harriet Gray Blackwell to Gray, December 8, 1955, letter held by author.

83. Gray to Wil Lou Gray Ogden, December 24, 1965, letter held by author.

84. *Dorland's Medical Dictionary*, 1407.

85. Ayres, *Let My People Learn*, 7.

86. This story appears in many accounts of Gray's early life. See Mabel Montgomery, *South Carolina's Wil Lou Gray*, 48; Bodie, *South Carolina Women*, 106.

87. Gray to Wil Lou Gray Ogden, April 13, 1965, letter held by author.

88. Ibid.

89. Emma Dial Gray, handwritten account of Sarah Dial in folder on William Gray's death, box 31, Wil Lou Gray Papers.

90. Box 31, Wil Lou Gray Papers.

91. Ayres, *Let My People Learn*, 10.

92. William Lafayette Gray to Gray, August 29, 1918, box 31, Wil Lou Gray Papers.

93. Julia Mood Peterkin was a contemporary of Wil Lou Gray and wrote to H. L. Mencken in 1926 that motherless children get "precious little real loving," an indication that she knew what it was like to be in that situation. She, like Gray, suffered a childhood of tragedy and displacement. Her father was a peer and a friend of Gray's father. See Robeson, "Ambiguity of Julia Peterkin."

94. Bettie Lou Snead, interview by author, Greenwood, S.C., January 11, 1996; Marigene Miller, interview by author, Columbia, April 14, 1994; Wil Lou Gray Ogden, interview by author, Whiteville, N.C., January 18, 1996. Betty Lou is the daughter of Cecil Gray and granddaughter of Robert Lee Gray, William's brother.

95. Elliott, Tolbert, and Gray, *Distinguished Women of Laurens County*, 119; Marigene Miller, interview by author, Columbia, March 12, 1994; Wil Lou Gray Ogden, interview by author, Whiteville, N.C., March 13, 1994; McNeely, "Her Accomplishments."

96. "Death Claims Gray Brothers in Two Days," *Laurens (S.C.) Advertiser*, n.d., clipping held by author. Quote by Wil Lou Gray in "South Carolina's Wil Lou Gray," *Senior Citizen Magazine*, 1964, 54.

97. Gray to Wil Lou Gray Ogden, September 2, 1964, letter held by author.

98. Blackwell, *Candle for All Time*, 83.

99. Ibid., 19.

100. Ibid., 82.

101. As was typical of men during this period, he had three young children and soon remarried. It is possible that Mary was chosen to fill Sarah's shoes before her death, evident by the hand William lent in grooming Mary from youth to adulthood.

102. Blackwell, *Candle for All Time*, 19.

103. Ibid., 82.

104. Ibid., 83.

105. Ibid.

106. Ibid., 119–28.

107. Ibid., 119.

108. Marigene Miller, interview by author, Columbia, June 21, 1996.

109. Marigene Miller, interview by author, Columbia, April 14, 1994; Wil Lou Gray Ogden, interview by author, Whiteville, N.C., April 12, 1995; Mrs. Albert Dial Gray Jr.,

interview by author, Whiteville, N.C., June 21, 1996. It was a known fact that Albert Dial did not care for Mary or his half-sister, Hattie. He considered them selfish and spoiled and avoided an intimate relationship with either of them. He had four children with Lillian, all of whom paid respect to Mary but admitted to never liking her. Dial Jr. did not attend college because his father blamed Wofford for exposing him to the vices of alcohol and gambling.

110. Marigene Miller, interview by author, Lake Waccamaw, N.C., June 23, 1996; Mrs. Albert Dial Gray Jr., interview by author, Whiteville, N.C., June 23, 1996. I confirmed this circumstance with Virginia Kea Council Gray in a phone interview conducted on May 15, 2010. She stated that the dislike of Mary may have been inspired by Albert Dial's wife, Lillian, rather than by way of him. Lillian was also Wil Lou Gray's childhood best friend.

111. Marigene Miller, interview by author.

112. Blackwell, *Candle for All Time*, 120.

113. Marigene Miller, interview by author.

114. Blackwell, *Candle for All Time*, 119.

115. "In Recognition of Outstanding Public Service." For a discussion of reconstituted families, see McGoldrick and Carter, "Forming a Remarried Family," 400.

116. "In Recognition of Outstanding Public Service."

117. Marigene Miller, interview by author, Columbia, August 5, 1995. Monkie (her nickname) said Gray received a marriage proposal from a man named Isaac Gray of Woodruff, S.C., but she turned him down. She did not want to marry because she did not love him, and she felt it would tie her down and limit her freedom. Kea Gray, Dial Jr.'s wife, said that she heard from Dial's mother, Lillian Caine, that Gray had been in love with a young man in her youth but her family did not approve of the relationship. Whether this young man was Isaac Gray is unknown. Kea Gray, interview by author, Whiteville, N.C., April 9, 1997.

118. Cook, *Eleanor Roosevelt*, 11.

119. Marigene Miller, interview by author, Columbia, March 12, 1994.

120. Evelyn Branch, interview by author, Columbia, August 25, 1995.

121. Darrell Crase and Dixie Crase, "Parental Death: Impact on Young Children," http://files.eric.ed.gov/fulltext/ED391597.pdf, accessed September 10, 2008. For writings on the effects of trauma and death on children see Krementz, *How It Feels*.

122. Kearl, *Endings*, cited in Crase and Crase, "Parental Death," 8.

123. Blackwell, *Candle for All Time*, 159.

124. Ibid., 119.

125. Bolick, *Laurens County Sketchbook*, 66. Bolick's book is an excellent source for general information about the people and buildings of Laurens. He displays sketches and paragraph summaries of special families, churches, people, and schools of the town. It is a simple book, but it creates a picture of where Gray lived in her youth through his descriptive sketches.

126. Ibid., 66.

127. Dabney, *Universal Education in the South*, 418.

128. See *Federal Census of South Carolina*, 1910, Population III, 658–59.

129. Solomon, *In the Company of Educated Women*, 64, qtd. in Johnson, *Southern Women at the Seven Sister Colleges*, 3.

130. Allen, "Laura Bragg and the Charleston Museum," 180n13. For transitions in women's lives between 1880 and 1920, see Rebecca Montgomery, *Politics of Education;* McCandless, *Past in the Present;* Gordon, *Gender and Higher Education;* Degler, *At Odds;* Margaret Wilson, *American Woman in Transition;* Higham, "Reorientation of American Culture"; Carroll Smith-Rosenberg, "The Female World of Love and Ritual" and "The New Woman as Androgyne: Social Disorder and Gender Crisis, 1870–1936," in Smith-Rosenberg, *Disorderly Conduct;* Rosenzweig, "'Anchor of My Life.'"

131. Johnson, *Southern Women at the Seven Sister Colleges,* 2.

132. Ibid., 3. Johnson states that one aspect of the determination of legitimacy was based on whether the school offered an Artium Baccalaureatus (A.B.) degree. Columbia College did offer this degree. For a discussion of the idea of the "true woman," see Welter, "Cult of True Womanhood." For a discussion of the evolution of this ideal in the South, see Scott, *Southern Lady.*

133. See Rosenzweig, *Anchor of My Life.*

134. "Services Held for Educator," *Columbia (S.C.) Record,* March 12, 1984; "Miss Wil Lou: Warrior for Equal Opportunity," *Columbia (S.C.) State,* March 13, 1984.

CHAPTER 2: AWAKENING

1. See Scott, *Southern Lady,* and Scott, *Natural Allies.* For a book that specifically addresses club ideology as it relates to race and region in South Carolina, see Johnson, *Southern Ladies, New Women.*

2. With so many reforms under way, Gray claimed illiteracy as her problem of choice. She said she did not have the energy beyond her work to eradicate illiteracy, although she supported suffrage. See "She Remembers," *Florence (S.C.) Morning News,* August 1969, clipping held by author; interview, Wil Lou Gray, June 14, 1974. For a history of the reform campaigns in the South in this period and a brief summary of southern progressive historiography, see Grantham, "Contours of Southern Progressivism"; Anne Firor Scott, "Progressive Wind"; Tindall, "Business Progressivism"; Tindall, *Persistent Tradition;* Tindall, *Emergence of the New South.*

3. "Can You Remember?" *Columbia College Alumnae Magazine,* 1970, 3.

4. Interview, Wil Lou Gray by Constance Ashton Myers, June 14, 1974, Southern Oral History Collection, Wilson Library Special Collections, University of North Carolina, Chapel Hill; transcript held by author.

5. *Columbia (S.C.) Advocate,* July 10, 1865, cited in Huff, *Tried by Fire,* 31.

6. Edwards and Gifford, *Gender and the Social Gospel.* This book provides a very good discussion of the historiography on the Social Gospel movement.

7. Huff, *Tried by Fire,* 75.

8. Archie Vernon Huff, Professor Emeritus, Furman University, interview by author, Greenville, S.C., July 31, 1995. See also Huff, *Tried by Fire.* Huff served as associate pastor of the Washington Street United Methodist Church from 1962 to 1965, during which time Wil Lou Gray was an active member of the congregation. Dr. Huff knew Gray well and received a piece of china hand painted by her as a wedding gift.

9. Eighmy, "Liberalism in the South," 372.

10. Interview, Wil Lou Gray by Constance Ashton Myers, June 14, 1974.

11. Gray to Tom (last name unknown), October 26, 1956, letter held by author.

12. The UDC was an outgrowth of other war memorial societies and hereditary clubs. Three hereditary clubs included many elite southern white women among their membership rolls: the UDC, the Colonial Dames (established in 1891), and the Daughters of the American Revolution (1890). Gray was a member of each of these organizations. Wolfe, *Daughters of Canaan*, 132; Blight, *Race and Reunion*.

13. Huff, *Tried by Fire*, 61.

14. Ibid., 71.

15. Ayres, *Let My People Learn*, 16.

16. Gray to Wil Lou Gray Ogden, May 13, 1959, letter held by author.

17. "Can You Remember?" 2; Mabel Montgomery, *South Carolina's Wil Lou Gray*, 4.

18. Huff, *Tried by Fire*, 62.

19. "Now Let's Plan for Big Things: Dr. Wil Lou Gray," *Columbia College Alumnae Magazine*, Winter 1969, 4; see also interview, Wil Lou Gray by Constance Ashton Myers, June 14, 1974.

20. "Now Let's Plan for Big Things," 4. Throughout her life Gray was conscientious about thrift. At the time of her death, her estate was valued at close to one million dollars. See Last Will and Testament, Wil Lou Gray, Probate Records, Richland County, Columbia. Copy held by author.

21. *Columbia (S.C.) State Magazine*, October 7, 1979, 8−9.

22. Freedman, "Benefits of Separate Female Organizations," 268.

23. Ibid., 266.

24. Ibid., 268, 271.

25. For a discussion of the history and purpose of the South Carolina women's club movement, see Johnson, *Southern Ladies, New Women;* Smedley, "Martha Schofield"; Taylor, "South Carolina and the Enfranchisement of Women"; Stackhouse, *Time Marches On.* For a more general history of the women's club movement and the suffrage struggle in the South, see Wheeler, *New Women of the New South*, and Anne Firor Scott, *Southern Lady.*

26. Jessie Laurence, speech on illiteracy and the American home, 1939, Jessie Huey Laurence Papers, Winthrop University Archives, Ida Dacus Library, Rock Hill, S.C.

27. Freeman, "Clubs to Parties," 322.

28. See Gordon, "Black and White Visions of Welfare."

29. On the YWCA see interview, Wil Lou Gray by Constance Ashton Myers, June 14, 1974. Gray joined the DAR in December 1909. National #76110, Chapter 3058SC, information located at http://services.dar.org/public/dar%5Fresearch/search__member /?Action=full&National__Number=76110, accessed December 10, 2010; application held by author. "If she was a member of one, she was a member of them all," states Wil Lou Gray Ogden, Gray's great-niece and namesake. She said Gray gave all of her female relatives the paperwork to join the organizations, but Ogden did not join any. Interview by author, January 1, 2011.

30. Blackwell, *Candle for All Time*, 166; Mabel Montgomery, *South Carolina's Wil Lou Gray*, 2. For a discussion of job opportunities for women at the turn of the century, see Anne Firor Scott, *Southern Lady;* Anne Firor Scott, *Natural Allies;* Antler, *Educated Woman and Professionalization;* and Campbell, *"Liberated" Woman of 1914.* Both DaMaris Ayres and Mabel Montgomery outline in detail Gray's educational career in their respective biographies. Gray began her work in rural South Carolina just as educational

reform was finding fertile ground in the state. The Southern Education Board's interest in southern schools and the emergence of health curricula were key components of the progressive educational wave that rolled across the South at the turn of twentieth century. For a history of the Southern Education Board, see Dabney, *Universal Education in the South;* Harlan, "Southern Education Board"; Kousser, "Progressivism."

31. Chafe, *Paradox of Change,* 99.

32. Ibid., 101, 111–12. I use *feminized* because teaching, nursing, librarian, and social work were considered acceptable jobs for women and extensions of their natural roles as caregivers, where law, medicine, and science were masculine fields and not recognized as women's work. See McCammon et al., "How Movements Win."

33. Mabel Montgomery, *South Carolina's Wil Lou Gray,* 2.

34. Chafe, *American Woman.* For a series of biographical sketches of important South Carolina women in this period, see Spruill, Littlefield, and Johnson, *South Carolina Women.*

35. Chafe, *American Woman,* 274.

36. Chafe, *American Woman.* See Woodward, *Origins of the New South;* Lander, *History of South Carolina;* Hardy, *Farm, Mill, and Classroom.*

37. Folder 4, box 1, Wil Lou Gray Papers. Gray lists the legislation on these issues and the role the teachers' association played in lobbying the General Assembly. See also Hardy, *Farm, Mill, and Classroom,* 22–26.

38. "Says Cry of South Is for Education," *New York Times,* January 12, 1904, http://query.nytimes.com/mem/archive-free/pdf?res=9B01E1DD1230EE32A25751C1A96 79C946597D6CF, accessed October 15, 2010.

39. Edward Cary, "Education and the South," *New York Times,* May 11, 1902, http://query.nytimes.com/mem/archive-free/pdf?res=9C0DEED6103DEE32A25752C1A96 39C946397D6CF, accessed October 15, 2010.

40. Box 1, Wil Lou Gray Papers.

41. Bailey, *Liberalism in the New South,* 135.

42. Montgomery, *Guide Book.* Folder 1, Correspondence In, 1900–1914, Wil Lou Gray Papers.

43. "Postwar Education in South Carolina," document located in folder 1, Correspondence In, 1900–1914, Wil Lou Gray Papers; "Report on Adult Education" (1922), 265.

44. "Postwar Education in South Carolina." See also Hudson, *Entangled by White Supremacy,* 349n12; *Acts and Joint Resolutions,* 52, 248–49, 452.

45. Knight, *Public Education in the South,* 160. In chapter 7 Knight provides a discussion of South Carolina's 1811 and 1835 laws that set the tone of education-related politics in the state until 1868, when a public school fund was established.

46. McPherson, "White Liberals and Black Power," 1357, 1376. For a history of the Freedmen's Bureau and Reconstruction's impact, see Eric Foner, *Reconstruction;* Woodward, *Origins of the New South;* Hahn, *Nation Under Our Feet;* Rabinowitz, "Half a Loaf."

47. For black education see Morris, *Reading, 'Riting, and Reconstruction;* Simkins, "Race Legislation in South Carolina"; Franklin, "Jim Crow Goes to School"; McPherson, "White Liberals and Black Power"; Kirby, "Black and White in the Rural South"; Berkeley, "Colored Ladies Also Contributed"; Devlin, "South Carolina and Black Migrations"; Wirt, *We Ain't What We Was.*

48. Qtd. in Bailey, *Liberalism in the New South*, 33.

49. Going, "South and the Blair Education Bill," 267.

50. *Wilmington (N.C.) Weekly Star*, January 14, 1887.

51. Bailey, *Liberalism in the New South*, 138; Dabney, *Universal Education in the South*, 3–18.

52. Bailey, *Liberalism in the New South*, 138.

53. Ibid., 142. For a history of Jeanes teachers in South Carolina, see Woodfaulk, "Jeanes Teachers."

54. Bailey, *Liberalism in the New South*, 135. For a history of the Southern Education Board, see Dabney, *Universal Education in the South*, 54–74; Harlan, "Southern Education Board"; and Kousser, "Progressivism," 169.

55. Bailey, *Liberalism in the New South*, 34.

56. Southern Education Foundation, http://www.southerneducation.org, accessed November 15, 2009. See also "Anna T. Jeanes, Philanthropist," *Cleveland Journal*, 1907, http://www.southerneducation.org, accessed November 15, 2009.

57. Grantham, *Southern Progressivism*, 246. See also Dabney, *Universal Education in the South;* Link, "Privies, Progressivism, and Public Schools"; and Grantham, "Contours of Southern Progressivism."

58. Grantham, *Southern Progressivism*, 152.

59. Dabney, *Universal Education in the South*, 65.

60. Mabel Montgomery, *South Carolina's Wil Lou Gray*, 2.

61. Interview, Wil Lou Gray by Constance Ashton Myers, June 14, 1974.

62. Ibid.

63. Her father financed her college education, but Gray saved her money and paid her own way through postgraduate course work. "Now Let's Plan for Big Things," 4.

64. Mabel Montgomery, *South Carolina's Wil Lou Gray*, 18–19. For more on Tate, see Grantham, *Southern Progressivism*, 270–72.

65. Interview, Wil Lou Gray by Constance Ashton Myers, June 14, 1974. Two years later, while a professor at Martha Washington College in Abingdon, Virginia, Gray conducted a class with the same title.

66. For information on Tate, see Dabney, *Universal Education in the South*, 223–29.

67. This vision included preparing teachers to teach in rural schools, establishing rural schools, and pushing for local taxation for public schools. The two problems they aimed to address: the lack of prepared teachers and the absence of community schools. See Dabney, *Universal Education in the South*, 54–73.

68. Hohner, "Southern Education in Transition."

69. Bailey, *Liberalism in the New South*, 140.

70. Dabney, *Universal Education in the South*, 120.

71. Ibid.

72. Eleanor Foxworth, "Sabre Anne McNeese White—Grandmother of Dr. D. B. Johnson," *News*, April 30, 2008, 12.

73. Mabel Montgomery, *South Carolina's Wil Lou Gray*, 6–9.

74. Interview, Wil Lou Gray by Constance Ashton Myers, June 14, 1974.

75. Dabney, *Universal Education in the South*, 226–30.

76. Elliott, Gray, and Tolbert, *Distinguished Women of Laurens County*, 116.

77. Mabel Montgomery, *South Carolina's Wil Lou Gray*, 15. See Harlan, *Booker T.*

Washington Papers, 8:486n1, 492, http://www.historycooperative.org/btw/Vol.8/html/
486.html, accessed January 12, 2010.

78. Harlan, *Booker T. Washington*, 296; Washington, "New Type of Rural School."
See also Harlan, "Southern Education Board." For a critique of Washington's view of
industrial education, see W. E. B. Du Bois, "Of Mr. Booker T. Washington and Others,"
in *The Souls of Black Folk* (1903), http://www.gutenberg.org/etext/408, accessed October 20, 2007.

79. Washington, "New Type of Rural School," 837. This article is very interesting
because Washington talks about his experimental school in Macon County, Alabama.
Here he incorporated the three R's with the daily chores of living. It was a work-study
program aimed to fit the child for life in the community and to give meaning to the exercises in the textbooks. Although black educational reform was dictated by the pervasive
white supremacy in the South, Washington's ideas defied racial barriers and influenced
educators across the South, particularly Gray. Her opportunity school mirrored Washington's work-study model, and she was successful in developing her program. She, like
Washington, found vocational education the best method to give a person an opportunity to learn while they continued to work in a trade. See Harlan, "Southern Education
Board," 189; Salmon, "50 Years in 40 Days," 171; Hardy, *Farm, Mill, and Classroom;* and
Simkins, "Race Legislation in South Carolina."

80. Harlan, *Booker T. Washington Papers*, 8:492.

81. Max Bennett Thrasher, *Tuskegee: Its Story and Its Work* (1901), http://books
.google.com, accessed September 10, 2008.

82. Superintendent of Education Report, 1919–33, General Assembly Reports and
Resolutions, SCDAH.

83. Mabel Montgomery, *South Carolina's Wil Lou Gray*, 15; "Can You Remember?"
Columbia College Alumnae Magazine, 1970, 1–7.

84. Gray did not receive a degree but took postgraduate courses.

85. College Catalog, 1907–8, Martha Washington College, Martha Washington College Papers, Special Collections, Kelly Library, Emory and Henry College, Emory, Virginia.

86. Ibid., "General Information," 12.

87. Ibid.

88. Ibid.

89. Ibid., 13. See also Curtis, *Three Quarters of a Century*, located at the Washington
County Historical Society, Abingdon, Virginia.

90. Schneider and Schneider, *American Women in the Progressive Era*, 52–53; Anne
Firor Scott, *Natural Allies*, 44, 60.

91. Grantham, *Southern Progressivism*, 269.

92. Ledger, Reel #2, Account Book, 1907–1910, Martha Washington College Papers.

93. College Catalog, 1907–8, 14.

94. Ibid.

95. Mabel Montgomery, *South Carolina's Wil Lou Gray*, 17.

96. College Catalog, 12.

97. Ibid., 19. Gray was twenty-five years old at the time.

98. Ayres, *Let My People Learn*, 34–45. Gray provided no insight or explanation as to
why she moved from teaching English literature to a graduate degree in political science.

99. Wil Lou Gray Columbia University transcript located in box 32, Wil Lou Gray Papers.

100. Daniel Hollis, Professor Emeritus, University of South Carolina, interview by author, August 15, 1996. Dr. Hollis said it was common for southerners to get accepted by Columbia even if they were not academically outstanding. He recalled his own experience and enjoyed the expression on the faces of many Ivy League colleagues when he told them of his academic mediocrity.

101. Dunning, *Reconstruction, Political and Economic*. See also Claude Bowers, *The Tragic Era: The Revolution after Lincoln* (Cambridge, Mass., 1929), v–vi, qtd. in Gerald Grob and Athan Billias, *Interpretations of American History: Patterns and Perspectives* (New York: Free Press, 1992), 415–420.

102. Grob and Billias, *Interpretations of American History*, 416.

103. Grantham, *Regional Imagination*, 79.

104. Grob and Billias, *Interpretations of American History*, 417. For the seminal work in Reconstruction historiography that has redefined and shaped the field since the 1988, see Foner, *Reconstruction*, and his concise version, *Short History of Reconstruction*. Foner's primary thesis is that Reconstruction failed because it did not fully integrate freed blacks into American society and protect their new freedoms granted via the Thirteenth, Fourteenth and Fifteenth Amendments. Although political and economic reforms were made, particularly the constitutional amendments, free blacks during Reconstruction were victims of a pervasive national racism, and despite the failure of the national state to protect and integrate them fully into American society, they actively forged their own communities and political and economic identities. Foner argues that even though Reconstruction did not achieve radical goals, it gave African Americans in the South a glimpse of participation in a free society. His work is considered the source of recent historical work in the field of memory studies.

105. Wil Lou Gray, "The Political Philosophy of John Codman Hurd," M.A. thesis, Department of Political Science, Columbia University, 1912.

106. Gray, "Political Philosophy of John Codman Hurd," 22.

107. Ibid., 2.

108. Ibid.

109. Ibid., 21.

110. Blight, *Race and Reunion*, 139.

111. Cooper, *Walter Hines Page*, iii.

112. See McRae, "White Womanhood, White Supremacy."

113. Chafe, *Paradox of Change*, 111, 112.

114. George Pitts was the Laurens County superintendent of education, and Gray worked under both Pitts and William K. Tate, the state superintendent of rural schools, until Tate's resignation in 1914 to head up Peabody Teachers College on the campus of Vanderbilt University. O. B. Martin became state superintendent of education and was replaced by John Swearingen in 1912. Swearingen would be an instrumental figure in the life and work of Gray. For a brief description of the work of Tate, see Grantham, *Southern Progressivism*, 146–72, and for a description of Gray's work as rural supervisor, see Mabel Montgomery, *South Carolina's Wil Lou Gray*, 21–28.

Chapter 3: The Making of a Professional

1. Historian Janet Hudson examines the World War I era in South Carolina (1914–24) and supplies two chapters that address general reforms and educational funding in this period. Her work offers an excellent racial, political, and economic context to Gray's early work with adult literacy and supplies the rationale and statistics on funding that explain why her work found support at this critical moment in the state's history. See Hudson, *Entangled by White Supremacy.*

2. For a summary of her work in this period, see "Report of the State Supervisor of Rural Schools," General Assembly Reports and Resolutions, Superintendent of Education, 1912–1916, SCDAH; folder 2, box 1, Correspondence In, 1914–16, Wil Lou Gray Papers. All of the references regarding Gray's papers, unless otherwise noted, are located in box 1 of her papers and in the folders dated between 1912 and 1936. The method of citation reflects how the records are stored.

3. Mabel Montgomery, *South Carolina's Wil Lou Gray*, 22.

4. Folder 1, box 1, Correspondence In, 1912–1914, Wil Lou Gray Papers.

5. Dabney, *Universal Education in the South*, 110. Although the effort was designed to help rural southern educators prepare to teach in their regions, educators from Puerto Rico and western states attended as well.

6. Ibid., 105.

7. See "Report on Adult Education" (1919–35).

8. Folder 4, box 1, Correspondence In, 1913, Wil Lou Gray Papers.

9. Wil Lou Gray's résumé, 1960, document held by author.

10. Ibid. See appendix for a copy of her résumé.

11. *Acts and Joint Resolutions*, 248–49.

12. It is important to note that in 1906 William Hand left his position as superintendent of the Chester schools to take a position as an instructor of secondary education at the University of South Carolina to reform high schools in the state. His salary was paid for with General Education Board funds. He organized an accreditation system and entrance examinations and is known as the father of the public school system in South Carolina. Between 1910 and 1914, 372 high school diplomas were issued. Gray was participating in his efforts to reform the secondary system in the state. See Dabney, *Universal Education in the South*, 420–21; Mabel Montgomery, *South Carolina's Wil Lou Gray*, 23–28. For a discussion of the hookworm campaign and the development of public sanitation in school curriculum, see Link, "Privies, Progressivism, and Public Schools."

13. Mabel Montgomery, *South Carolina's Wil Lou Gray*, 28; Elliott, Gray, and Tolbert, *Distinguished Women of Laurens County*, 116. For Tate's salary information, see Dabney, *Universal Education in the South*, 229. There is a 1914 pamphlet on rural education compiled by Tate and Gray, but the author was unable to locate the material. For a description of Tate, see Grantham, *Southern Progressivism*, 271. Grantham says, "Tate was one of the most successful rural supervisors." For a discussion of the educational philosophy behind Peabody College, where Tate taught after leaving his position in South Carolina, see Force, *Payne at Peabody*, and Hoffschwelle, "Science of Domesticity."

14. Grantham, *Southern Progressivism*, 271.

15. Folder 1, Correspondence In, 1912–14, Wil Lou Gray Papers.

16. Folder 2, Correspondence In, 1912–14, Wil Lou Gray Papers.

17. For information about the SIA in state records, see Superintendent of Education Report, 1919–33, General Assembly Reports and Resolutions, SCDAH.

18. Wil Lou Gray to John Swearingen, June 12, 1913, box 1, Correspondence In, 1912–14, Wil Lou Gray Papers.

19. *Forty-Eighth Annual Report of the State Superintendent of Education* (1915), 30. Too, as mentioned earlier, William Tate found her work worthy of discussion in his lectures at Peabody.

20. Folder 2, Correspondence In, 1914–16, Wil Lou Gray Papers.

21. William Lafayette Gray served on the community Board of Trustees in Laurens.

22. Gray, "Evolution of Adult Elementary Education."

23. William Hays Simpson, *Life in Mill Communities* (1943), 46, located at http://books.google.com/books?id=CpsdTj3mqgsC&printsec=frontcover&source=gbs__v2__summary__r&cad=0#v=onepage&q&f=false, accessed October 18, 2006. This book also has a summary of the work Gray conducted in the state of South Carolina between 1918 and 1940.

24. Stewart, *Moonlight Schools*, 16. For a more recent history of Stewart, see Baldwin, *Cora Wilson Stewart*.

25. McNeely, "Her Accomplishments," 15

26. Ibid. See Simon, "Appeal of Cole Blease"; Link, "Progressive Movement in the South"; and Anne Firor Scott, "Progressive Wind," 53.

27. Gray, *Night School Experiment*, 5–6.

28. Ibid.

29. Ibid., 1.

30. After 1919 Gray would consistently plead with the General Assembly to deal with black illiteracy and ask that tax money be used to aid in the eradication of the problem.

31. Prior to the war, the Smith-Lever Act of 1914 officially established the Cooperative Extension Service, which in South Carolina used federal, state, and local funds to undertake agricultural extension work through Clemson College. Objectives were to make better farms and homes, increase willingness by adults and youth to be better citizens, and organize groups that could improve the welfare of the community, like the 4-H Clubs and the Corn and Tomato Clubs. Gray used extension services to assist in her work.

32. McNeely, "Her Accomplishments," 15.

33. William Workman, "Her Friends Know Wil Lou Gray Won't Really Retire," *Greenville (S.C.) News*, August 11, 1957.

34. *Forty-Eighth Annual Report of the State Superintendent of Education* (1915), 30–31.

35. Gray, "Evolution of Adult Elementary Education," 3. See "50 Years in 40 Days: The Advances Made by Governor Manning and the Legislature of South Carolina," *Survey*, April 3, 1915, 13. The appropriation applied to the 1916 fiscal year. This money enabled school workers to enroll five thousand people over the age of fourteen in mill schools and in rural night schools. See Hardy, *Farm, Mill, and Classroom*, 40.

36. Ayres, *Let My People Learn*, 58.

37. "Big Decrease in Illiteracy Here," 1917, Correspondence Out, 1919, Wil Lou Gray Papers.

38. Ibid.

39. John Swearingen to Gray, July 6, 1917.

40. Folder 2, box 1, Correspondence In, 1914–16, Wil Lou Gray Papers.

41. Ibid.

42. M. Bates Stephens, state superintendent of education in Maryland, to Gray, May 21, 1917, box 1, Correspondence In, 1917, Wil Lou Gray Papers.

43. Ibid.

44. Gray to Adelaide Ayer, December 9, 1917, box 1, Correspondence In, 1917, Wil Lou Gray Papers.

45. Folder 2, Correspondence In, 1914–16, Wil Lou Gray Papers.

46. Ayres, *Let My People Learn*, 67.

47. Folder 2, Correspondence In, 1918, Wil Lou Gray Papers.

48. Gertrude M. Stevens to Gray, November 14, 1917, Correspondence In, 1917, Wil Lou Gray Papers.

49. Folder 2, Correspondence In, 1918, Wil Lou Gray Papers.

50. Ayres, *Let My People Learn*, 64.

51. The South Carolina Women's Council of Defense was the women's division of the South Carolina Council of Defense, the public relations and propaganda branch of the state during World War I. David Coker chaired the organization. It increasingly took on the responsibility of policing pro-German activities and organizations within the state. It disbanded at the end of the war. South Carolina State Council of Defense Records, SCDAH.

52. South Carolina Illiteracy Commission, *Appeal in Behalf*, 1.

53. Mabel Montgomery, *South Carolina's Wil Lou Gray*, 33, and Stackhouse, *Time Marches On*, 20.

54. Hereafter the South Carolina Illiteracy Commission is cited as SCIC.

55. Qtd. in Clarke, introduction to *American Women and the World War*.

56. *Republican Motherhood* is a term used to define the expectation that women in the early Republic had the responsibility to raise children to uphold the values of republicanism and become good citizens. See Kerber, "Republican Mother," and Kerber, *Women of the Republic*.

57. Helen Beebe, letter to state chairman of the Literacy Committee, General Federation of Women's Clubs, 1928, box 2, folder 84, Wil Lou Gray Papers.

58. Mrs. A. O. Granger, "The Effect of Clubwork in the South," *Annals of the American Academy of Political and Social Science* 28 (1906): 56.

59. Harold A. Ehrensperger, "Governor's Messages," *American Political Science Review* 13 (1919): 275.

60. United States Bureau of the Census, *Negro Population 1790–1815*, vol. 915 (Washington, D.C.: U.S. Bureau of the Census, 1918), 21; *Sixty-Third Annual Report of the State Superintendent of Education* (1931), 78. The problem was terminal. By 1930 South Carolina exchanged places with Louisiana as the state with the highest percentage of "negro illiteracy" at 26.9 percent. I want to add that this may not have been accurate

because the 1910 census stated that 25.7 percent of the total population of 1,515,400 was illiterate. See *Thirteenth Census of the United States*, Supplement for South Carolina, SCDAH.

61. Ehrensperger, "Governor's Messages," 276.

62. This was probably due to the immensity of the problem. Gray to family, December 20, 1961, letter held by author.

63. "Report on Adult Education" (1922), 238. Gray summarized the history if the organization in her report to the General Assembly in 1922. Her dates differ slightly from those records by fellow SCIC member Mabel Montgomery. The six original members of the first commission were John Clinkscales, Gray, L. O. Patterson, Mrs. Walter Duncan, John Swearingen, and George Brown.

64. Stackhouse, *Time Marches On*, 26.

65. Mabel Montgomery, *South Carolina's Wil Lou Gray*, 34.

66. "Report on Adult Education" (1922), 239.

67. Mabel Montgomery, *South Carolina's Wil Lou Gray*, 34.

68. "Report on Adult Education" (1922), 239.

69. South Carolina Illiteracy Commission, *Appeal in Behalf*, 3. In 1930 South Carolina was the most illiterate state in the Union and lacked an enforced compulsory attendance law until 1937. See "Report on Adult Education" (1931).

70. Helsly, "'Voices of Dissent,'" 91, 140.

71. Hickel, "'Justice and the Highest Kind of Equality,'" 749.

72. Mabel Montgomery, *South Carolina's Wil Lou Gray*, 33.

73. Hickel, "'Justice and the Highest Kind of Equality.'"

74. Mass mailing on behalf of illiteracy to local civic groups by Julia Selden, March 18, 1918, folder 4, box 1, Wil Lou Gray Papers.

75. Folder 18, box 1, Wil Lou Gray Papers. See also Dorgan et al., *Oratory of Southern Demagogues;* Hickel, "'Justice and the Highest Kind of Equality,'" 749, and Ford, "Rednecks and Merchants."

76. Stackhouse, *Time Marches On*, 3. The South Carolina Federation of Women's Clubs is hereafter cited as SCFWC.

77. See West, "Weaving Their White Magic."

78. Mabel Montgomery, Mrs. James Coker, Wil Lou Gray, and Julia Selden were members of the SCFWC and involved in both the SCIC and the Women's Council of Defense.

79. Clarke, "Women's Committee Created," in *American Women in the World War.*

80. Ibid.

81. Ibid.

82. Clarke, "South Carolina and Other States," in *American Women and the World War.*

83. Edmunds, *Episcopal Church of the Advent.*

84. She took two classes at Converse in 1901; phone interview with Dr. John Harrison, Converse College, October 18, 2005. A Julia Selden of Uniontown, Alabama, appears in the 1895–96 catalog as a student and also in the 1896–97 catalog at the Livingston Female Academy; e-mail from Sheila Blackmon Limerick, Archives and Special Collections Librarian, Julia Tutwiler Library, University of West Alabama, Livingston, February 9, 2010.

85. *Cemetery Records of Spartanburg County* (Spartanburg, S.C.: Spartanburg Historical Society, 1976). Book located in the South Caroliniana Library, Columbia; Edmunds, *Episcopal Church of the Advent.*

86. None of Hettie's children married. See *Thirteenth Census of the United States,* 1910. The home was torn down some time since 1994.

87. Delta Kappa Gamma, *Pioneer Teachers,* 47.

88. "Miss Selden's Own Story," paper clipping, box 24, Wil Lou Gray Papers.

89. Gray, "Evolution of Adult Elementary Education."

90. Julia Selden to Gray, September 16, 1918, box 2, Wil Lou Gray Papers.

91. *Forty-Eighth Annual Report of the State Superintendent of Education* (1915), 30–31. Gray's written account of her experiment was issued by the State Department of Education in 1915. See Gray, "Night School Experiment." In her official report, Gray mentions Stewart's Moonlight Schools but does not mention Selden's earlier effort to establish adult night schools in neighboring Spartanburg.

92. Gray, "Evolution of Adult Elementary Education."

93. Delta Kappa Gamma, *Pioneer Teachers,* 47.

94. Ibid. It is important to note that Gray's position as supervisor of adult schools grew out of her work as field worker for the Illiteracy Commission.

95. Bilanchone, *Lives They Lived; Federal Census of Spartanburg County,* 1910 and 1920, http://www.ancestry.com; Delta Kappa Gamma, *Pioneer Teachers,* 58, and Bodie, *South Carolina Women.*

96. Box 24, Wil Lou Gray Papers; Delta Kappa Gamma, *Pioneer Teachers,* 47.

97. Mary E. Anderson, "Late Miss Julia Selden Pioneer in Work for Adult Illiterates," *Columbia (S.C.) State.* Her article was based on an essay about Selden, allegedly published in the *New York Evening Post* in July 1922 as "A Commencement That's Different," that outlined Selden's night schools. The essay notes that her great-uncle was Gov. Thomas Bennett, who was instrumental in establishing the first grade school in the state. Found in Illiteracy Scrapbook, box 24, Wil Lou Gray Opportunity School Archives.

98. Delta Kappa Gamma, *Pioneer Teachers,* 47. It is unknown whether the state or a civic organization planted the trees. Gonzales Square was created in memory of Ambrose Gonzales's brother Narciso, who cofounded the *State* with his brother. In 1903 he was shot in broad daylight by Lt. Gov. James Tillman, nephew of Ben Tillman, and died. Tillman was acquitted. See Edgar, *South Carolina,* 468. I have found additional reference to these trees in Gray's "Report on Adult Education" in the State Superintendent of Education Reports, and it is likely located in the reports after 1933, when she organized pilgrimages to the State House and Charleston. She mentions taking the group by the square to honor the memory of these supporters of adult education.

99. I attempted to locate the trees at the site but was unsuccessful.

100. Julia Selden to Patterson Wardlaw, May 10, 1918, folder 4, box 2, Wil Lou Gray Papers. All letters, unless otherwise noted, are found in this location, and letters will be noted by last name only after first reference. In 1906 Spartanburg claimed to have 165 buildings, 3,010 teachers, and 16,232 students. See Edgar, *South Carolina,* 464.

101. Selden to Wardlaw, March 10, 1918.

102. Selden to Wardlaw, March 29, 1918.

103. Ibid.

104. Wardlaw to Selden, March 13, 1918, Correspondence Out, 1915–30, Wil Lou Gray Papers.

105. Selden to Wardlaw, March 18, 1918.

106. Ibid. Wardlaw communicated with commission members in February 1918, even though the group did not formally meet until June 22, 1918.

107. Wardlaw to Selden, March 23, 1918.

108. Selden to Wardlaw, March 29, 1918.

109. Clarke, "South Carolina and Other States." The executive body in South Carolina was composed of "Mrs. F. Louise Mayes, Greenville, chairman; Mrs. Richard I. Manning, Columbia, 1st vice chairman; Mrs. J. L. Coker, Hartsville, 2nd vice chairman; Mrs. E. C. von Tresckow, Camden, secretary; Mrs. R. E. Stackhouse, Spartanburg treasurer; Mrs. W. C. Cathcart, Columbia, publicity committee; Executive Committee: Mrs. F. Louise Mayes, Mrs. Richard I. Manning, Mrs. J. L. Coker, Mrs. E. C. von Tresckow, Mrs. R. E. Stackhouse, Mrs. W. C. Cathcart, Miss Jane B. Evans, Mrs. Ben Hagood, Mrs. J. W. Allen, Mrs. Mary C. McCanna, Mrs. Joseph Sprout, Mrs. Harriet Caldwell, Mrs. Robert Mixon, Mrs. J. D. Chapman, Mrs. Waller Duvall, Mrs. J. L. McWhirter, Mrs. Harriet P. Lynch, Mrs. Ernest Pringle, Miss Minnie M. Gee, Mrs. Mary Slattery, Mrs. Andrew Bramlett, Mrs. I. O. J. Kreps, Miss Katie Lee."

110. Selden to Wardlaw, April 10, 1918; Wardlaw to Selden, April 16, 1918.

111. Wardlaw to Selden, April 16, 1918.

112. Ibid.

113. Selden to Wardlaw, May 10, 1918.

114. Megginson, "Black South Carolinians in World War I," 153.

115. "Report on Adult Education" (1922), 240.

116. Three excellent books that illustrate the organization of the black community in this period are Hahn, *Nation Under Our Feet*; Higginbotham, *Righteous Discontent*; and Bass and Poole, *Palmetto State*. For a discussion of rape and lynching and white women's perceptions, see Hall, *Revolt against Chivalry*.

117. See Blight, *Race and Reunion*, for a discussion of the white supremacist narrative of the past.

118. Wardlaw to R. D. Webb, August 31, 1918.

119. South Carolina Sunday School Convention Poster, box 1, folder 4, Wil Lou Gray Papers.

120. Selden to Wardlaw, May 10, 1918.

121. Ibid.

122. Wil Lou Gray Papers, box 24.

123. Webb to Wardlaw, May 16, 1918, box 1, folder 4, Wil Lou Gray Papers.

124. Document 4, box 1, 1918, Wil Lou Gray Papers.

125. Newspaper clipping in a letter, Webb to Wardlaw, May 16, 1918. Resolution by Illiteracy Commission of South Carolina, May 1918, Wil Lou Gray Papers.

126. *Columbia (S.C.) State*, 1918.

127. Ibid.

128. Wardlaw to Selden, June 12, 1918.

129. Ibid.

130. Selden to Wardlaw, July 10, 1918.

131. Selden to Wardlaw, July 17, 1918.

132. See biographical sketch of Coker in Edgar, *South Carolina Encyclopedia.*

133. David Coker to Selden, July 15, 1918, box 1, Correspondence Out, 1915–30, Wil Lou Gray Papers. Historian Janet Hudson illustrates that Selden and Coker corresponded during the war about black work and economy. Selden's letters revealed a view of black people that was negative. See Hudson, *Entangled by White Supremacy,* 98–99.

134. Coker to Selden, July 15, 1918.

135. Ibid.

136. Selden to Wardlaw, July 17, 1918.

137. Wardlaw to Selden, July 19, 1918.

138. Coker to Selden, July 22, 1918.

139. Selden to Wardlaw, August 5, 1918.

140. Wardlaw to Selden, August 7, 1918.

141. Wil Lou Gray, "What Should a Superintendent," 255.

142. Wardlaw to Gray, July 23, 1918.

143. Wardlaw to Gray, July 24, 1918.

144. Wardlaw to Gray, August 3, 1918.

145. Ayres, *Let My People Learn,* 72.

146. Wardlaw to Gray, September 4, 1918.

147. John Swearingen to Gray, June 16, 1939, folder 259, box 24, Wil Lou Gray Papers.

148. W. J. Holloway to Gray, September 12, 1918.

149. South Carolina Illiteracy Commission, *Appeal in Behalf,* 1.

150. Wardlaw to Gray, September 10, 1918.

151. Ibid.

152. Selden to Gray, September 16, 1918. Both women were thirty-five years old.

153. Selden to Wardlaw, September 20, 1918.

154. Selden to Wardlaw, October 5, 1918.

155. Bodie, *South Carolina Women,* 105.

156. Selden to Wardlaw, October 31, 1918.

157. Ibid.

158. Selden to Gray, November 1, 1918.

159. Hardy, *Farm, Mill, and Classroom,* 43.

160. Box 2, Wil Lou Gray Papers.

161. E-mail from Jenny Williams, February 16, 2011; Emma Julia Selden matriculation record, e-mail, March 1, 2010, from Kim Fulmer, George Washington University registrar.

162. See Joan Scott, "Gender," and Bonnie G. Smith, *Gender of History.*

163. See Hudson, *Entangled by White Supremacy,* for a detailed history of reform and World War I in South Carolina. Gray draped her progressive impulse in the traditional decorum associated with a southern upper-class woman that worked to offset any offense that could be read into the methods by which she orchestrated her "agendas." I too use this to indicate Gray's dual image of the professional and southern lady. She had to work with men as an unmarried, self-sufficient woman in the South and get along with women in the public (male) and private (female) sectors, an ability she skillfully cultivated throughout her career. On the ideology of true womanhood and the notions that undergirded southern female behavior, see Wolfe, *Daughters of Canaan,* 6; Blair, *Clubwoman as Feminist;* Anne Firor Scott, *Southern Lady;* Anne Firor Scott, "New Woman

in the New South"; Welter, "Cult of True Womanhood"; Johnson, "'Drill into Us'"; and Spruill, *New Woman of the New South,* for some overviews of this ideology.

164. Kuhlman, *Petticoats and White Feathers;* Bercaw, *Gender and the Southern Body Politic;* Frankel and Dye, *Gender, Class, Race, and Reform.*

165. Gray notes the training of teachers in the majority of her reports to the General Assembly between 1919 and 1935. See "Report on Adult Education" (1919–35). Gray used teacher institutes and summer training sessions as ways to prepare teachers to teach adults. They were also taught to use the materials she designed.

166. Hudson, *Entangled by White Supremacy,* 63.

167. "Report on Adult Education" (1920), 209.

168. Bright Williamson to Gray, April 12, 1923, copy held by author. For biographical data on Williamson, see Snowden, *History of South Carolina,* 157.

169. Box 2, Wil Lou Gray Papers.

170. Cora Wilson Stewart, comment about Wil Lou Gray, National Education Association Reports of Committees on Illiteracy, 153–54, folder 2, box 24, Wil Lou Gray Papers.

Chapter 4: Commodifying Literacy

1. Lois Shawver, "Provisional Definitions of Common Postmodern Terms from A to D," http://users.california.com/~rathbone/local2.htm, accessed September 10, 2009.

2. D'Errico, "Remarx."

3. "Report on Adult Education" (1922), 238.

4. The Illiteracy Commission became the South Carolina State Advisory Committee on Adult Education and operated until the 1960s. The governor appointed the members of the commission for four-year terms. Hardy, *Farm, Mill, and Classroom,* 43.

5. "Report on Adult Education" (1923), 238.

6. "Report on Adult Education" (1922), 239.

7. "Report on Adult Education" (1921), 266.

8. "Report on Adult Education" (1923), 131.

9. Lack of skilled teachers for all levels of education was a universal problem in the South. For a discussion of the origins of this problem see Rebecca Montgomery, *Politics of Education,* 24–28. See also Edward Cary, "Education and the South," *New York Times,* May 11, 1902; "Southern Education," *New York Times,* July 12, 1912.

10. "Report on Adult Education" (1921), 263.

11. "Report on Adult Education" (1924), 80.

12. Wil Lou Gray, "A Community Project in Adult Elementary Education," July 20, 1929, 2, Wil Lou Gray Papers.

13. "Report on Adult Education" (1928), 30.

14. Cora Wilson Stewart, comment about Gray, National Education Association Reports of Committees on Illiteracy, 153–54, box 24, Wil Lou Gray Papers.

15. "Report on Adult Education" (1930), 35.

16. Ibid.

17. In 1926 Gray wrote a civics text for adult students, *Elementary Studies in Civics for the Pupils of South Carolina,* while attending a summer session at Columbia University.

Her professor, Dr. Albert Shields, reviewed the book and wrote the introduction. Gray was the only student in the class. See Mabel Montgomery, *South Carolina's Wil Lou Gray*, 39–40. She also wrote with her stepmother *The Bible Story Reader* used in adult schools as an instructional text.

18. "Report on Adult Education" (1930), 36.

19. "Report on Adult Education" (1921), 263.

20. "Report on Adult Education" (1927), 26.

21. Archie Vernon Huff, interview by author, Greenville, S.C., July 31, 1995. Huff's description of this type of education stemmed from a discussion of southern liberalism and the ingrained prejudices that accompanied this type of progress.

22. *University Weekly News* (University of South Carolina), "Illiteracy Issue," October 24, 1923, Correspondence Out, Wil Lou Gray Papers.

23. Ibid.

24. John Swearingen, "Time for Action Says Swearingen" (1919), Correspondence Out, 1919–1925, Wil Lou Gray Papers.

25. Note Gray's "Report on Adult Education" for 1919–25.

26. "Report on Adult Education" (1921), 208–10.

27. Bright Williamson to Gray, April 12, 1923, copy held by author.

28. "Report on Adult Education" (1919–25).

29. Clark, "Country Newspaper," 4.

30. Ibid., 3.

31. Patterson Wardlaw, "Our Program of Progress in Education," *South Carolina Education*, April 1922, Correspondence Out, Wil Lou Gray Papers.

32. Marion Wright, "Horry's Great Campaign," *South Carolina Education*, 1922, Correspondence Out, Wil Lou Gray Papers.

33. "Our State Needs Educated Men and Women" (broadside), *Saluda (S.C.) Standard*, May 28, 1925.

34. Box 24, Wil Lou Gray Papers.

35. It is important to note that labor strikes had occurred in the state in 1919 and had minimal impact. See Simon, *Fabric of Defeat*.

36. "Report on Adult Education" (1923), 240.

37. Foreword, 1929, Wil Lou Gray Papers, copy held by author.

38. Berthoff, "Southern Attitudes toward Immigration," 360.

39. South Carolina had .4 percent foreign-born population in 1920. Hawk, *Economic History of the South*, 503.

40. J. B. Felton to Gray, July 30, 1919; cited in Cristina Nelson, "Waging Warfare with the Darkness of Ignorance: The Work of Educators Wil Lou Gray and Mary Elizabeth Frayser, South Carolina Reformers," draft copy of thesis, Department of History, University of North Carolina, 63. Copy held by author.

41. Hope and Gray, *Night and Adult Schools*, 6; box 21, Wil Lou Gray Papers. United States Bureau of the Census, *Negro Population 1790–1915*, vol. 915 (Washington, D.C.: U.S. Bureau of the Census, 1918), 21.

42. Ibid.

43. Ibid. See Gray, "Adult Night Schools Do Much in the State to Reduce Adult Illiteracy," Correspondence Out, Wil Lou Gray Papers.

44. John Swearingen, "Time for Action Says Swearingen—Every Man Should Help

Fight on Illiteracy" (1919), newspaper clipping, Correspondence Out, Wil Lou Gray Papers.

45. "Report on Adult Education" (1922), 257.

46. Demagogues used this same fear tactic to garner support. During World War I Coleman Blease was notorious for anti-immigrant language. It can be inferred that Gray and her state comrades built upon this existing framework in their desire to rally support for statewide literacy. Fear tactics used by demagogues were seen as despicable, yet when Gray used the same approach it was okay because the expected outcome was beneficial to the state. She appropriated the fear tactic and shaped it to benefit her literacy campaign. What this reveals is the knowledge among the powerful of what media tactics worked to sway public opinion.

47. Patterson Wardlaw, "Duty of State to Adult Illiterate," Correspondence Out, 1919–30, Wil Lou Gray Papers.

48. Ibid. There are hundreds of newspaper articles in the Correspondence Out reels of the Wil Lou Gray papers. Most are cut out with no date, but all document the illiteracy campaigns in the first decade of her work.

49. *South Carolina Education,* April 1922, newspaper clipping, Correspondence Out, Wil Lou Gray Papers.

50. Gray, "Community Project in Adult Elementary Education," 1.

51. *South Carolina Education,* April 1922, newspaper clipping, Correspondence Out, Wil Lou Gray Papers.

52. Ibid.

53. G. M. Gilbert, "Dictators and Demagogues," *Journal of Social Issues* 11 (1955), 51–53, qtd. in Cal M. Logue and Howard Dorgan, "The Demagogue," in Dorgan et al., *Oratory of Southern Demagogues,* 4.

54. Qtd. in Hawk, *Economic History of the South,* 512.

55. Ibid.

56. Ibid., 513.

57. Folder 18, box 1, Wil Lou Gray Papers. See Dorgan et al., *Oratory of Southern Demagogues;* Hickel, "'Justice and the Highest Kind of Equality'"; and Ford, "Rednecks and Merchants."

58. Link, *Paradox of Southern Progressivism,* xii.

59. Ibid.

60. Kett, "Women and the Progressive Impulse," 172.

61. Ibid., 170.

62. Ibid., 173.

63. Ibid., 175.

64. Fink, *Progressive Intellectuals,* 4.

65. Ibid., 3.

66. Gray, "State Wide Campaign Aimed at Wiping Out the Stamp of Illiteracy," Correspondence Out, 1919, Wil Lou Gray Papers.

67. "Report on Adult Education" (1930), 35.

68. Simon, *Fabric of Defeat.* Simon argues that their power as a political class ended after World War II: "Business leaders continued to be the preeminent force in the capital after World War II. Over the next decade, they consolidated their grip on power, turning the state government into a virtual professional booster association that marketed

South Carolina to investors as a paradise of cheap labor, sunny skies, and warm smiles. Despite some organizational gains during the World War II, a union represented few textile workers in 1948. Although they made more money than ever before, they had no say on the shop floor and no voice when it came to hiring and firing. Factories remained dangerous places; the air was thick with layers of deadly lint, and the fast-moving machines were a constant threat to limbs and fingers" (237).

69. "Report on Adult Education" (1922), 257.

70. Ibid., 252.

71. Frankel and Dye, *Gender, Class, Race, and Reform;* Kuhlman, *Petticoats and White Feathers;* Bercaw, *Gender and the Southern Body Politic.*

72. By the 1920 election, women were allowed to vote in South Carolina by legislative act but were specifically denied the right to serve on juries even though the state had not ratified the Nineteenth Amendment. Women also needed literacy to exercise their right to vote properly. See Bland, "Fighting the Odds," and Shankman, "Jury of Her Peers."

73. Harvey Neufeldt to Mary Mac Ogden, e-mail, April 19, 2010, transcript held by author.

74. In 1918 New York and South Carolina were the only two states to employ full-time supervisors of adult schools. See Knowles, *Adult Education Movement.* See Hardy, *Farm, Mill, and Classroom,* 44. Gray was actually appointed in 1918 but assumed her position in January 1919.

75. *Southern Christian Advocate,* June 29, 1922, Illiteracy Scrapbook, Wil Lou Gray Opportunity School Archive.

76. "'Lay-By' Schools," *New York Times,* January 23, 1921.

77. "Report on Adult Education" (1923), 127.

78. Gray, "South Carolina's Program," 84; "Report on Adult Education" (1922).

79. "Report on Adult Education" (1922), 103. Because of this success, the "lay-by" schools continued for a decade, but due to a curtailment in state appropriations for the program, they ceased after 1929.

80. "Report on Adult Education" (1925), 81.

81. Ibid., 98.

82. Ibid., 81.

83. "Report on Adult Education" (1920), 205; "Report on Adult Education" (1925), 80.

84. "Report on Adult Education" (1925), 80.

85. Ibid.

86. "Report on Adult Education" (1921), 253.

87. Ibid.

88. See Cohen, *Making a New Deal.*

89. "Report on Adult Education" (1920), 204.

90. Ibid., 205.

91. President of Gossett Mill to J. D. Hill, June 27, 1929; copy held by author.

92. R. J. Alderman to Gray, August 29, 1928, Wil Lou Gray Papers.

93. Wil Lou Gray, "Meeting the Challenge of Illiteracy," *California Federation News,* March 1931, 10, Illiteracy Scrapbook, Wil Lou Gray Opportunity School Archive.

94. Ibid., 11.

95. Ibid.

96. Hardy, *Farm, Mill, and Classroom*, 114.

97. See Mabel Montgomery, *South Carolina's Wil Lou Gray*, 42, and Akerson and Neufeldt, "Alabama's Illiteracy Campaign for Black Adults."

98. William Emerson, "She Spells Opportunity with the Three R's," *Collier's Magazine*, March 29, 1952, 49.

99. Blackwell, "Wil Lou Gray, Educator," 12.

100. Interview, Wil Lou Gray, February 11, 1975, Museum of Education, South Carolina Educational Television.

101. Blackwell, "Wil Lou Gray, Educator," 12.

102. "Crusader Wil Lou Gray Has Fought to Wipe Out Illiteracy in South Carolina," *Columbia (S.C.) State Magazine*, October 7, 1979.

103. Doug Williams, *Columbia (S.C.) State Magazine*, August 28, 1983, 5.

104. "Report on Adult Education" (1923), 127.

105. Wil Lou Gray, "South Carolina's Program," 84. For a summary of Gray's adult education program, see Lander, *History of South Carolina*, 137–38; Hardy, *Farm, Mill, and Classroom*.

106. Correspondence Out, roll 738, 1921, Wil Lou Gray Papers.

107. Wil Lou Gray to anonymous, September 23, 1919.

108. State Superintendent Report, 1915.

109. "Report on Adult Education" (1922), 251.

110. Interview, Wil Lou Gray, February 11, 1975, Museum of Education, South Carolina Educational Television.

111. "Report on Adult Education" (1922), 252.

112. Erin Kohn, "Brief Sketch of the History of the Opportunity School," *South Carolina Independent*, June 9, 1938, clipping located in Illiteracy Scrapbook, Wil Lou Gray Opportunity School Archive.

113. Ibid.

114. "Report on Adult Education" (1923), 129.

115. Box 1, folder 18, 1922, Wil Lou Gray Papers.

116. *Southern Christian Advocate*, June 29, 1922, Illiteracy Scrapbook, Wil Lou Gray Opportunity School Archive. The *Southern Christian Advocate* was the official publication for the Methodist Conferences in South Carolina, Georgia, and Florida.

117. Kohn, "Brief Sketch."

118. Gray, "South Carolina's Program," 84. For a discussion of the evolution of southern education and the Southern Education Board, a body that served as a mediator between northern philanthropic funds and southern institutions, see Dabney, *Universal Education in the South;* Grantham, *Southern Progressivism*, 246–74.

119. *Sixty-Third Annual Report of the State Superintendent of Education* (1931), 76–87; Lander, *History of South Carolina*, 137; Hardy, *Farm, Mill, and Classroom*, 96.

120. Mabel Montgomery, *South Carolina's Wil Lou Gray*, 46–52; Gray, "South Carolina's Program," 82.

121. "Report on Adult Education" (1920).

122. Gray, *Elementary Studies in Civics*.

123. "Report on Adult Education" (1924), 130.

124. "Report on Adult Education" (1922), 258.

125. Ibid.

126. Gray, "Community Project in Adult Elementary Education," 3.

127. Erin Kohn, "South Carolina's Unique Adult Schools," *Interstate Bulletin*, November–December 1927, box 21, folder 1549, Wil Lou Gray Papers.

128. "Report on Adult Education" (1928), 255.

129. *Sixty-Third Annual Report of the State Superintendent of Education* (1931), 76, SCDAH.

130. *Sixty-Fourth Annual Report of the State Superintendent of Education* (1932), 56, SCDAH.

131. Wil Lou Gray, "Challenging Statistical Facts," box 3, folder 194, Wil Lou Gray Papers.

132. "Report on Adult Education" (1926), 52.

133. Ibid.

134. Ibid., 51.

135. "Report on Adult Education" (1921), 253.

136. Foreword, 1929, Wil Lou Gray Papers.

137. Gray, "Community Project in Adult Elementary Education," 1.

138. "Report on Adult Education" (1921), 263.

139. Ibid., 251.

140. Ibid.

141. Ibid.

142. "Report on Adult Education" (1928), 37.

143. Report to the Superintendent, box 24, 1924–25, Wil Lou Gray Papers.

144. Gray to William Watts Ball, January 27, 1938, William Watts Ball Papers, Duke University Special Collections. This is also quoted by Alethea Washington, "Current Trends and Events in Negro Education: Rural Education," *Journal of Negro Education* 7 (1938): 99.

145. John Mills Lemmon, "Compulsory Education and Its Effect on Making of Character," M.A. thesis, University of South Carolina, 1914, cited in Littlefield, "'I am only one,'" 119.

146. In South Carolina the black population in 1920 totaled 181,422, with an illiteracy rate of 38.7 percent. In 1930 the black population was 156,065, with an illiteracy rate of 26.9 percent. See Hope and Gray, *Night and Adult Schools*, 6.

147. "Report on Adult Education" (1921), 257.

148. Ibid.

149. "Report on Adult Education" (1920–24).

150. "Report on Adult Education" (1920), 205.

151. Ibid., 202. It is important to note that philanthropic efforts to improve black education in the state were carried out by the Rosenwald Fund between 1917 and 1932. More than five hundred schools were built in rural South Carolina to aid black education. It is estimated that one-third of all black children in this period attended a Rosenwald school. When the school equalization movement began in South Carolina in 1951 to thwart integration, these schools closed as black education was consolidated and new black schools were built by the state. It is estimated that the state spent $100 million on K-12 school construction between 1951 and 1960, and the total number of black high schools increased from 80 to 145. See the links pertaining to Rosenwald schools

"South Carolina African Americans—Historically Black Schools and Libraries," *SCI-WAY*, http://www.sciway.net/afam/sc-historically-black-schools.html, accessed March 1, 2011. It is estimated that of the four thousand Rosenwald schools built by the 1930s in all fifteen southern states, two-thirds were built in counties where Jeanes teachers were employed. See Littlefield, "'I am only one,'" 117.

152. Report to the Superintendent, 1924–25, box 24, Wil Lou Gray Papers.

153. Folder 1549, box 21, Wil Lou Gray Papers. For a list of state appropriations allotted for adult education from 1919 to 1935, see folder 189, box 3, Wil Lou Gray Papers.

154. "Report on Adult Education" (1925), 258; folder 1549, box 21, Wil Lou Gray Papers.

155. It is argued that the Jeanes teachers were instrumental in changing white superintendents' negative attitudes about black teachers and education. The organization, communication, and expert leadership of these teachers changed the perception of black education in the interwar period. Many black educators by 1940 claimed that in 1920 it would have been hard to get a white county superintendent to visit a black school, but that changed during the interwar period due to the hard work of Jeanes teachers. See Littlefield, "'I am only one,'" 108, and Woodfaulk, "Jeanes Teachers."

156. Report to the Superintendent, 1924–25, box 24, Wil Lou Gray Papers.

157. "Report on Adult Education" (1926), 51.

158. Ibid., 49.

159. For statistics on lynching in South Carolina from 1880 to 1940, see Moore, *Carnival of Blood*.

CHAPTER 5: DEMOCRACY IN BLACK AND WHITE

1. Interview, Gray by Constance Ashton Myers, June 14, 1974, Constance Ashton Myers Collection, South Caroliniana Library, University of South Carolina, Columbia; a tape of this interview is held by the Southern Oral History Collection, Wilson Library, University of North Carolina, Chapel Hill.

2. Gray, Gray, and Tilton, *Opportunity Schools;* "Reviews," *Peabody Journal of Education* (November 1932): 188; Cartwright, "Research Projects and Methods"; "Educational News and Editorial Comment," *Elementary School Journal* 33 (1932): 3; "Educational News and Editorial Comment," *School Review* 40 (1932): 481–96.

3. Brearley and Montgomery, *Facing Facts in South Carolina,* 10, pamphlet located in folder of undated material, box 21, Wil Lou Gray Papers.

4. For a history of the eugenics movement in the South, see Larson, *Sex, Race, and Science*. Larson argues that clubwomen were the chief advocates of the eugenics movement in the South. He suggests that their support led to the establishment of institutions for the feebleminded (epileptics, insane, retarded, and criminally insane) in every southern state by 1921. He further states that once the institutions were established, southern clubwomen advocated forced sterilization of the feebleminded inside these institutions. Louisiana was the only southern state where this legislative aim was thwarted by Catholic legislators who found the idea morally reprehensible.

5. Peterkin meant struggle as a universal, ongoing process of change in the world. Peterkin, "What and Why I Have Written?" unpublished sketch, folder 28-613-7, Julia Mood Peterkin Papers, South Carolina Historical Society, Charleston.

6. Peterkin and Ulmann, *Roll, Jordan, Roll,* 16.

7. See Sullivan, *Days of Hope;* Hall, "Long Civil Rights Movement"; Gilmore, *Defying Dixie.*

8. Hall, "Long Civil Rights Movement," 1243.

9. For a summary analysis of Gray's experiment, see Willis, "First Fifty Years"; Gray, Gray, and Tilton, *Opportunity Schools.*

10. Cartwright, "Research Projects and Methods," 514.

11. L. L. Bernard, "Culture and Environment II: The Continuity of Nature and Culture," *Social Forces* 9 (1930): 44; Cartwright, "Research Projects and Methods," 514. Gray also served as vice president of the National Education Association's Adult Education Division in 1929. Folder 1550, box 22, Wil Lou Gray Papers.

12. Director of Rural Education to Frank Bachman, December 11, 1925, Wil Lou Gray Papers. Gray received a master of arts degree in political science from Columbia University in 1911 and pursued graduate study in education at Teachers College in 1916 and 1924. See Wil Lou Gray résumé, document held by author. For a summary history of her studies, see Mabel Montgomery, *South Carolina's Wil Lou Gray.*

13. Gray's official title at the time was state supervisor of night schools and later adult education supervisor. See George Smith, *Documents on the Early Beginnings.*

14. Gray, "South Carolina's Program," 84; Gray to Dr. J. B. Nash, April 21, 1930, box 4, folder 218, Wil Lou Gray Papers.

15. *Sixty-Third Annual Report of the State Superintendent of Education* (1931), 76–87, SCDAH.

16. Gray, Gray, and Tilton, *Opportunity Schools of South Carolina,* 19.

17. It is plausible that Gray met Thorndike while a graduate student at Columbia in 1916 and again in 1924. He also served as a speaker along with Gray at the National Education Association's conference on illiteracy in 1924.

18. Gray, Gray, and Tilton, *Opportunity Schools of South Carolina,* 87.

19. Morse Cartwright to F. P. Keppel, January 21, 1931, Carnegie Corporation Collection, Rare Books and Manuscripts Library, Columbia University, New York.

20. Grant application, "Training Illiterates to Read," Carnegie Corporation Collection.

21. Box 3, Wil Lou Gray Papers; See *Sixty-Third Annual Report of the State Superintendent of Education* (1931), 76–87.

22. Gray, Gray, and Tilton, *Opportunity Schools of South Carolina,* 32.

23. Ibid., 89.

24. Carrie McCully Patrick, "Negro School to Close at Seneca," *Columbia (S.C.) State,* n.d., Illiteracy Scrapbook, Wil Lou Gray Opportunity School Archive.

25. "The Beginning of the Opportunity School as Written by Dr. Wil Lou Gray in 1923," in George Smith, *Documents on the Early Beginnings,* 32.

26. Two hundred eighty-eight students attended the summer camp, almost double the experimental one hundred. See box 4, folder 267, Wil Lou Gray Papers.

27. Untitled clipping, July 27, 1931, Illiteracy Scrapbook, Wil Lou Gray Opportunity School Archive.

28. Box 2, folder 137, Wil Lou Gray Papers.

29. *Sixty-Third Annual Report of the State Superintendent of Education* (1931), 76–87.

30. "Reviews," *Peabody Journal of Education,* November 1932, 188.

31. Box 4, folder 267, Wil Lou Gray Papers.

32. Box 24, Wil Lou Gray Papers.

33. Gray, Gray, and Tilton, *Opportunity Schools of South Carolina*, 90.

34. Smith, "Mary McLeod Bethune's 'Last Will and Testament,'" 112.

35. Olema Wiggins to Gray, August 19, 1931, box 3, Wil Lou Gray Papers.

36. Newspaper clipping, September 1931, Illiteracy Scrapbook, Wil Lou Gray Opportunity School Archive.

37. "Reviews," 188; Cartwright, "Research Projects and Methods," 514; "Educational News and Editorial Comment," 3; "Educational News and Editorial Comment," 481–96.

38. For movie scripts as cultural texts, see May, *Big Tomorrow*, and for "print-capitalism" see Benedict Anderson, *Imagined Communities*.

39. Keppel to Gray, January 11, 1932, Carnegie Corporation Collection.

40. "Reports of State Officers Boards and Committees to the General Assembly of the State of South Carolina," January 14, 1936, 2:48, SDAH; "Report on Adult Education" (1920), 205.

41. "Reports of State Officers Boards and Committees," 2:49.

42. Ibid.

43. Ibid.

44. Program, April 14, 1935, folder 185, box 3, Wil Lou Gray Papers.

45. Biography of Channing H. Tobias located at "Channing H. Tobias: An Inventory of His Papers," Kautz Family YMCA Archives, http://special.lib.umn.edu/findaid/html/ymca/yusa0007.phtml, accessed December 5, 2010.

46. There was a large black professional class in Columbia at the time. See Hine, "Corporeal and Ocular Veil."

47. Channing Tobias to Gray, April 3, 1935, folder 185, box 3, Wil Lou Gray Papers.

48. "Reports of State Officers Boards and Committees," 2:50.

49. Hope and Gray, *Night and Adult Schools*, 33.

50. The grounds of the South Carolina State House contain numerous Confederate monuments, and the Confederate flag is present by a Confederate monument as of 1962.

51. Folder 220, box 4, Wil Lou Gray Papers.

52. Hardy, *Farm, Mill, and Classroom*, 96–97n39; *Seventy-First Annual Report of the State Superintendent of Education* (1938–39), 37.

53. Olin Johnston to Gray, December 17, 1936, box 4, folder 217, Wil Lou Gray Papers.

54. Gray to William Watts Ball, January 27, 1938, William Watts Ball Papers, Duke University Special Collections. This is also quoted by Alethea Washington, "Current Trends and Events in Negro Education: Rural Education," *Journal of Negro Education* 7 (1938): 99.

55. *A Study of Educational Inequalities in South Carolina* (1936), documentary film located at http://www.archive.org/details/naacp__south__carolina, accessed January 10, 2010.

56. Folder 214, box 4, Wil Lou Gray Papers.

57. "Our Chance to Stand Higher," n.d., newspaper clipping, Illiteracy Scrapbook, box 24, Wil Lou Gray *Papers*.

58. Untitled newspaper clipping, n.d., Echoes Illiteracy Scrapbook, Box 24, Wil Lou Gray Opportunity School Archive.

59. Folder 214, box 4, Wil Lou Gray Papers.

60. Folder 214, box 4, Wil Lou Gray Papers.

61. John Groves to Gray, July 19, 1936, folder 214, box 4, Wil Lou Gray Papers.

62. Folder 214, box 4, Wil Lou Gray Papers.

63. Ibid.

64. Emma Gillard to Gray, December 10, 1936, folder 216, box 4, Wil Lou Gray Papers.

65. J. E. Blanton to Gray, September 3, 1936, folder 215, box 4, Wil Lou Gray Papers.

66. Blanton to Gray, September 16, 1936, folder 215, box 4, Wil Lou Gray Papers.

67. In 1919 the state appropriated twenty-five thousand dollars for her work and increased the amount over the course of the twenties to a high mark of close to sixty thousand dollars, which declined between 1930 and 1940 to just fifteen thousand. See "Report on Adult Education" (1930–40).

68. Gray to Bernard Baruch, October 2, 1939, folder 259, box 4, Wil Lou Gray Papers.

69. Huff, *Tried by Fire*, 99; Archie Vernon Huff, interview by author, July 31, 1995. Huff relayed to me the actual story Gray told to him. He said that Blease so objected to the visit by Bethune that he slammed his gold-handled cane on the floor of the sanctuary foyer and said, "I will not worship with a goddamn nigger in the pulpit."

70. See Fink, *Progressive Intellectuals*, for a discussion of the relationship between Septima Clark and Gray. See also Charron, *Freedom's Teacher*.

71. Interview, Modjeska Simkins by Jacquelyn Dowd Hall, Southern Oral History Collection, University of North Carolina, transcript located at http://docsouth.unc .edu/sohp/G-0056-2/G-0056-2.xml, accessed January 5, 2008. Simkins referred to the South Carolina Opportunity School, established in 1947 and known today at the Wil Lou Gray Opportunity School. Gray's year-round adult school was for whites only.

72. See Synnott, "Crusaders and Clubwomen."

73. Interview, Simkins by Hall.

74. Gray to Dr. William Cooper, April 14, 1949, Miller F. Whittaker Library, Archives and History Center, South Carolina State University, Orangeburg.

75. Program, Seventh Annual Conference, Adult Education and the Negro, South Carolina State College, Orangeburg, April 6–9, 1949, Miller F. Whittaker Library, Archives and History Center. For information about the organization of the tribute, see also Cooper to Miller F. Whittaker, March 7, 1949; Whittaker to Cooper, March 16, 1949.

76. Gray to Cooper, April 14, 1949.

CONCLUSION

1. Grantham, *Southern Progressivism*, 154–74.

2. George M. Smith, *Opportunity Schools*, 6.

3. "Reports of State Officers Boards and Committees to the General Assembly of the State of South Carolina," January 14, 1936, 2:44, SCD A H.

4. Ibid.

5. Ibid., 44.

6. Ibid., 48. "Report on Adult Education" (1920), 205.

7. George Smith, *Opportunity Schools*, 5.

8. "Reports of State Officers Boards and Committees to the General Assembly of the State of South Carolina," January 14, 1936, vol. 2, 47.

9. Erin Kohn, "Brief Sketch of the History of the Opportunity School," *South Carolina Independent*, June 9, 1938, Illiteracy Scrapbook, Wil Lou Gray Opportunity School Archive.

10. Folder 214, box 4, Wil Lou Gray Papers.

11. Ibid.

12. Draft copy of letter to Eleanor Roosevelt from Wil Lou Gray, n.d., folder 67, box 22, Wil Lou Gray Papers. The response to this note from M. H. McIntyre, the assistant secretary to the president, to Gray, December 22, 1936, is located in folder 218, box 4, Wil Lou Gray Papers.

13. Ibid.

14. She was invited to Newfoundland in 1930 to educate teachers about adult education. See George Smith, *Opportunity Schools*, 6.

15. Hope and Gray, *Night and Adult Schools*, 6. This pamphlet was published yearly by the two and included information about the census. By 1935 they ramped up their efforts to raise public awareness about the need to have a literate state by 1940. In the 1930 census there were 938,774 white and 793,681 black people in the state.

16. Folder 67, box 22, Wil Lou Gray Papers.

17. For information about her speeches at the NEA conferences in the 1920s and the presence of leaders such as Thorndike and Alderman at these meetings, see folders 1550 and 1551, box 21, Wil Lou Gray Papers.

18. Gray retired as supervisor of adult education for the State Department of Education, handing the position to her cousin Marguerite Tolbert. She became the director of the South Carolina Opportunity School. She retired in 1958 but took an active role in seeking financial support from both former alumni and general patrons.

19. "The Opportunity School Gets $50,000 Grants for Scholarships," (*Columbia, S.C.*) *Journal*, December 11, 1968.

20. Ibid.

21. Ibid.

22. *Carolina Pioneer*, November 25, 1956.

23. James F. Miles, "Wil Lou Gray—Noblesse Oblige," Opportunity School Founder's Day address, November 26, 1963, transcript held by author.

24. This phrase is often associated with historian Sara Evans, who made it famous in her book *Personal Politics: The Roots of Women's Liberation in the Civil Rights Movement and the New Left*, but Carol Hanisch coined the phrase in 1969. See Hanisch, "The Personal Is Political: The Women's Liberation Movement Classic (with a new explanatory introduction)," *Women of the World, Unite! Writings of Carol Hanisch*, http://www.carolhanisch.org/CHwritings/PIP.html, accessed October 15, 2009. Many feminist writers agree that to give one individual the credit for the phrase is pointless when it represents the crystallization of ideas that predate the second-wave movement. "Clearly the ideas that gave rise to the 'personal is political' predate feminism, but feminism crystallized these concepts as they referred to the particular oppression of women," states sociologist Benita Roth. Comment at "'The Personal Is Political': Origins of the Phrase," http://userpages.umbc.edu/~korenman/wmst/pisp.html, accessed March 12, 2010.

25. Laverne Prosser, "Wil Lou Gray's Story Important," *Charleston (S.C.) News and Courier,* April 5, 1964.

26. Gray, photocopied letter to family, June 29, 1960, letter held by author.

27. Kessler-Harris, *In Pursuit of Equity,* 4; "Biographical Data, Wil Lou Gray, Teacher and Educator," in George Smith, *Documents on the Early Beginnings.*

28. Harvey Neufeldt to Mary Mac Ogden, e-mail, April 19, 2010, transcript held by author.

29. Sawer, "Gender, Metaphor and the State," 120. Sawer offers an excellent discussion of social liberal thought in the period between 1900 and World War I and the feminization of the public sphere.

30. Blackwell, "Wil Lou Gray, Educator," 12. DaMaris Ayres developed her article from this essay; see Ayres, "Crusader: Wil Lou Gray Has Fought to Wipe Out Illiteracy in South Carolina," *Columbia (S.C.) State Magazine,* October 7, 1979, 9.

31. Gray, *Elementary Studies in Civics,* 54.

32. Ibid., 6, 8.

33. Blackwell, "Wil Lou Gray, Educator," 13.

34. *Carolina Pioneer,* July 13, 1957, 3.

35. Ibid.

36. Draft of Superintendent Report, 1925, box 24, Wil Lou Gray Papers.

37. *Carolina Pioneer,* November 25, 1956.

38. Gray, "South Carolina's Program," 84.

39. M. B. Hall to Gray, February 5, 1935, Correspondence In, 1935, Wil Lou Gray Papers.

40. Lois M. Quinn, "An Institutional History of the GED," http://www4.uwm.edu/eti/reprints/GEDHistory.pdf, accessed February 20, 2010; Knight, *Public Education in the South,* 446.

41. Hardy, *Farm, Mill, and Classroom,* 98. For information about South Carolina's compulsory attendance law, see pages 47, 65, 189.

42. Ibid., 98. See also Quinn, "Institutional History of the GED."

43. Hardy, *Farm, Mill, and Classroom,* 189.

44. Ibid., 139–86.

45. Evelyn Branch, interview by author, Columbia, August 23, 1995; 2007.

46. The absence of opinions or clear positions about controversial topics such as segregation and suffrage in the period I examine suggests that Gray was aware of the consequences that overt challenges to traditional practice might have on her job. She had to work, and she supported her father and mother-in-law with the help of her brother during the Depression. Gray's salary ranged from $1800 to $2750 per year between 1919 and 1935. See folder 189, box 3, July 11, 1935, Wil Lou Gray Papers.

47. Gray to Harriet Blackwell, June 3, 1963, letter held by author.

Bibliography

Manuscripts

Carnegie Corporation Collection. Rare Books and Manuscripts Library, Columbia University, New York.

Constance Ashton Myers Collection. South Caroliniana Library, University of South Carolina, Columbia.

Eunice Temple Ford Stackhouse Papers. South Caroliniana Library, University of South Carolina, Columbia.

Frank Durham Papers. South Caroliniana Library, University of South Carolina, Columbia.

Gannon Center for Women and Leadership Archives, Loyola University, Chicago, http://orpheus.it.luc.edu/orgs/gannon/archives/completelist.cfm, accessed April 15, 2005.

Illiteracy Commission Collection. South Caroliniana Library, University of South Carolina, Columbia.

James F. Miles Papers, 1929–85. South Caroliniana Library, University of South Carolina, Columbia.

John E. Swearingen Papers. South Caroliniana Library, University of South Carolina, Columbia.

Julia Mood Peterkin Vertical Files Collection, 1927–36. South Caroliniana Library, University of South Carolina, Columbia.

Laura Mood Papers, 1905–66. South Caroliniana Library, University of South Carolina, Columbia.

Lucretia P. Hale Papers, 1820–1900. Part of the Complete Peterkin Papers. 1960. Special Collections, South Caroliniana Library, University of South Carolina, Columbia.

Mary Elizabeth Frayser Papers. Dacus Library, Winthrop University, Rock Hill, South Carolina.

Martha Washington College Records, 1905–20. Emory and Henry College, Abingdon, Virginia.

Nathaniel Barksdale Dial Papers, 1862–1914. Duke University Special Collections, Durham, North Carolina.

Patterson Wardlaw Papers. South Caroliniana Library, University of South Carolina, Columbia.

Rebecca Dial Papers, 1922–60. South Caroliniana Library, University of South Carolina, Columbia.

Seneca Institute Records. Clemson University Special Collections, Clemson, South Carolina.

Southern Oral History Program Collection, 1973–2005 (general abstract). University of North Carolina, Chapel Hill.

South Carolina Federation of Women's Clubs Papers. Dacus Library, Winthrop University, Rock Hill, South Carolina.

Wil Lou Gray Opportunity School Archives, West Columbia, South Carolina.

Wil Lou Gray Papers, boxes 1–34. South Caroliniana Library, University of South Carolina, Columbia. Correspondence Out documents on microfilm, rolls 746–48.

Wil Lou Gray to Albert Dial Gray Jr. and extended family, 1936–72. Collection of Mrs. Albert Dial Gray, Whiteville, North Carolina. Letters held by author.

Wil Lou Gray to Wil Lou Gray Ogden, 1958–78. Letters held by author.

William Knox Tate Papers, 1894–1952. South Caroliniana Library, University of South Carolina, Columbia.

Documents

Acts and Joint Resolutions of the General Assembly of the State of South Carolina Passed at the Regular Session of 1919. Columbia: Bryan, 1919.

Brearley, H. C., and Mabel Montgomery. *Facing Facts in South Carolina.* Columbia: South Carolina State Department of Education, 1937.

Clarke, Ida Clyde. *American Women and the World War,* New York: Appleton, 1918, http://www.lib.byu.edu/estu/World War I/comment/Clarke/Clarke01.htm, accessed October 25, 2005.

Church and Cemetery Records. First Methodist Church of Laurens, South Carolina; Spartanburg, South Carolina.

Columbia College Criterion and Yearbook, 1899–1904.

Federal Census of the United States, Slave Schedule: Laurens County, South Carolina, 1810–1850. South Carolina State Archives, Columbia. Microfilm. Roll 865.

Federal Census of South Carolina 1880–1940. South Carolina Department of Archives and History, Columbia.

Matriculation Record, Wil Lou Gray. Columbia University, New York, 1910–17.

Matriculation Record, Wil Lou Gray. Winthrop University, Rock Hill, SC, 1905.

The Gray Family Journal. Genealogy of Gray family compiled by Marguerite Tolbert, Columbia, 1937. Revised by Wil Lou Gray Ogden, Danville, Virginia, 1976. Some material taken from "The Nash Family Book," an unpublished genealogy. Pamphlet owned by author.

Gray, Wil Lou. *Elementary Studies in Civics for the Pupils of South Carolina.* Rev. ed. Columbia: State Company, 1927.

———. "Evolution of Adult Elementary Education in South Carolina." *Adult Elementary Education Interstate Bulletin* 2 (1927): 3.

———. *A Night School Experiment in Laurens County, South Carolina.* Columbia: State Department of Education, 1915.

———. "South Carolina's Program for Belated Learners." *Journal of the Association of University Women* 23 (1930): 80–85.

———. "What Should a Superintendent or Supervising Teacher Do When Visiting a School?" In *Proceedings of the Seventeenth Conference for Education in the South and the Twenty-Fifth Annual Meeting of the Southern Educational Association,* 255–58. N.p.: The Committee, 1914.

Gray, Wil Lou, and Marguerite Tolbert. *A Brief Manual for Adult Teachers in South Carolina.* Columbia: State Department of Education, 1944.

Gray, William, Wil Lou Gray, and J. Warren Tilton. *The Opportunity Schools of South Carolina—An Experimental Study.* New York: American Association for Adult Education, 1932.

Hope, James, and Wil Lou Gray. *Night and Adult Schools.* Columbia: State Department of Education, 1935.

"Report on Adult Education," 1919–36, Superintendent of Education Report, General Assembly Reports and Resolutions, South Carolina Department of Archives and History.

Smith, W. Roy. *South Carolina as a Royal Province.* New York: Macmillan, 1903.

South Carolina Illiteracy Commission. *An Appeal in Behalf of the Work of the Illiteracy Commission of South Carolina.* Columbia: McCaw, 1918.

Snowden, Yates. *History of South Carolina.* Chicago: Lewis, 1920.

BOOKS

Abbott, Shirley. *Womenfolks: Growing Up Down South.* New Haven: Ticknor & Fields, 1983.

Anderson, Benedict. *Imagined Communities: Reflections on the Origins and Spread of Nationalism.* London: Verso, 1983.

Anderson, James. *The Education of Blacks in the South, 1860–1935.* Chapel Hill: University of North Carolina Press, 1988.

Anderson, Margaret. *My Thirty Years' War: The Autobiography: Beginnings and Battles to 1930.* New York: Horizon, 1969.

Antler, Joyce. *The Educated Woman and Professionalization: The Struggle for a New Feminine Identity, 1890–1920.* New York: Garland, 1987.

Ascoli, Peter. *Julius Rosenwald: The Man Who Built Sears and Roebuck and Advanced the Cause of Black Education in the American South.* Bloomington: Indiana University Press, 2006.

Ashmore, Harry. *An Epitaph for Dixie.* New York: Norton, 1958.

Ayers, Edward. *The Promise of the New South: Life after Reconstruction.* New York: Oxford University Press, 1992.

———. *Vengeance and Justice: Crime and Punishment in the Nineteenth Century American South.* New York: Oxford University Press, 1984.

Ayres, DaMaris. *Let My People Learn*. Greenwood, S.C.: Attic, 1988.

Bailey, Hugh. *Liberalism in the New South: Southern Social Reform and the Progressive Movement*. Coral Gables, Fla.: University of Miami Press, 1969.

Baldwin, Yvonne Honeycutt. *Cora Wilson Stewart and Kentucky's Moonlight Schools: Fighting for Literacy in America*. Lexington: University of Kentucky Press, 2006.

Ball, William Watts. *A Boy's Recollection of the Red Shirt Campaign of 1876*. Columbia: State Company, 1911.

————. *The State That Forgot: South Carolina's Surrender to Democracy*. Indianapolis: Bobbs-Merrill, 1932.

Bass, Jack, and W. Scott Poole. *The Palmetto State: The Making of Modern South Carolina*. Columbia: University of South Carolina Press, 2009.

Baxandall, Rosalyn, Linda Gordon, Linda Perlman Gordon, and Susan Reverby, eds. *America's Working Women: A Documentary History 1600 to the Present*. New York: Norton, 1995.

Beam, Lura. *He Called Them by the Lightning: A Teacher's Odyssey in the Negro South, 1908–1919*. New York: Bobbs-Merrill, 1967.

Bercaw, Nancy, ed. *Gender and the Southern Body Politic: Essays and Comments*. Jackson: University Press of Mississippi, 2000.

Bilanchone, Linda. *The Lives They Lived: A Look at the Women in the History of Spartanburg*. Spartanburg, S.C.: Altman, 1981.

Blackwell, Harriet Gray. *A Candle for All Time*. Richmond: Dietz, 1959.

Blair, Karen. *The Clubwoman as Feminist: True Womanhood Defined, 1868–1914*. New York: Holmes & Meier, 1980.

Blight, David. *Race and Reunion: The Civil War in American Memory*. Cambridge, Mass.: Belknap Press of Harvard University Press, 2001.

Bodie, Idella. *South Carolina Women: They Dare to Lead*. Orangeburg, S.C.: Sandlapper, 1981.

Bolick, Julian. *A Laurens County Sketchbook*. N.p.: Privately published, 1973.

Brownell, Blaine, and David Goldfield, eds. *The City in Southern History: The Growth of Urban Civilization in the South*. Port Washington, N.Y.: Kennikat, 1977.

Brundage, W. Fitzhugh. *Lynching in the New South: Georgia and Virginia, 1880–1930*. Urbana: University of Illinois Press, 1993.

————, ed. *Under Sentence of Death: Lynching in the South*. Chapel Hill: University of North Carolina Press, 1997.

————, ed. *Where These Memories Grow: History, Memory, and Southern Identity*. Chapel Hill: University of North Carolina Press, 2000.

Bullock, Henry Allen. *A History of Negro Education in the South from 1619 to the Present*. Cambridge, Mass.: Harvard University Press, 1967.

Burts, Robert Milton. *Richard Irvine Manning and the Progressive Movement in South Carolina*. Columbia: University of South Carolina Press, 1974.

Butler, Judith. *Gender Trouble: Feminism and the Subversion of Identity*. New York: Routledge, 1990.

Byerly, Victoria. *Hard Times, Cotton Mill Girls: Personal Histories of Womanhood and Poverty in the South*. Ithaca, N.Y.: ILR, 1986.

Cabell, George W. *The Negro Question: A Selection of Writings on Civil Rights in the South*. New York: Doubleday, 1885.

Campbell, Barbara K. *The "Liberated" Woman of 1914: Prominent Women in the Progressive Era*. Ann Arbor: University of Michigan Press, 1979.

Carrigan, William D. *The Making of a Lynching Culture: Violence and Vigilantism in Central Texas, 1836–1916*. Urbana: University of Illinois Press, 2004.

Carter, Dan. *The Politics of Rage: George Wallace, the New Conservatism and the Transformation of American Politics*. Baton Rouge: Louisiana State University Press, 2000.

Cash, W. J. *The Mind of the South*. New York: Knopf, 1941.

Chafe, William. *The American Woman: Her Changing Social, Economic, and Political Roles: 1920–1970*. London: Oxford University Press, 1972.

———. *The Paradox of Change: American Women in the Twentieth Century*. London: Oxford University Press, 1991.

Charron, Katherine Mellen. *Freedom's Teacher: The Life of Septima Clark*. Chapel Hill: University of North Carolina Press, 2009.

Clark, Septima. *Echo in My Soul*. New York: Dutton, 1962.

Clayton, Bruce. *The Savage Ideal: Intolerance and Intellectual Leadership in the South, 1890–1914*. Baltimore: Johns Hopkins University Press, 1972.

Cohen, Lizabeth. *Making a New Deal: Industrial Workers in Chicago, 1919–1939*. Cambridge: Cambridge University Press, 1990.

Collins, Patricia Hill. *Black Feminist Thought: Knowledge, Consciousness, and the Politics of Empowerment*. New York: Routledge, 2000.

———. *Fighting Words: Black Women and the Search for Justice*. Minneapolis: University of Minnesota, 1998.

Cook, Blanche Wiesen. *Eleanor Roosevelt*, vol. 1, *1884–1933*. London: Penguin Books, 1992.

Cooper, Anna Julia. *A Voice from the South by a Black Woman of the South*. Xenia, Ohio: Aldine, 1892. Rpt., New York: Oxford University Press, 1988.

Cooper, John Milton, Jr. *Walter Hines Page: The Southerner as American, 1855–1918*. Chapel Hill: University of North Carolina Press, 1977.

Cooper, William J., and Thomas Terrill. *The American South: A History*, vol. 11. Lanham, Md.: Rowman & Littlefield, 2009.

Cott, Nancy. *The Bonds of Womanhood: "Women's Sphere" in New England, 1780–1835*. New Haven: Yale University Press, 1977.

Cott, Nancy, and Elizabeth Pleck, eds. *A Heritage of Her Own*. New York: Simon & Shuster, 1979.

Cox, Karen. *Dixie's Daughters: The United Daughters of the Confederacy and the Preservation of Confederate Culture*. Gainesville: University Press of Florida, 2003.

Crawford, Fiona Goff. *State Government*. New York: Holt, 1931.

Curtis, Claude. *Three Quarters of a Century at Martha Washington College*. Bristol, Vir.: King, 1928.

Dabbs, James McBride. *Haunted by God: The Cultural and Religious Experience of the South*. Richmond: Knox, 1972.

———. *The Road Home*. Philadelphia: Christian Press, 1960.

———. *Who Speaks for the South?* New York: Funk & Wagnalls, 1964.

Dabney, Charles. *Universal Education in the South*. Chapel Hill: University of North Carolina Press, 1936.

Dailey, Jane, Glenda Elizabeth Gilmore, and Bryant Simon, eds. *Jumpin' Jim Crow:*

Southern Politics from the Civil War to Civil Rights. Princeton: Princeton University Press, 2000.

Degler, Carl. *At Odds: Women and the Family in America from the Revolution to the Present.* New York: Oxford University Press, 1980.

Delta Kappa Gamma. *Pioneer Teachers of South Carolina.* Rock Hill, S.C.: Whiting, 1958.

Dial, Rebecca. *True to His Colors: A Story of South Carolina's Senator Nathaniel Barksdale Dial.* New York: Vantage, 1974.

Dorgan, Howard, et al., eds. *The Oratory of Southern Demagogues.* Baton Rouge: Louisiana State University Press, 1981.

Drago, Edmund L. *Hurrah for Hampton! Black Red Shirts in South Carolina during Reconstruction.* Fayetteville: University of Arkansas Press, 1998.

Dunbar, Anthony. *Against the Grain.* Charlottesville: University of Virginia Press, 1981.

Durham, Frank, ed. *The Collected Short Stories of Julia Peterkin.* Columbia: University of South Carolina Press, 1970.

Dunning, William. *Reconstruction, Political and Economic: 1865–1877.* New York: Harper, 1907.

Edgar, Walter. *South Carolina: A History.* Columbia: University of South Carolina Press, 1998.

———, ed. *The South Carolina Encyclopedia.* Columbia: University of South Carolina Press, 2006.

Edmunds, John, Jr. *The Episcopal Church of the Advent.* Spartanburg, S.C.: Reprint Company, 1988.

Edwards, Wendy Diechmann, and Carolyn De Swarte Gifford, eds. *Gender and the Social Gospel.* Chicago: University of Illinois, 2003.

Egerton, John. *The Americanization of Dixie.* New York: *Harper's Magazine* Press, 1974.

Elliott, Irene, Wil Lou Gray, and Marguerite Tolbert. *South Carolina's Distinguished Women of Laurens County.* Columbia: Bryan, 1972.

Etheridge, E. W. *The Butterfly Caste: A Social History of Pellagra in the South.* Westport, Conn.: Greenwood, 1972.

Evans, Maurice. *Black and White in the Southern States; A Study of the Race Problem in the United States from a South African Point of View.* New York: Longmans, Green, 1915.

Fink, Leon. *Progressive Intellectuals and the Dilemmas of Democratic Commitment.* Cambridge, Mass.: Harvard University Press, 1997.

Foner, Eric. *Reconstruction: America's Unfinished Revolution, 1863–1877.* New York: Perennial Classics, 2002.

———. *A Short History of Reconstruction, 1863–1877.* New York: Harper & Row, 1990.

Force, William. *Payne at Peabody: An Apostle of Education.* Nashville: Vanderbilt University Press, 1985.

Foster, Gaines. *Ghosts of the Confederacy: Defeat, the Lost Cause, and the Emergence of the New South, 1865–1913.* New York: Oxford University Press, 1987.

Fox-Genovese, Elizabeth. *Within the Plantation Household: Black and White Women in the Old South.* Chapel Hill: University of North Carolina Press, 1988.

Frankel, Noralee, and Nancy S. Dye, eds. *Gender, Class, Race, and Reform in the Progressive Era.* Lexington: University Press of Kentucky, 1991.

Frayser, Walter J., Frank Saunders Jr., and Jon Wakelyn. *The Web of Southern Social Relations.* Athens: University of Georgia Press, 1985.

Gibbs, Margaret. *The DAR*. New York: Holt, Reinhart & Winston, 1969.

Gilmore, Glenda. *Defying Dixie: The Radical Roots of Civil Rights, 1919–1950*. New York: Norton, 2008.

———. *Gender and Jim Crow: The Politics of White Supremacy in North Carolina, 1896–1920*. Chapel Hill: University of North Carolina Press, 1996.

Glazer, Penina, and Miriam Slater. *Unequal Colleagues: The Entrance of Women into the Professions, 1890–1940*. New Brunswick, N.J.: Rutgers University Press, 1987.

Gordon, Lynn. *Gender and Higher Education in the Progressive Era*. New Haven: Yale University Press, 1990.

Grantham, Dewey. *The Regional Imagination: The South and Recent American History*. Nashville: Vanderbilt University Press, 1979.

———. *The South and the Sectional Image*. New York: Harper & Row, 1967.

———. *Southern Progressivism: The Reconciliation of Progress and Tradition*. Knoxville: University of Tennessee Press, 1983.

Graydon, Nell. *Tales of Columbia*. Columbia: Bryan, 1964.

Habermas, Jürgen. *The Structural Transformation of the Public Sphere: An Inquiry into a Category of Bourgeois Society*. Cambridge, Mass.: MIT Press, 1989.

Hackney, Sheldon. *Magnolias without Moonlight: The American South from Regional Confederacy to National Integration*. New Brunswick, N.J.: Transaction, 2005.

———. *Populism to Progressivism in Alabama*. Princeton: Princeton University Press, 1969.

Hahn, Steven. *A Nation under Our Feet: Black Political Struggles in the Rural South from Slavery to the Great Migration*. Cambridge, Mass.: Belknap Press of Harvard University Press, 2003.

Hale, Grace Elizabeth. *Making Whiteness: The Culture of Segregation in the South, 1890–1940*. New York: Pantheon Books, 1998.

Hall, Jacquelyn Dowd. *Revolt against Chivalry: Jessie Daniel Ames and the Women's Campaign against Lynching*. New York: Columbia University Press, 1979.

Harding, Sandra. *The Science Question in Feminism*. Ithaca: Cornell University Press, 1986.

Hardy, Norfleet. *Farm, Mill, and Classroom: A History of Tax Supported Adult Education in South Carolina to 1960*. Columbia: Bryan, 1967.

Harlan, Louis. *Booker T. Washington: The Wizard of Tuskegee, 1901–1915*. London: Oxford University Press, 1983.

———, ed. *The Booker T. Washington Papers*. 14 vols. Urbana: University of Illinois Press, 1972–89.

Harrison, Robert. *Congress, Progressive Reform and the New American State*. Cambridge: Cambridge University Press, 2004.

Haskin, Sara Estelle. *Women and Missions in the Methodist Episcopal Church, South*. Nashville: Methodist Publishing House, 1920.

Hawk, Emory Q. *Economic History of the South*. New York: Prentice-Hall, 1934.

Hayes, Jack Irby. *South Carolina and the New Deal*. Columbia: University of South Carolina Press, 2001.

Higginbotham, Evelyn Brooks. *Righteous Discontent: The Women's Movement in the Black Baptist Church, 1880–1920*. Cambridge, Mass.: Harvard University Press, 1993.

Hine, Darlene Clark. *HineSight: Black Women and the Reconstruction of American History.* New York: Carlson, 1994.

———. *"We Specialize in the Wholly Impossible": A Reader in Black Women's History.* New York: Carlson, 1995.

Hobsbawm, Eric. *The Invention of Tradition.* Cambridge: Cambridge University Press, 1992.

Holt, Thomas. *Black over White: Negro Political Leadership in South Carolina during Reconstruction.* Urbana: University of Illinois Press, 1977.

Hudson, Janet G. *Entangled by White Supremacy: Reform in World War I–Era South Carolina.* Lexington: University Press of Kentucky, 2009.

Huff, A. Vernon. *Tried by Fire.* Columbia: Bryan, 1975.

Hughes, Athol, ed. *The Inner World and Joan Riviere: Collected Papers, 1920–1958.* London: Karnac Books, 1991.

Jacobson, Matthew Frye. *Barbarian Virtues: The United States Encounters with Foreign Peoples at Home and Abroad, 1876–1917.* New York: Hill & Wang, 2000.

Johnson, Joan Marie. *Southern Ladies, New Women: Race, Region, and Clubwomen in South Carolina, 1890–1930.* Gainesville: University Press of Florida, 2004.

———. *Southern Women at the Seven Sister Colleges: Feminist Values and Social Activism, 1875–1915.* Athens: University of Georgia Press, 2008.

Jones, Beverly. *Quest for Equality: The Life of Mary Eliza Church Terrel 1863–1950.* Chapel Hill: University of North Carolina Press, 1980.

Jones, Jacqueline. *Labor of Love, Labor of Sorrow: Black Women, Work, and the Family from Slavery to the Present.* New York: Random House, 1985.

Kearl, Michael C. *Endings: A Sociology of Death and Dying.* New York: Oxford University Press, 1989.

Kerber, Linda. *No Constitutional Right to Be Ladies: Women and the Obligations of Citizenship.* New York: Hill & Wang, 1998.

———. *Women of the Republic: Intellect and Ideology in Revolutionary America.* Chapel Hill: University of North Carolina Press, 1980.

Kessler-Harris, Alice. *In Pursuit of Equity: Women, Men and the Quest for Economic Citizenship.* New York: Oxford University Press, 2003.

———. *Out to Work: A History of Wage Earning Women in the United States.* New York: Oxford University Press, 1982.

———. *A Woman's Wage: Historical Meanings and Social Consequences.* Lexington: University Press of Kentucky, 1990.

Key, V. O., Jr. *Southern Politics in State and Nation.* New York: Knopf, 1949.

Kirby, Jack Temple. *Darkness at the Dawning: Race and Reform in the Progressive South.* Philadelphia: Lippincott, 1972.

Knight, Edgar Wallace. *Public Education in the South.* Boston: Ginn, 1922.

Knowles, M. S. *The Adult Education Movement in the United States.* New York: Holt, Rinehart & Winston, 1962.

Kolmar, Wendy, and Frances Bartkowski. *Feminist Theory: A Reader.* New York: McGraw-Hill, 2005.

Kousser, Morgan. *The Shaping of Southern Politics: Suffrage Restrictions and the Establishment of the One Party South, 1880–1910.* New Haven: Yale University Press, 1974.

Krementz, Jill. *How It Feels When a Parent Dies*. New York: Knopf, 1982.

Kuhlman, Erika A. *Petticoats and White Feathers: Gender Conformity, Race, the Progressive Peace Movement, and the Debate over War, 1895–1919*. Westport, Conn.: Greenwood, 1997.

Lagemann, Ellen C. *A Generation of Women: Education in the Lives of Progressive Reformers*. Cambridge, Mass.: Harvard University Press, 1979.

Lander, Ernest. *A History of South Carolina 1865–1960*. Chapel Hill: University of North Carolina Press, 1960.

Landess, Thomas. *Julia Peterkin*. Boston: Twayne, 1976.

Larson, Edward J. *Sex, Race, and Science: Eugenics in the Deep South*. Baltimore: Johns Hopkins University Press, 1995.

Leland, John A. *A Voice from South Carolina*. Charleston: Walker, Evans & Cogswell, 1879.

Lerner, Gerda. *The Grimke Sisters from South Carolina: Pioneers for Women's Rights and Abolition*. New York: Oxford University Press, 1967.

Link, William. *The Paradox of Southern Progressivism, 1880–1930*. Chapel Hill: University of North Carolina Press, 1992.

Lumpkin, Katharine Du Pre. *The Making of a Southerner*. New York: Knopf, 1947.

Martin, C. J. *The Development of Negro Higher Education in South Carolina*. Columbia: State Department of Education, 1949.

May, Larry. *The Big Tomorrow: Hollywood and the Politics of the American Way*. Chicago: University of Chicago Press, 2000.

McCandless, Amy. *The Past in the Present: Women's Higher Education in the American South*. Tuscaloosa: University of Alabama Press, 1999.

McClellan, Edward. *Schools and the Shaping of Character: Moral Education in America 1607–Present*. Bloomington: Indiana University Press, 1992.

McLaurin, Melton. *Celia: A Slave*. New York: Harper Collins, 1999.

Miller, Page, ed. *Reclaiming the Past: Landmarks of Women's History*. Bloomington: Indiana University Press, 1992.

Mitchell, Broadus. *Depression Decade: From New Era through New Deal, 1929–1941*. New York: Reinhart, 1947.

———. *The Industrial Revolution in the South*. Baltimore: Johns Hopkins Press, 1930.

Montgomery, Rebecca. *The Politics of Education in the New South: Women and Reform in Georgia, 1890–1930*. Baton Rouge: Louisiana State University Press, 2006.

Montgomery, Mabel. *South Carolina's Wil Lou Gray*. Columbia: Vogue, 1963.

———. *Worth While South Carolinians*. Columbia: State, 1934.

Montgomery, Warner M. *Forest Acres*. Charleston, S.C.: Arcadia, 2010.

Moore, John Hammond. *Carnival of Blood: Dueling, Lynching, and Mob Violence in South Carolina, 1880–1920*. Columbia: University of South Carolina, 2006.

Morris, Robert C. *Reading, 'Riting, and Reconstruction: The Education of the Freedmen in the South, 1861–1870*. Chicago: University of Chicago Press, 1981.

Neuhaus, Richard John. *To Empower People: The Role of Mediating Structures in Public Policy*. Washington, D.C.: American Enterprise Institute for Public Policy Research, 1977.

Nicholls, William. *Southern Tradition and Regional Progress*. Chapel Hill: University of North Carolina Press, 1960.

Nieman, Donald G., ed. *From Slavery to Sharecropping: White Land and Black Labor in the Rural South, 1865–1900*. New York: Garland, 1994.

Nixon, Raymond. *Henry W. Grady: Spokesman of the New South*. New York: Knopf, 1943.

Norton, Mary Beth, ed. *Major Problems in American Women's History*. Lexington, Mass.: Heath, 1989.

Penn, Rosalyn Terborg. *African American Women and the Struggle for the Vote, 1850–1920*. Bloomington: Indiana University Press, 1998.

Peterkin, Julia Mood. *Black April*. Indianapolis: Bobbs-Merrill, 1927.

———. *Scarlet Sister Mary*. Indianapolis: Bobbs-Merrill, 1928.

Peterkin, Julia Mood, and Doris Ulmann. *Roll, Jordan, Roll*. New York: Ballou, 1933.

Pfeifer, Michael J. *Rough Justice: Lynching and American Society, 1874–1947*. Urbana: University of Illinois Press, 2004.

Poole, W. Scott. *Never Surrender: Confederate Memory and Conservatism in the South Carolina Upcountry*. Athens: University of Georgia Press, 2004.

Rable, George C. *But There Was No Peace: The Role of Violence in the Politics of Reconstruction*. Athens: University of Georgia Press, 1984.

Reynolds, Katherine C., and Susan Schramm. *A Separate Sisterhood: Women Who Shaped Southern Education in the Progressive Era*. New York: Lang, 2002.

Roller, David, and Robert Twyman, eds. *The Encyclopedia of Southern History*. Baton Rouge: Louisiana State University Press, 1979.

Rosenzweig, Linda. *The Anchor of My Life: Middle-Class American Mothers and Daughters, 1880–1920*. New York: New York University Press, 1993.

Schneider, Dorothy, and Carl Schneider. *American Women in the Progressive Era: 1910–1920*. New York: Facts on File, 1993.

Scott, Anne Firor. *Making the Invisible Woman Visible*. Urbana: University of Illinois Press, 1984.

———. *Natural Allies: Women's Associations in American History*. Urbana: University of Illinois Press, 1991.

———. *One Half the People: The Fight for Woman Suffrage*. Urbana: University of Illinois Press, 1982.

———. *The Southern Lady: From Pedestal to Politics, 1830–1930*. Chicago: University of Chicago Press, 1970.

Scott, Joan. *Gender and the Politics of History*. New York: Columbia University Press, 1999.

The Scrapbook: A Compilation of Historical Facts about Places and Events of Laurens County, South Carolina. Laurens, S.C.: Laurens County Historical Society, 1982.

Simpson, Lewis, ed. *I'll Take My Stand: The South and the Agrarian Tradition*. Baton Rouge: Louisiana State University Press, 1977.

Simon, Bryant. *A Fabric of Defeat: The Politics of South Carolina Millhands, 1910–1948*. Chapel Hill: University of North Carolina Press, 1998.

Skelton, Caroline Nabors. *Godfrey Ragsdale: From England to Henrico County, Virginia: One Documented Line of Descent Covering 350 Years in America*. Franklin Springs, Ga.: Advocate, 1969.

Smith, Bonnie. *The Gender of History: Men, Women, and the Practice of History*. Cambridge, Mass.: Harvard University Press, 1998.

Smith, George. *Documents on the Early Beginnings of the South Carolina Opportunity School.* N.p., 1999.

———. *The Opportunity Schools and the Founder Wil Lou Gray.* Columbia: Wil Lou Gray Opportunity School, 2000.

Smith, John David, ed. *Disenfranchisement Proposals and the Ku Klux Klan.* Vol. 9, pt. 1, of *Anti-Black Thought, 1863–1925.* New York: Garland, 1993.

Smith, Lillian. *Strange Fruit: A Novel.* New York: Reynal & Hitchcock, 1944.

Smith-Rosenberg, Carroll. *Disorderly Conduct: Visions of Gender in Victorian America.* New York: Oxford University Press, 1985.

Solomon, Barbara. *In the Company of Educated Women: A History of Women and Higher Education in America.* New Haven: Yale University Press, 1985.

Sosna, Morton. *In Search of the Silent South.* New York: Columbia University Press, 1977.

Spears, R. Wright. *One in the Spirit: Ministry for Change in South Carolina.* Columbia: Bryan, 1997.

Spruill, Marjorie. *The New Woman of the New South.* London: Oxford University Press, 1993.

Spruill, Marjorie J., Valinda Littlefield, and Joan M. Johnson, eds. *South Carolina Women: Their Lives and Times.* Vol. 2. Athens: University of Georgia Press, 2010.

Stackhouse, Eunice. "Mary E. Frayser: Pioneer Social and Research Worker in the South and Leader in Women's Organization in South Carolina." Unpublished manuscript, 1944.

———. *Time Marches On, 1898–1939.* Columbia: South Carolina Federation of Women's Clubs, 1939.

Stewart, Cora Wilson. *Moonlight Schools for the Emancipation of Adult Illiterates.* New York: Dutton, 1922.

Stubblefield, H. W. *Towards a History of Adult Education in America.* London: Croom-Helm, 1988.

Stubblefield, H. W., and Patrick Keane. *Adult Education in the American Experience: From the Colonial Period to the Present.* San Francisco: Jossey-Bass, 1994.

Sullivan, Pat. *Days of Hope: Race and Democracy in the New Deal Era.* Chapel Hill: University of North Carolina Press, 1996.

Tatum, Noreen. *A Crown of Service: A Story of Women's Work in the Methodist Episcopal Church South from 1878–1940.* Nashville: Parthenon, 1960.

Tétreault, Mary Ann, and Robin L. Teske, eds. *Partial Truths and the Politics of Community: Feminist Approaches to Social Movements, Community, and Power.* 2 vols. Columbia: University of South Carolina Press, 2003.

Tindall, George Brown. *The Emergence of the New South, 1913–1945.* Baton Rouge: Louisiana State University Press, 1967.

———. *The Persistent Tradition in New South Politics.* Baton Rouge: Louisiana State University Press, 1975.

Tolnay, Stewart E., and E. M. Beck. *A Festival of Violence: An Analysis of Southern Lynchings, 1882–1930.* Urbana: University of Illinois Press, 1995.

Trelease, Alan. *White Terror: The Ku Klux Klan Conspiracy and Southern Reconstruction.* New York: Harper & Row, 1971.

Twelve Southerners. *I'll Take My Stand: The South and the Agrarian Tradition.* New York: Harper & Row, 1930.

Ulrich, Laurel Thatcher. *Well Behaved Women Seldom Make History.* New York: Vintage Books, 2007.

Vicinus, Martha. *Independent Women: Work and Community for Single Women, 1850–1920.* Chicago: University of Chicago Press, 1985.

Wallace, David Duncan. *A History of South Carolina.* New York: Lewis, 1920.

———. *A History of South Carolina—Biographical.* 4 vols. New York: American Historical Society, 1935.

———. *A History of the South Carolina Teacher's Association.* Columbia: South Caroliniana Library, 1924.

———. *History of Wofford College.* Nashville: Vanderbilt University Press, 1951.

———. *South Carolina: A Short History, 1520–1948.* Columbia: University of South Carolina Press, 1961.

Ware, Susan. *Holding Their Own: American Women in the 1930s.* Boston: Twayne, 1982.

Weber, Lynn. *Understanding Race, Class, Gender, and Sexuality: A Conceptual Framework.* Boston: McGraw-Hill, 2001.

Wesley, Charles. *A History of the National Association of Colored Women's Clubs: A Legacy of Service.* Washington, D.C.: Association, 1984.

Wheeler, Marjorie Spruill. *New Women of the New South: The Leaders of the Woman Suffrage Movement in the Southern States.* New York: Oxford University Press, 1993.

Whisnant, David. *All That Is Native and Fine: The Politics of Culture in an American Region.* Chapel Hill: University of North Carolina Press, 1983.

Wiebe, Robert. *The Search for Order, 1877–1920.* New York: Hill & Wang, 1967.

Wiener, Jonathan. *Social Origins of the New South.* Baton Rouge: Louisiana State University Press, 1978.

Williams, Susan Millar. *A Devil and a Good Woman Too: The Lives of Julia Peterkin.* Athens: University of Georgia Press, 1997.

Williamson, Joel. *The Crucible of Race: Black/White Relations in the American South since Emancipation.* New York: Oxford University Press, 1984.

Wilson, Charles Reagan. *Baptized in Blood: The Religion of the Lost Cause, 1865–1920.* Athens: University of Georgia Press, 1980.

Wilson, Margaret. *The American Woman in Transition, 1870–1920.* New York: Greenwood Press, 1979.

Wirt, Frederick M. *We Ain't What We Was: Civil Rights in the New South.* Durham, N.C.: Duke University Press, 1997.

Wolfe, Margaret Ripley. *Daughters of Canaan: A Saga of Southern Women.* Lexington: University Press of Kentucky, 1995.

Wood, Amy. *Lynching and Spectacle: Witnessing Race Violence in America, 1890–1940.* Chapel Hill: University of North Carolina Press, 2011.

Woodward, C. Vann. *The Burden of Southern History.* Baton Rouge: Louisiana State University Press, 1970.

———. *The Origins of the New South: 1877–1913.* Baton Rouge: Louisiana State University Press, 1951.

———. *The Strange Career of Jim Crow.* New York: Oxford University Press, 1955.

Workman, William. *The Case for the South.* New York: Devon-Adair, 1960.

ARTICLES AND SECTIONS OF BOOKS

Abrams, Richard. "The Failure of Progressivism." In *The Shaping of the Twentieth Century: Interpretive Essays*, edited by Richard Abrams and Lawrence Levine, 203–15. Boston: Little, Brown, 1971.

Akerson, James, and Harvey Neufeldt, "Alabama's Illiteracy Campaign for Black Adults, 1915–1930: An Analysis." *Journal of Negro Education* 54 (1985): 189–95.

Allen, Louise Anderson. "Laura Bragg and the Charleston Museum." In *Founding Mothers and Others: Women Educational Leaders during the Progressive Era*, ed. Alan R. Sandovnik and Susan Semel, 177–201. New York: Palgrave, 2002.

Baker, Bruce E. "Under the Rope: Lynching and Memory in Laurens County, South Carolina." In *Where These Memories Grow: History, Memory, and Southern Identity*, ed. W. Fitzhugh Brundage, 319–46. Chapel Hill: University of North Carolina Press, 2000.

Bartley, Numan. "In Search of the New South: Southern Politics after Reconstruction." *Reviews in American History* 10 (1982): 150–63.

———. "The South and Sectionalism in American Politics." *Journal of Politics* 38 (1976): 239–57.

Beeby, James M. "Red Shirt Violence, Election Fraud, and the Demise of the Populist Party in North Carolina's Third Congressional District, 1900." *North Carolina Historical Review* 85 (2008): 1–28.

Bernard, L. L. "Culture and Environment II: The Continuity of Nature and Culture." *Social Forces* 9 (1930): 39–48.

Berkeley, Kathleen. "Colored Ladies Also Contributed: Black Women's Activities from Benevolence to Social Welfare, 1866–1896." In *The Web of Southern Social Relations: Women, Family, and Education*, edited by Walter J. Fraser Jr., R. Frank Saunders Jr., and Jon Wakelyn, 181–203. Athens: University of Georgia Press, 1985.

Bernard, L. L. "Culture and Environment II: The Continuity of Nature and Culture." *Social Forces* 9 no. 1 (1930): 42–48.

Berthoff, Rowland T. "Southern Attitudes toward Immigration, 1865–1914." *Journal of Southern History* 17 (1951): 328–60.

Blackwell, Harriet Gray. "Wil Lou Gray, Educator." *Holland's: The Magazine of the South*, December 1938.

Bland, Samuel. "Fighting the Odds: Militant Suffragists in South Carolina." *South Carolina Historical Magazine*, January 1981, 37–48.

Bollet, Alfred Jay. "Politics and Pellagra: The Epidemic of Pellagra in the US in the Early Twentieth Century." *Yale Journal of Biology and Medicine* 65 (1992): 211–21.

Brown, Elsa Barkley. "'What Has Happened Here': The Politics of Difference in Women's History and Feminist Politics." *Feminist Studies* 18 (1992): 295–312.

Brown, Sterling. "The American Race Problem as Reflected in American Literature." *Journal of Negro History* 8 (1939): 275–90.

———. "The Negro Character as Seen by White Authors." *Callalloo* 14/15 (1982): 55–89.

Bryce, James. "Thoughts on the Negro Problem." *North American Review,* December 1891, 641–60.

Burnside, Ronald. "Racism in the Administration of Governor Cole Blease." *Proceedings of the South Carolina Historical Association* (1965): 43–47.

Butler, Judith. "Gender and Performance." In *Body and Flesh: A Philosophical Reader,* ed. Donn Welton, 27–45. Oxford: Blackwell, 1998.

Carlson, Shirley J. "Black Ideals of Womanhood in the Late Victorian Era." *Journal of Negro History* 77 (1992): 61–73.

Cartwright, Morse A. "Research Projects and Methods in Educational Sociology." *Journal of Educational Sociology* 5 no. 8 (1932): 514–20.

Clark, Thomas D. "The Country Newspaper: A Factor in Southern Opinion, 1865–1930." *Journal of Southern History* 14 (1948): 3–33.

Davis, Allen. "The Social Workers and the Progressive Party, 1912–1916." *American Historical Review* 69 (1964): 671–88.

———. "Welfare, Reform, World War I." *American Quarterly* 19 (1967): 516–33.

D'Errico, Peter. "Remarx: Corporate Personality and Human Commodification." *Rethinking M.A.RXSIM* 9 (1996/97): 99–113, http://www.umass.edu/legal/derrico/corporateperson.html.

Dill, Bonnie Thornton. "The Dialectic of Black Womanhood." *Signs* 4 (1979): 543–55.

Dollar, Charles M. "The South and the Fordney McCumber Tariff of 1922: A Study in Regional Politics." *Journal of Southern History* 39 (1973): 45–66.

Eighmy, John Lee. "Liberalism in the South during the Progressive Era." *Church History* 38 (1969): 359–72.

Fikes, Robert. "Adventures in Exoticism: The 'Black Life' Novels of White Writers." *Western Journal of Black Studies* 26 (2002): 6–15.

Flower, Dean. "Eudora Welty and Racism." *Hudson Review* 60 (2007): 325–32, http://www.hudsonreview.com/flowerSu07.pdf.

Ford, Lacy. "Rednecks and Merchants: Economic Development and Social Tensions in the South Carolina Upcountry, 1865–1900." *Journal of American History* 71 (1984): 294–318.

Franklin, John Hope. "Jim Crow Goes to School: The Genesis of Legal Segregation in Southern Schools." *South Atlantic Quarterly* 58 (1959): 225–35.

Freedman, Estelle. "The Benefits of Separate Female Organizations." In *Major Problems in American Women's History,* edited by Mary Beth Norton. Lexington, Mass.: Heath, 1989.

Freeman, Sarah. "Clubs to Parties: North Carolina Advancement and the New Deal." *North Carolina Historical Review* 68 (1991): 320–39.

Geertz, Clifford. "Thick Description: Toward an Interpretive Theory of Culture." In *The Interpretation of Cultures,* 3–32. New York: Basic Books, 1973.

Gilbert, G. M. "Dictators and Demagogues." *Journal of Social Issues* 11 (1955): 51–53.

Gilmore, Glenda. "Gender and the Origins of the New South." *Journal of Southern History* 67 (2001): 769–88.

Going, Allen J. "The South and the Blair Education Bill." *Mississippi Valley Historical Review* 44 (1957): 267–90.

Gordon, Linda. "Black and White Visions of Welfare: Women's Welfare Activism, 1890–1945." *Journal of American History* 78 (1991): 559–90.

Grantham, Dewey. "The Contours of Southern Progressivism." *American Historical Review* (1981): 1035–59.

Hall, Jacquelyn Dowd. "The Long Civil Rights Movement and the Political Uses of the Past." *Journal of American History* 91 (2005): 1233–63.

———. "'The Mind That Burns in Each Body': Women, Rape, and Racial Violence." In *Powers of Desire: The Politics of Sexuality*, edited by Ann Snitow, Christine Stansell, and Sharon Thompson, 328–49. New York: Monthly Review Press, 1983.

Hall, Jacquelyn Dowd. "Open Secrets: Memory, Imagination and the Refashioning of the Southern Identity." *American Quarterly* 80 (1998): 109–24.

———. "Partial Truths." *Signs* 14 (1989): 908–24.

———. "Second Thoughts: On Writing a Feminist Biography." *Feminist Studies* 13 (1987): 19–37.

Harlan, Louis. "The Southern Education Board and the Race Issue in Public Education." *Journal of Southern History* 23 (1957): 189–202.

Hesse-Biber, Sharlene Nagy, and Michelle L. Yaiser. "Feminist Approaches to Research as a Process: Reconceptualizing Epistemology, Methodology, and Method." In *Feminist Perspectives on Social Research*, edited by Sharlene Nagy Hesse-Biber and Michelle L. Yaiser, 3–26. New York: Oxford University Press, 2004.

Hickel, K. Walter. "'Justice and the Highest Kind of Equality Require Discrimination': Citizenship, Dependency, and Conscription in the South, 1917–1919." *Journal of Southern History* 66 (2000): 749–80.

Higginbotham, Evelyn Brooks. "African American Women's History and the Metalanguage of Race." *Signs* 17 (1992): 251–74.

———. "Beyond the Sound of Silence: Afro-American Women in History." *Gender and History* 1 (1989): 50–67.

Higham, John. "The Reorientation of American Culture in the 1890s." In *Writing American History: Essays on Modern Scholarship*, ed. John Higham, 73–102. Bloomington: University of Indiana Press, 1970.

Hine, Darlene Clark. "The Corporeal and Ocular Veil: Dr. Matilda A. Evans (1872–1935) and the Complexity of Southern History." *Journal of Southern History* (2004): 3–34.

———. "Black Women's History, White Women's History: The Juncture of Race and Class." In *HineSight: Black Women and the Reconstruction of American History*, 49–58. New York: Carlson, 1994.

———. "Lifting the Veil, Shattering the Silence: Black Women's History in Slavery and Freedom." In *The State of Afro-American History*, edited by Darlene Clark Hine. Baton Rouge: Louisiana State University Press, 1986.

———. "Rape and the Inner Lives of Black Women: Thoughts on the Culture of Dissemblance." In *HineSight: Black Women and the Reconstruction of American History*. New York: Carlson, 1994.

Hoffschwelle, Mary. "The Science of Domesticity: Home Economics at George Peabody College for Teachers, 1914–1939." *Journal of Southern History* 57 (1991): 659–80.

Hohner, Robert. "Southern Education in Transition: William Waugh Smith, the Carnegie Foundation, and the Methodist Church." *History of Education Quarterly* 27 (1987): 181–203.

Hollis, David. "Cole Blease: The Years between the Governorship and the Senate, 1915–1924." *South Carolina Historical Magazine*, January 1979, 1–17.

Hutchinson, George. "Mediating 'Race' and 'Nation': The Cultural Politics of the Messenger." *African American Review* 28 (1994): 531–38.

Irish, Marian D. "Recent Political Thought in the South." *American Political Science Review* 46 (1952): 121–41.

Johnson, Joan Marie. "'Drill into Us ... the Rebel Tradition': The Contest over Southern Identity in Black and White Women's Clubs, South Carolina, 1898–1930." *Journal of Southern History* 66 (2000): 525–62.

Jones, Allen. "Political Reform in the Progressive Era." *Alabama Review* 21 (1968): 173–94.

Kantrowitz, Stephen. "Ben Tillman and Hendrix McLane, Agrarian Rebels: White Manhood, 'The Farmers,' and the Limits of Southern Populism." *Journal of Southern History* 66 (2000): 497–524.

Kerber, Linda. "The Republican Mother: Women and the Enlightenment—An American Perspective." In *Toward an Intellectual History of Women: Essays by Linda K. Kerber*, 41–62. Chapel Hill: University of North Carolina Press, 1997.

"Separate Spheres, Female Worlds, Woman's Place: The Rhetoric of Women's History." *Journal of American History* 75 (1988): 9–39.

Kett, Joseph. "Women and the Progressive Impulse in Southern Education." In *The Web of Southern Social Relations: Women, Family and Education*, ed. Walter Fraser, R. Frank Saunders Jr., and Jon Wakelyn, 166–80. Athens: University of Georgia Press, 1985.

Kirby, Jack Temple. "Black and White in the Rural South, 1915–1954." *Agricultural History* 58 (1984): 411–22.

Kousser, J. Morgan. "Progressivism—For Middle Class Whites Only: North Carolina Education, 1880–1910." *Journal of Southern History* 46 (1980): 169–94.

Lemons, J. Stanley. "Black Stereotypes as Reflected in Popular Culture, 1880–1920." *American Quarterly* 29 (1977): 102–16.

Link, Arthur. "The Progressive Movement in the South, 1870–1914." *North Carolina Historical Review* 23 (1946): 172–95.

Link, William. "Privies, Progressivism, and Public Schools: Health Reform and Education in the Rural South, 1909–1920." *Journal of Southern History* 54 (1988): 623–42.

Luthin, Reinhard H. "Some Demagogues in American History." *American Historical Review* 57 (1951): 22–46.

Mandle, Jay. "The Re-establishment of the Plantation Economy in the South, 1865–1910." *Review of Black Political Economy* 3 (1973): 68–88.

McCammon, Holly, Karen Campbell, Ellen Granberg, and Christine Mowery. "How Movements Win: Gendered Opportunity Structures and U.S. Women's Suffrage Movements, 1866 to 1919." *American Sociological Review* 66 (2001): 47–70.

McGoldrick, Monica, and Betty Carter, "Forming a Remarried Family." In *The Changing Family Life Cycle: A Framework for Family Therapy*, ed. Betty Carter and Monica McGoldrick, 399–429. Boston: Allyn & Bacon.

McNeely, Patricia. "Her Accomplishments Began with a Barrel of Flour." *Sandlapper Magazine*, January 1970, 15–16.

McPherson, James. "White Liberals and Black Power in Negro Education, 1865–1915." *American Historical Review* 75 (1970): 1357–86.

McRae, Elizabeth Gillespie. "White Womanhood, White Supremacy, and the Rise of Massive Resistance." In *Massive Resistance: Southern Opposition to the Second Reconstruction,* ed. Clive Webb, 181–202. New York: Oxford University Press, 2005).

Megginson, W. J. "Black South Carolinians in World War I: The Official Roster as a Resource for Local History, Mobility, and African-American History." *South Carolina Historical Magazine,* April 1995: 153–73.

Moore, James Tice. "The Historical Context for 'Redeemers Reconsidered.'" In *Origins of the New South Fifty Years Later: The Continuing Influence of a Historical Classic,* ed. John Boles and Bethany Johnson, 131–43. Baton Rouge: Louisiana State University Press, 2003.

———. "Redeemers Reconsidered: Change and Continuity in the Democratic South, 1870–1900." In *Origins of the New South Fifty Years Later: The Continuing Influence of a Historical Classic,* ed. John Boles and Bethany Johnson, 109–30. Baton Rouge: Louisiana State University Press, 2003.

Newbold, N. C. "Common Schools for Negroes in the South." *Annals of the American Academy of Political and Social Science* 140 (1928): 209–23.

Poole, W. Scott. "Religion, Gender, and the Lost Cause in South Carolina's 1876 Governor's Race: 'Hampton or Hell!'" *Journal of Southern History* 68 (2002): 573–98.

Pryse, Marjorie. "Trans/Feminist Methodology: Bridges to Interdisciplinary Thinking." *NWSA Journal* 12 (2000): 109.

Rabinowitz, Howard. "Half a Loaf: The Shift from White to Black Teachers in the Negro Schools of the Urban South, 1865–1890." *Journal of Southern History* 40 (1974): 565–95.

Riviere, Joan. "Womanliness as a Masquerade." In *Feminist Theory: A Reader,* ed. Wendy Kolmar and Frances Bartkowski, 146–49. New York: McGraw-Hill, 2005.

Robeson, Elizabeth. "The Ambiguity of Julia Peterkin." *Journal of Southern History* 61 (1995): 762–86.

Robison, Daniel. "From Tillman to Long: Some Striking Leaders of the Rural South." *Journal of Southern History* 3 (1937): 289–310.

Rosenzweig, Linda W. "'The Anchor of My Life': Middle-Class American Mothers and College-Educated Daughters, 1880–1920." *Journal of Social History* 25 (1991): 5–25.

Salmon, Thomas. "50 Years in 40 Days: The Advances made by Governor Manning and the Legislature of South Carolina." *Survey* 34 (1915): 13–14.

Sawer, Marian. "Gender, Metaphor and the State." *The World Upside Down: Feminisms in the Antipodes,* special issue, *Feminist Review* no. 52 (1996): 119–20.

Scott, Anne Firor. "After Suffrage: Southern Women in the Twenties." *Journal of Southern History* 30 (1964): 298–318.

———. "Most Invisible of All: Black Women's Voluntary Associations." *Journal of Negro History* 56 (1990): 3–22.

———. "The New Woman in the New South." *South Atlantic Quarterly* 61 (1962): 473–83.

———. "A Progressive Wind from the South, 1906–1913." *Journal of Southern History* 29 (1963): 53–70.

Scott, Joan. "Gender: A Useful Category of Historical Analysis." *American Historical Review* 91 (1986): 1053–75.

Shankman, Arnold. "A Jury of Her Peers: The South Carolina Woman and Her Campaign for Jury Service." *South Carolina Historical Magazine*, April 1980, 102–21.

Shaw, Stephanie. "Black Club Women and the Creation of the National Association of Colored Women." In *"We Specialize in the Wholly Impossible": A Reader in Black Women's History*, edited by Darlene Clark Hine, Wilma King, and Linda Reed. New York: Carlson, 1995.

Simkins, Francis. "The Everlasting South." *Journal of Southern History* 13 (1947): 307–22.

———. "Race Legislation in South Carolina since 1865." *South Atlantic Quarterly* 20 (1921): 61–71.

Simon, Bryant. "The Appeal of Cole Blease of South Carolina: Race, Class and Sex in the New South." *Journal of Southern History* 62 (1996): 57–87.

Singal, Daniel Joseph. "Ulrich B. Phillips: The Old South as the New." *Journal of American History* 63 (1977): 871–91.

Sklar, Kathryn Kish. "Organized Womanhood: Archival Sources on Women and Progressive Reform." *Journal of American History* 75 (1988): 176–83.

Smedley, Katharine. "Martha Schofield and the Rights of Women." *South Carolina Historical Magazine* 85 (1986): 195–210.

Smith, Elaine. "Mary McLeod Bethune's 'Last Will and Testament': A Legacy for Race Vindication." *Journal of Negro History* 84 no 1–4 (1996): 105–22.

Spivey, Herman E. "Southern Literary Culture." *South Atlantic Bulletin* 13 (1947): 1–8.

Stone, Clarence. "Bleasism and the 1912 Election in South Carolina." *North Carolina Historical Review* (1963): 71.

Synnott, Marcia. "Crusaders and Clubwomen: Alice Norwood Spearman Wright and Her Women's Network." In *Throwing Off the Cloak of Privilege: White Southern Women in the Civil Rights Era*, edited by Gail Murray, 49–76. Gainesville: University Press of Florida, 2004.

Taylor, Antoinette Elizabeth. "South Carolina and the Enfranchisement of Women: The Early Years." *South Carolina Historical Society* 85 (1986): 115–26.

Tindall, George Brown. "Business Progressivism: Southern Politics in the Twenties." *South Atlantic Quarterly* 62 (1963): 92–106.

Tunnell, Ted. "Creating 'the Propaganda of History': Southern Editors and the Origins of *Carpetbagger* and *Scalawag*." *Journal of Southern History* 72 (2006): 789–822.

Vincent, Melvin J. "Regionalism and Fiction." *Social Forces* 14 (1936): 335–40.

Ward, Dorothy Haizlip. "The Dial Family of Laurens County." In *The Scrapbook: A Compilation of Historical Facts about Places and Events of Laurens County, South Carolina*, edited by William P. Jacobs, 162–65. Laurens, S.C.: Laurens County Historical Society, 1982.

Washington, Booker T. "The New Type of Rural School." *Survey* (1913): 837.

Watson, Richard. "A Testing Time for Southern Congressional Leadership: The War Crisis, 1917–1918." *Journal of Southern History* 44 (1978): 3–40.

Weaver, Valerie. "The Failure of Civil Rights 1875–1883 and Its Repercussions." *Journal of Negro History* 54 (1985): 368–82.

Weber, Lynn. "A Conceptual Framework for Understanding Race, Class, Gender and Sexuality." *Psychology of Women's Quarterly* 22 (1998): 13–32.

Welter, Barbara. "The Cult of True Womanhood, 1820–1860." *American Quarterly* 1 (1966): 151–74.

Whites, Leanne. "The DeGraffeinreid Controversy: Class, Race, and Gender in the North and South." *Journal of Southern History* 54 (1988): 449–78.

Wiener, Jonathan M. "Planter Persistence and Social Change, 1850–1970." *Journal of Interdisciplinary History* 7 (1976): 235–60.

Wilson, C. "The Religion of the Lost Cause: Ritual and Organization of the Southern Civil Religion, 1865–1920." *Journal of Southern History* 46 (1980): 219–38.

Wilson, Francille. "'This Past Was Waiting for Me When I Came': The Contextualization of Black Women's History." *Feminist Studies* 22 (1996): 346–61.

Woodward, C. Vann. "In Search of the Southern Identity." In *The Burden of Southern History*, 3–25. Baton Rouge: Louisiana State University Press, 1968.

Zuczek, Richard. "The Last Campaign of the Civil War: South Carolina and the Revolution of 1876." *Civil War History* 42 (1996): 18–31.

THESES AND DISSERTATIONS

Brice, James Taylor. "The Use of Executive Clemency under Coleman Livingston Blease Governor of South Carolina, 1911–1915." Ph.D., University of South Carolina, 1965.

Burnside, Ronald Danton. "The Governorship of Coleman Livingston Blease, 1911–1915." Ph.D., University of Indiana, 1963.

Carter, Wingard. "State Support for the Public Schools in South Carolina." M.A., University of South Carolina, 1936.

Coley, Bertie Iola. "The Educational Programs of the South Carolina Federation of Women's Clubs, 1898–1938." M.A., University of South Carolina, 1938.

Davis, Sidney Thomas. "Woman's Work in the Methodist Church." Ph.D., University of Pittsburgh, 1963.

Devlin, George Alfred. "South Carolina and Black Migrations, 1865–1930." Ph.D., University of South Carolina, 1984.

Feimster, Crystal Nicole. "'Ladies and Lynching': The Gendered Discourse of Mob Violence in the New South, 1880–1930." Ph.D., Princeton University, 2000.

Finnegan, Terence Robert. "At the Hands of Parties Unknown: Lynching in Mississippi and South Carolina, 1881–1940." Ph.D., University of Illinois at Urbana-Champaign, 1993.

Gage, Mary Cox. "Julia Peterkin: A Study of the Early Writing." M.A., Fairleigh Dickinson University, 1978.

Gilmore, Glenda. "Gender and Jim Crow: Women and the Politics of White Supremacy in North Carolina, 1896–1920." Ph.D., University of North Carolina, 1992.

Gray, Wil Lou. "The Political Philosophy of John Codman Hurd." M.A., Columbia University, 1912.

Harris, Carmen. "'A Ray of Hope for Liberation': Blacks in the South Carolina Extension Service, 1915–1970." Ph.D., Michigan State University, 2002.

Helsly, Terry Lynn. "'Voices of Dissent': The Anti-War Movement and the State Council of Defense in South Carolina, 1916–1918." M.A., University of South Carolina, 1974.

Henry, Louis Lee. "Julia Peterkin: A Biographical and Critical Study." Ph.D., Florida State University, 1965.

Leake, Janet. "A Survey of Negro Public Schools of Columbia, South Carolina." M.A., University of South Carolina, 1932.

Littlefield, Valinda. "'I am only one, but I am one': Southern African-American Women Schoolteachers, 1884–1954." Ph.D., University of Illinois at Urbana-Champaign, 2003.

Lupold, John Samuel. "The Nature of South Carolina Progressives, 1914–1916." M.A., University of South Carolina, 1968.

Mitchell, Sandra Corley. "Conservative Reform: South Carolina's Progressive Movement, 1915–1929." M.A., University of South Carolina, 1979.

Mixon, Kenneth Wayne. "The Senatorial Career of Coleman Livingston Blease, 1925–1931." Ph.D., University of South Carolina, 1970.

Motley, Mary Mac. "The Making of South Progressive: South Carolina's Wil Lou Gray, 1883–1920." M.A., University of North Carolina, Wilmington, 1997.

Nelson, Cristina R. "'A Virgin Field to Work Out Our Own Salvation': The Work of Wil Lou Gray and Mary Elizabeth Frayser, Progressive South Carolina Educators." M.A., University of North Carolina, 1996.

Lewis, Nghana Tamu. "Politics from the Pedestal: Modernity, Cultural Intervention, and the Myth of Southern Womanhood, 1920–1945." Ph.D., University of Illinois at Urbana-Champaign, 2001.

Robeson, Elizabeth. "A World of My Own Making: The Dualism of Julia Peterkin." M.A., Columbia University, 1992.

Slaunwhite, Jerry Lockhar. "The Public Career of Nathaniel Barksdale Dial." Ph.D., University of South Carolina, 1978.

Smith, Selden Kennedy. "Ellison DuRant Smith: A Southern Progressive, 1909–1929." Ph.D., University of South Carolina, 1970.

Thompson, Harold Dean. "Minerva Finds a Voice: The Early Career of Julia Peterkin." Ph.D., Vanderbilt University, 1987.

West, Elizabeth. "Weaving Their White Magic: Avenues of Feminine Patriotism in World War I South Carolina." M.A., University of South Carolina.

Willis, James Truett. "The First Fifty Years of the South Carolina Opportunity School." Ed.D., University of Georgia, 1973.

Wood, Amy Louise. "Spectacles of Suffering: Witnessing Lynching in the New South, 1880–1930." Ph.D., Emory University, 2002.

Woodfaulk, Courtney Sanabria. "The Jeanes Teachers of South Carolina: The Emergence, Existence, and Significance of Their Work." Ph.D., University of South Carolina, 1992.

Yates, Irene. "Conjures and Cures in the Novels of Julia Peterkin." Ph.D., University of South Carolina, 1946.

Index

Cain, John J., 33
Caine, Lillian ("Mama Lyl"), xiii
Calhoun, John C., 2
Carnegie Corporation, 92, 106, 107, 110, 112
Carnegie Foundation, 104, 105, 124
Carney, Mabel, 106, 124
Carter, Dan, 18
Cartwright, Morse, 107
Carver, George Washington, 112
Chamberlain, Daniel, 17, 140n52
Chamberlain, George E., 59
child labor laws, 16, 22, 31, 34, 90, 127
Christianity: 66, 67, 83; see also Methodism;
    Methodist Episcopal Church (general)
Christopher, Dora, 25
Christopher, Jerome, 25
Christopher, Laura Gray, 25
Christopher, Lula, 25
Christopher, Robert, 25
Civil War, 1, 13, 14, 18, 32, 47, 48, 55, 82, 130
Civilian Conservation Corps, 7, 122, 123,
    136n47
Clark, Thomas, 81
Clemson College. see Clemson University
Clemson Opportunity School, 122
Clemson University, 2, 16, 105, 106, 108, 109,
    110, 151n31
Cleveland, Grover, 21
Clinton Male High School, 16
Clinton Mill, 89
Clover Mill, 89
Clyburn, James, 130
Cohen, Lizabeth, 89
Coker, David, 68, 69, 152n51
Coker, James (Mrs.), 60, 65, 153n78
Collins, Patricia Hill, 11
Columbia College, xiii, xiv, 2, 26, 29
Columbia University, 3, 6, 31, 105
Communist Party, 105
Compulsory Attendance Law, 55, 74, 81, 90,
    95, 96, 127, 139n35
Confederate battle flag, 1, 165n50
Conference for Christian Education. see
    Conference for Education
Conference for Education, 38, 44, 70
continuation school, 88, 89
Cook, Blanche Wiesen, 28
Coolidge, Calvin, 124
Cooper, John Milton, Jr., 49
Cooper, Robert Archer, 74
Cooper, William, 119
cotton industry, 6, 15, 20, 25
credit system, 21
crop liens, 21
Cullen, Countee, 112

Cunningham, Ann Pamela, 112
Curry, J. L. M., 38

D. W. Alderman & Sons Company, 90
D'Ericco, Peter, 76
Dabbs, James McBride, 137n1
Dabney, Charles, 39, 52
Daughters of the American Revolution
    (DAR), 10, 35, 91, 144–45n12
Democratic Party, xiii, 17, 18, 21, 130
Denver Opportunity School (CO), 91, 130n32
Depression, 8, 9
Dial, Albert, 14, 18, 20, 21, 23, 141n70,
    142–43n109
Dial, Chrystie Abercrombie, 14
Dial, Hastings (grandfather), 14
Dial, Hastings (grandson), 14
Dial, Henry Arthur, 137–38n7
Dial, Martin, 14
Dial, Mary Hudgens, 14
Dial, Nathaniel, 18, 21, 22, 141n70
Dial, Rebecca Abercrombie, 14, 80
Dial's Methodist Church, 14
Dixiecrats, 130
Du Bois, W. E. B., 45, 112
Dunbar, Paul, 112
Dunklin, Jim, 26
Dunning, William Archibald, 47–48

Edmunds, Samuel Henry, 60
Eighmy, John, 32
Election Law (1882), 18
electricity, 16, 23
Enforcement Act (1871), 17
Equalizing Act to Guarantee a Seven Months'
    Term (1917), 37
eugenics, 104, 163n4

Farmers Union, 64
Fillis (enslaved), 14
Fink, Leon, 85
folk schools, 6, 91, 135n38
Ford, Lacy, 21
Fort Jackson, 33
Freedman, Estelle, 34
Freedman's Bureau, 37
Freeman, Sarah Wilkerson, 35
Fund for Rudimentary Schools for Southern
    Negroes, 38
Future Teachers of America Club, xi

Gaffney Manufacturing Company, 89, 90
Geertz, Clifford, 4
gender norms, 10, 11–12, 27–28, 30, 66, 86,
    100, 120